Sunset

COMPLETE HOME STORAGE

By the Editors of Sunset Books

SUNSET BOOKS INC.
President, Chief Executive Officer: Stephen J. Seabolt
VP, Chief Financial Officer: James E. Mitchell
VP, Manufacturing Director: Lorinda Reichert
Director, Sales & Marketing: Richard A. Smeby
Editorial Director: Bob Doyle
Director of Finance: Lawrence J. Diamond
Production Director: Lory Day
Retail Sales Development Manager: Becky Ellis
Art Director: Vasken Guiragossian

Complete Home Storage was produced in conjunction with
ST. REMY MULTIMEDIA INC.
President/Chief Executive Officer: Fernand Lecoq
President/Chief Operating Officer: Pierre Léveillé
Vice President, Finance: Natalie Watanabe
Managing Editor: Carolyn Jackson
Managing Art Director: Diane Denoncourt
Production Manager: Michelle Turbide

Staff for this Book:
Senior Editors: Jim McRae, Pierre Home-Douglas
Assistant Editor: Jennifer Ormston
Writers: Stacey Berman, Jim Hynes, Rob Lutes,
    Adam van Sertima
Art Directors: Jean Pierre Bourgeois, Odette Sévigny
Designer: Jean-Guy Doiron
Picture Editor: Linda Castle
Contributing Illustrators: Gilles Beauchemin, Michel Blais,
    François Daxhelet, Jacques Perrault
Production Coordinator: Dominique Gagné
System Coordinator: Éric M. Beaulieu
Scanner Operators: Martin Francoeur, Sara Grynspan
Technical Support: Jean Sirois
Proofreader: Judy Yelon
Indexer: Linda Cardella Cournoyer
Other Staff: Lorraine Doré, Robert Labelle, Giles Miller-Mead,
    Valery Pigeon, Mathieu Raymond-Beaubien

Book Consultants:
Jon Arno
Don Vandervort

COVER:
Design: Robin Weiss
Photography: Michael Garland

Design credits:
p. 13 (right) IKEA Home Furnishings
p. 52 (bottom) Jacques Lamarche
p. 55 (bottom, right) Lelia Romandini
p. 83 (bottom) IKEA Home Furnishings
p. 89 (all) LeeRowan, a Newell Company
p. 90 (bottom) IKEA Home Furnishings
p. 97 (top) IKEA Home Furnishings
p. 100 (right) IKEA Home Furnishings
p. 111 (bottom right) IKEA Home Furnishings
p. 128 (top) Jean Chappell
p. 128 (bottom) Ron Bogley
p. 129 (top) John Hamilton, George Kelce
p. 139 (top) Sears Roebuck and Co.
p. 139 (bottom) Rubbermaid Inc.
p. 149 (bottom) Rubbermaid Inc.
p. 150 (right) James Elliott Bryant
p. 151 (top) The Hastings Group
p. 152 (top) Karlis Rekevics
p. 153 (bottom) Glenn D. Brewer
p. 154 (top) Universal Gym Equipment Inc.
p. 165 (top) Rubbermaid Inc.
p. 165 (bottom) Suncast Corporation
p. 166 (bottom) Donald Wm. MacDonald
p. 168 (top) Buzz Bryan
p. 168 (bottom) Armstrong and Sharfman

First printing April 1997
Copyright © 1997
Published by Sunset Books Inc.
    Menlo Park, CA 94025.

ISBN 0-376-01765-1
Library of Congress Catalog Card Number: 96-071706
Printed in the United States

For more information on *Complete Home Storage* or any other
Sunset Book, call 1-800-643-8030, ext. 544.

CONTENTS

PLANNING FOR HOME STORAGE

It seems that there is never enough room in a home to accommodate growing storage needs. As hard as we try, photo albums accumulate to the point of taking over shelves, sports gear piles up and dominates closets, and bulk food items overflow cabinets and pantries. Of course, methods for dealing with these storage concerns vary from individual to individual and from home to home, but the common goal is to have a clutter-free living environment. You've met your goal when you have found a practical place for everything, and everything is in its place.

Beginning in this chapter, and continuing throughout the book, you'll find efficient ways to begin organizing or reorganizing for storage needs. Specific solutions for each room of the house, offering a space by space storage plan, is found on page 11. If you do need to hire a professional, first read the useful information on page 14. And to learn how to store hazards safely, see page 15.

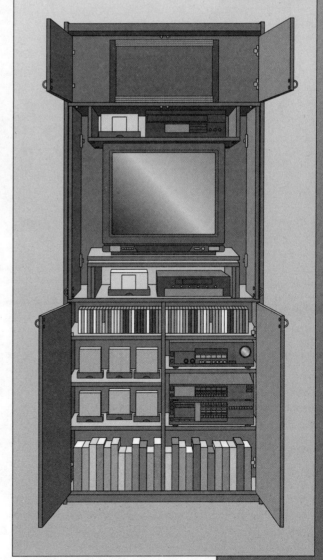

A complete media cabinet is perfect for contemporary needs—room for electronic entertainment equipment and accessories like video and audiocassettes all in a single, beautiful unit that doesn't take up too much space. Find out more about electronics storage on page 13.

GETTING STARTED

Most of us live with many more possessions than we can comfortably manage without an organized storage system. Properly placed, belongings stay tidy, safe from damage, and conveniently accessible. This book will help you make the most of your storage space, allowing you to tailor it to your specific needs.

In the process, you'll also discover potential storage areas that you never knew existed.

RETHINKING YOUR SPACE

Before you begin building new storage units you need to step back for a few minutes and consider your own

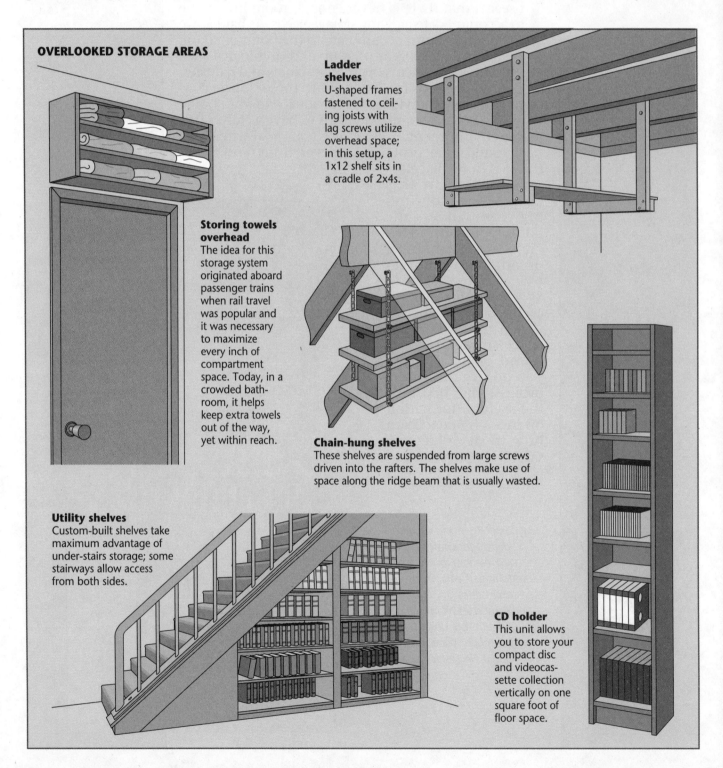

OVERLOOKED STORAGE AREAS

Ladder shelves
U-shaped frames fastened to ceiling joists with lag screws utilize overhead space; in this setup, a 1x12 shelf sits in a cradle of 2x4s.

Storing towels overhead
The idea for this storage system originated aboard passenger trains when rail travel was popular and it was necessary to maximize every inch of compartment space. Today, in a crowded bathroom, it helps keep extra towels out of the way, yet within reach.

Chain-hung shelves
These shelves are suspended from large screws driven into the rafters. The shelves make use of space along the ridge beam that is usually wasted.

Utility shelves
Custom-built shelves take maximum advantage of under-stairs storage; some stairways allow access from both sides.

CD holder
This unit allows you to store your compact disc and videocassette collection vertically on one square foot of floor space.

particular storage needs and how best to deal with them. That means coming up with an organized, carefully considered plan. First of all, you will need to examine what you own and what you really need to keep. Then, plan where in the house these objects can be most conveniently kept, and buy or build any new storage units that are needed. Finally, organize these objects in a neat and logical way. In the rest of this book, we'll show you how to create new storage units. But, on this page, we'll provide tips on making sure you make the best use of the new storage space you'll uncover.

Cutting down on clutter: The first step in meeting your storage needs is to figure out what belongings you can do without. Of course, this may be the hardest part for most people. When it comes to storing belongings, especially those with which we have an emotional attachment, sentimental feelings usually conflict with any plans for organization. There's no point, however, in creating new storage space for unnecessary or old objects. Start with small areas—a closet or toolbox—that you can sort through in a short period of time. Plan on selling or giving away what you can. Here are a few reasons to get rid of clutter:
• Clutter costs time. It has to be cleaned and shuffled about, and it keeps you from getting at the things you need.
• Clutter costs money. Creating new storage space for things you feel you must store is costly.
• Clutter tends to multiply. If an area is already messy, it's tempting to shove in one more object.
• Clutter can be dangerous. Poorly stored objects can fall on a child; toxic substances can remain hidden in the mess rather than being safely stored.
• If an item is broken, it may be cheaper to replace when needed than to repair it.
• For all the odds and ends we keep "just in case," it's probably easier to replace the few we end up needing than to store them all indefinitely.

Active, seasonal, and dead storage: Storage usually falls into one of these three categories: Active storage includes things you need access to regularly, such as sewing supplies or food; keep it separate from other storage. Seasonal storage is typically out-of-season clothes and sports equipment. Dead storage includes things that are rarely needed, such as toys waiting for the next child or memorabilia that might be pulled out every 20 years. Basements, kitchens, dens, bedrooms, and attached garages are usually the best choices for active storage. An attic is ideal for dead or seasonal storage. When sitting down to plan what goes in which room, there are a few points you may want to keep in mind:

• For active storage, keep things close to where they are used most often. If you usually do your mending in the living room, for example, why not find a place near the couch or armchair for your sewing supplies?
• Make sure that storage spaces in the garage and basement are well lit, particularly since some of these spots double as activity areas, such as for laundry rooms or workshops.
• Plan to set up a catchall bin for items that are needed frequently.

Building and buying new storage units: Before adding new storage units, make sure you're using the existing space efficiently. New units should suit the space available as well as the objects you plan to store there.
• Make a scale drawing of the area to plan the space. Self-adhesive notepaper is a handy idea for scale cutouts of furniture that can then be moved around on the plan.
• For storing large objects on shelves, such as cardboard boxes, dollhouses, and bulk food items, make sure the shelves are deep enough so that the objects don't topple off.
• Make sure shelves are sturdy enough for the load they'll have to bear. Longer spans should be supported with brackets.
• Make deep storage areas accessible with lazy Susans and pullout units.
• Divide up vertical spaces with stacking bins or baskets or wall-mounted shelves.
• In a dusty area, such as a workshop, or for storing books, documents, and other objects that need to be kept particularly clean, consider using closed cabinets and drawers.

Using the new space: Finally, you're ready to use your new storage space. The following considerations are important when installing each object in its new home:
• Keep those things you use the most at the front of drawers and shelves.
• Store only lightweight objects high overhead.
• Take into account the height of the members of your household when deciding what should go where (page 9).
• Make sure all dead storage is clearly labeled on a surface that will be visible once the boxes are piled up. This will allow for easy identification if you have to access the items.
• As much as possible, avoid storing items next to household utilities such as electrical service panels and water heaters.
• When storing breakable items such as dishes, make sure to mark the boxes and avoid piling anything on top of them.

FURNITURE FOR STORAGE

Various sorts of furniture and wall systems can be used to handle storage concerns in the home. The type of unit used often depends on the room: A bedroom armoire is ideal for clothes; a living room wall system is practical for home entertainment electronics; a china hutch keeps dinnerware organized in the dining room. An example of each, as well as other storage units, is shown below.

One of the main advantages of this type of storage is that you can add or replace a unit as situations change. Alternatively, you can modify an existing piece by lowering or raising its shelves or refitting its drawers.

MOVABLE VS. BUILT-IN STORAGE UNITS

Furniture can be freestanding or built-in. The freestanding category includes both single furniture pieces, such as armoires and chests, and modular wall systems that are expandable or have interchangeable parts. Built-ins are custom-fit to specific areas in your home and can be built and installed by a professional or an ambitious do-it-yourselfer.

Furniture: Movable and built-in furniture have their advantages and disadvantages. Movable units can be placed wherever storage needs arise and they can be taken with you when you move away. A drawback, however, is that when buying ready-made or ready-to-assemble furniture, you may not always be able to get exactly the size and configuration you want. Wall

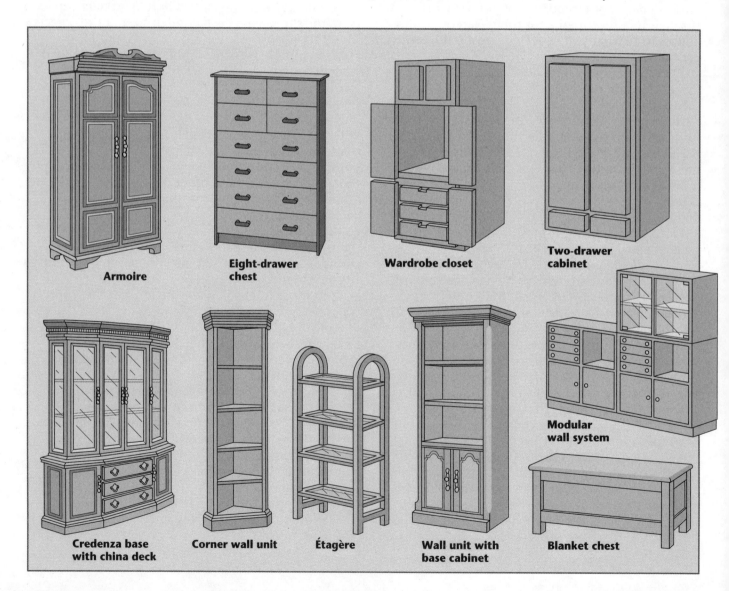

Armoire

Eight-drawer chest

Wardrobe closet

Two-drawer cabinet

Credenza base with china deck

Corner wall unit

Étagère

Wall unit with base cabinet

Modular wall system

Blanket chest

units are often the exception because they can be fitted with specialized components, but they can't meet every need.

Built-ins: Use built-ins for odd-size spaces in your home where other furniture can't fit—such as under staircases, over doorways, and around windows. They also save a considerable amount of floor space when built into existing walls.

As an added benefit, built-ins look almost seamless in a room, complementing the existing architectural style in a highly efficient manner. When custom built, however, these storage units can be very costly, depending on size, materials, and the complexity of the design.

Although being able to tailor the piece to match your existing space is the main advantage of built-in units, you can add premade items as needed.

STORING IN STYLE

Storage furniture should be more than functional—it must look good in the room. Whether using premade or custom-built units, you can create a look to match any decor, style, or personal preference. American country pieces, for example, typically have simple lines with sparse, unpretentious detailing. Contemporary pieces are strong and sophisticated, with form often taking precedence over decoration.

Color can be used to express style, too. For a sleek, sophisticated appearance, choose either matte or shiny black storage units. Wood tones are more traditional, but a piece painted white will also enhance the formal tone of a traditionally decorated room. For a fresh, contemporary look, consider bright colors—either monotones or a variety of colors—in one unit or area.

MATERIALS
Most wall and other storage systems are made of a veneer of wood or laminate over particleboard or plywood core—very few are solid wood. Keep in mind that wood and laminates differ in both look and properties.

Wood: Whether solid wood, or veneer over panels, wood gives a warm, natural look. Solid wood is more durable and elegant, but much more expensive than wood-veneered panels, which require less handwork and will not shrink or swell with seasonal changes in relative humidity.

Woods are classified as either hardwoods or softwoods. Hardwoods come from deciduous trees, softwoods from conifers. Hardwoods are generally more expensive, hold fasteners better, and are more resistant to wear than softwoods. Choose light-toned oak, ash,

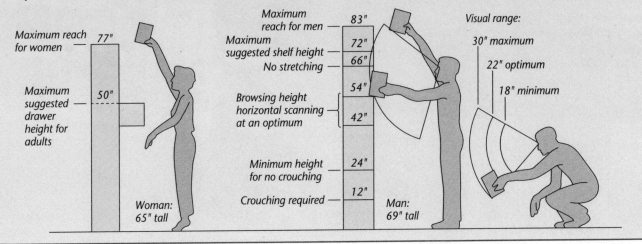

IDEAL SHELF HEIGHT FOR ADULT REACH

As the years go by and you accumulate more and more items, you'll need to find new places to store them—especially if you aren't in the habit of getting rid of old belongings. To keep everything within reach, yet maintain a sense of order in your home, shelving units—attached directly to walls, or within wall systems—are ideal.

The illustration below will give you an idea of how high to place shelves and other storage units. It depicts bookcase

and shelf adaptations to accommodate the average-sized woman and man. Remember that you must take into account factors such as visual range and esthetic appeal.

Place regularly used items from around eye level to waist height and less-used objects on the highest and lowest shelves. You can add to these units as needed—a better solution than planning a new layout or buying more storage items.

Maximum reach for women — 77"

Maximum suggested drawer height for adults — 50"

Woman: 65" tall

Maximum reach for men — 83"

Maximum suggested shelf height — 72"

No stretching — 66"

54"

Browsing height horizontal scanning at an optimum — 42"

Minimum height for no crouching — 24"

Crouching required — 12"

Man: 69" tall

Visual range:
30" maximum
22" optimum
18" minimum

and maple, and dark-toned cherry, walnut, and mahogany. Most softwoods are easier to tool, and more readily available than hardwoods. Popular softwoods include fir and pine. If you would like to paint or stain your wood storage furniture, see the ideas on wood finishes on page 189.

Laminate: Because they're durable, easy to clean, and available in many colors and patterns, plastic laminates are popular surfacing materials for storage systems. In general, laminates come in one of three forms: The cheapest and least durable is a brittle vinyl or paper surface film, while at the other end of the spectrum high-pressure laminate is very durable and most expensive. In between, melamine—special paper impregnated with melamine resin—is the most popular because it is fairly durable and affordable.

SIZE CONSIDERATIONS

Whether you're commissioning custom cabinetry or buying a manufactured wall system, knowing the sizes and the shapes of the objects you want to organize will help you design or buy an appropriate unit and ensure that those items will fit properly in it.

Shelf height: The illustration on page 9 shows norms for fitting shelving to people. While they're not inflexible rules, these are generally accepted standards that you may want to follow when planning your storage areas and systems. Don't place shelves out of reach—note that the recommended height for the highest shelf is 6 feet, unless you have a ladder or stool to help you reach its contents.

Shelf size: Think in terms of linear footage when figuring your shelving needs. A single 6-foot-long shelf offers 6 linear feet of storage. A tall unit with six shelves, each 6 feet long, offers 36 linear feet of storage.

To get a rough idea of the linear footage of shelving you need, simply measure the linear footage of the books, records, and other items you intend to store. Allow extra room for expansion and open display space.

Shelf depth and height: They depend on the size of the stored objects. Adjustable shelves are the most flexible; for fixed shelves, measure the books and other items, then add an inch or two for head space. See below for more on spacing common storage articles on shelves.

Shelf length: This depends on the shelf material and the weight of the objects that it will support. Ask a carpenter for more help.

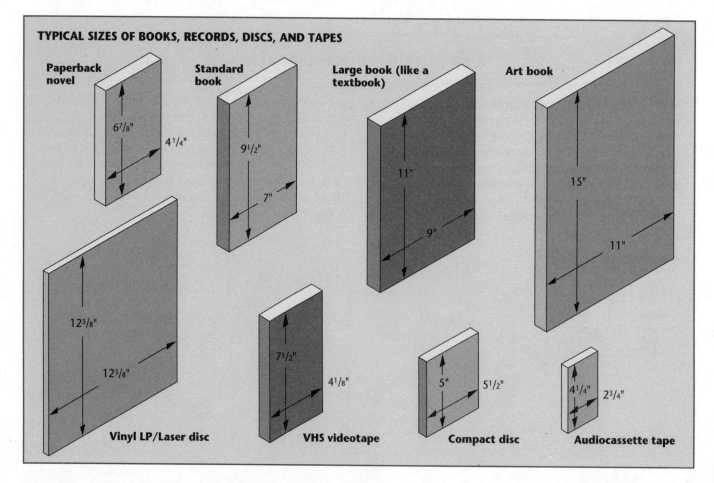

TYPICAL SIZES OF BOOKS, RECORDS, DISCS, AND TAPES

Paperback novel — $6^7/_8$", $4^1/_4$"

Standard book — $9^1/_2$", 7"

Large book (like a textbook) — 11", 9"

Art book — 15", 11"

Vinyl LP/Laser disc — $12^3/_8$", $12^3/_8$"

VHS videotape — $7^1/_2$", $4^1/_8$"

Compact disc — 5", $5^1/_2$"

Audiocassette tape — $4^1/_4$", $2^3/_4$"

SOLUTIONS FOR DIFFERENT ROOMS

Each room in the house has its own particular purpose—and its own individual storage needs. Different spaces and different layouts mean that you need to tackle each room independently and come up with specific solutions based on your needs and the design of the room. Here are some ideas for storage in rooms ranging from the basement to the attic.

KITCHENS

Quite possibly the most-used room in the home, the kitchen is also an area where proper storage is a must. With the right planning, you can keep months' worth of bulk food products close by—in deep pantries and cupboards, under sinks, and on built-in shelves. Cooking utensils, pots, pans, and baking supplies should also be stored in areas where they will be most handy.

Unused kitchen wall space, even an area just a few feet wide, can accommodate a mini-office equipped with shelving for cookbooks, a desktop, and drawers. Under a window or along an unused wall, a small wall unit can expand available display and storage area.

An armoire, hutch, or other freestanding cupboard or cabinet with glass or solid doors provides plenty of space for china and glassware and also helps keep them dust-free. Built-in units that include drawers, adjustable shelves, and cabinets are also good organizers. Stacks of dishes can be very heavy, so be sure shelves are strong and well supported. Ideas for kitchens start on page 33.

BEDROOMS

In recent years, bedrooms have become much more than just rooms to sleep in. They often house video and audio gear, fitness equipment, home office areas, library corners, and more.

Because space is limited in most bedrooms, wall systems and other add-ons that store both clothing and other gear are particularly useful. In a bedroom, a large wall unit can take the place of conventional dressers.

Assess your space: Perhaps the closets could be used more efficiently, or perhaps drawers are too large for what they are storing. Make decisions as to whether you want to spend the money to buy extra furniture or add-on bins, or dedicate precious weekend and evening time to building your own units. Maybe an easier solution is just to reorganize. Closet organizers, as discussed beginning on page 87, are a wonderful way to solve the problem of limited storage space, time, and budget.

CHILDREN'S ROOMS

The most important thing to keep in mind when planning children's rooms is that needs change with age. Don't outfit these rooms with furniture pieces that are suited only for a particular age group—fill your children's rooms with items that can be adapted as the youngsters grow. For example, you can modify a rolling cart from a diaper and toy storage unit to accommodate an infant, to a versatile computer stand for the growing adolescent. See page 95 for more on how to ensure the versatility of children's furniture. And it's never too soon to consider that items such as low bookshelves, a desk, and drawers encourage your children to be neat and organized.

BATHROOMS

It seems as if there's never enough space for soaps, shampoos, razors, toothbrushes, and other bathroom essentials. But look again. Even on the tightest budget, anyone can attach shelves to bare walls; mount soap, washcloth, and shampoo bins on the inside of shower doors; and reorganize the space under the sink. Plan to keep frequently used items readily available—in shallow drawers, prominently displayed on shelves, or at the front of cabinets. For more on how to use your bathroom space more efficiently, turn to page 104.

DINING AREAS

There are few more useful additions to a dining room than a wall system featuring deep cabinets, drawers, and shelves to hold dishes, glassware, serving pieces, and even tablecloths. You may choose the more traditional alternative of a china cabinet. There is also the option of adding an armoire or a hutch to your dining room for items such as fancy tablecloths, linens, and napkins. For greater efficiency, you can even combine units with a countertop to create a functional buffet-style serving area.

Where space is at a premium, a dining room that's used only part-time for dining can serve other roles as well. A wall system outfitted with a fold-down desk, file drawers, and cabinets can provide efficient office space that's easily camouflaged when company arrives. Or how about a cabinet filled with audio equipment wired to speakers throughout the house?

If your dining area is part of a large kitchen or an extension of your living room, a wall system, whether it reaches to the ceiling or is just waist high, can effectively divide the space and create the effect of a separate dining room. Shelves, hutches, and bins can supply both storage space, and a place to display family pictures, keepsakes, and other items.

For dish and glassware display, consider a single shelf that runs along a wall at eye level or just above head height—perhaps at the same height as the tops of windows. For a few dollars, interior lighting in china cabinets with glass shelves can highlight prized possessions such as fine china heirlooms.

If you live in an area prone to earthquakes, choose dining room cabinets and display cases with doors that can be locked or latched closed.

LIVING AREAS

Whether your family congregates in an informal living room, a family room, a den, or a family kitchen, that's the place where such activities as game playing, reading, watching television, and listening to music occur. Every one of these activities involves paraphernalia. It's easy to understand why such areas seem to attract clutter.

Because they're so versatile, modular wall systems are especially popular in family living areas. Equipped with adjustable shelving, cabinets, drawers, television bays, and other specialty options, these units can organize myriad objects. But virtually any piece of storage furniture or built-in can help contain the clutter. You can buy or build cabinet systems such as a base for a television set with drawers that open to reveal ideal storage spots for videocassettes, VCR head cleaner supplies, and movie and other entertainment-related magazines. For help organizing electronic equipment and their accessories, see page 13.

In more formal living areas, use wall systems that combine open shelving and cabinets to exhibit art objects and prized collections as well as to conceal audio equipment and other accessories.

Keep books on open shelving where they can be easily seen and reached. In general, it's best to place heavy books and reference works on the lower tiers of a shelf system. Art books can go at eye level, and paperbacks can be arranged on higher shelves. Coffee tables and other low pieces of furniture are also handy places to keep books and magazines—they give guests something to do when waiting for dinner or your company.

Unless you recycle them regularly, magazines can quickly overwhelm their designated storage space. For easy reference, consider special binders or magazine holders that slide onto shelves like books. Or buy inexpensive wicker baskets, or other handy storage bins, and keep magazines in a neat pile near couches. You can also store magazines in flat stacks, ideally behind cabinet doors. Ensure shelves are strong and well supported enough to handle heavy magazine stacks.

How you display special pieces such as heirlooms, fine china, and sentimental family favorites depends on how much you plan to protect them from theft and breakage, and whether you want to accent their worth by using subtle lighting techniques, for example. A ready-made or built-in storage unit with glass shelves, sliding glass doors, and interior lighting allows you to enjoy your collection and, at the same time, keep it safe, secure, and clean. Some collectibles can be kept on open shelves, whereas you might find it safer and less nerve-racking to store them in drawers and cabinets when a lot of people come to visit at once—especially if they include children.

GARAGES, BASEMENTS, AND ATTICS

These rooms are usually considered the primary storage spaces in the home, where display and presentation take second place to efficiency. Use shelves and cabinets to keep tools, laundry supplies, and other necessities organized. Always lock up dangerous supplies and sharp objects, and, as much as possible, try to keep young children out of these areas.

 ASK A PRO

HOW CAN I MOISTUREPROOF A CABINET?

Cabinets are a great place to keep old books, documents, photos, and even items you will need to access often, such as textbooks, cookbooks, and bulk food items that are too large to fit in the kitchen. But your efforts are useless if moisture is allowed to seep in and damage the contents.

To protect a storage cabinet from basement dampness, raise it 3 to 4 inches off the floor on a treated wood base and place it against furring strips fastened to the wall. Spread heavy polyethylene sheeting under and behind the cabinet to provide added protection; fasten it to the upper strip to keep it in place.

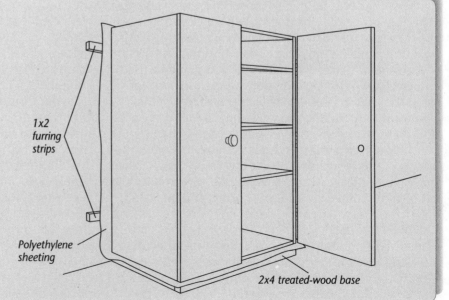

1x2 furring strips

Polyethylene sheeting

2x4 treated-wood base

ORGANIZED ELECTRONICS

Today's homes are equipped with a large enough variety of electronics that families don't ever have to leave their dens for a complete entertainment experience. Large-screen televisions, compact discs, movie laser discs, VCRs, and video games are everywhere. The problem rests in how to store these units efficiently.

Fortunately, you can store electronic supplies in anything from ready-made media cabinets to storage furniture, and from modular to custom units. In doing so, it's important to keep ventilation in mind: open-backed shelves and cabinets vent built-up heat. Or you can cut holes in the back and top of cabinets and media centers, or use exhaust fans for ventilation. You can also route lighting and electronic wires through these holes.

Be sure shelf and platform materials are strong enough to support equipment. For lighter loads, consider pullout and swiveling shelves *(below)*. Drawers allow efficient storage of small items like cassette tapes, as do special organizers you can buy—these keep accessories in order on shelves or in cabinets.

Consult specialists who work at home electronics stores for more help with planning and installation.

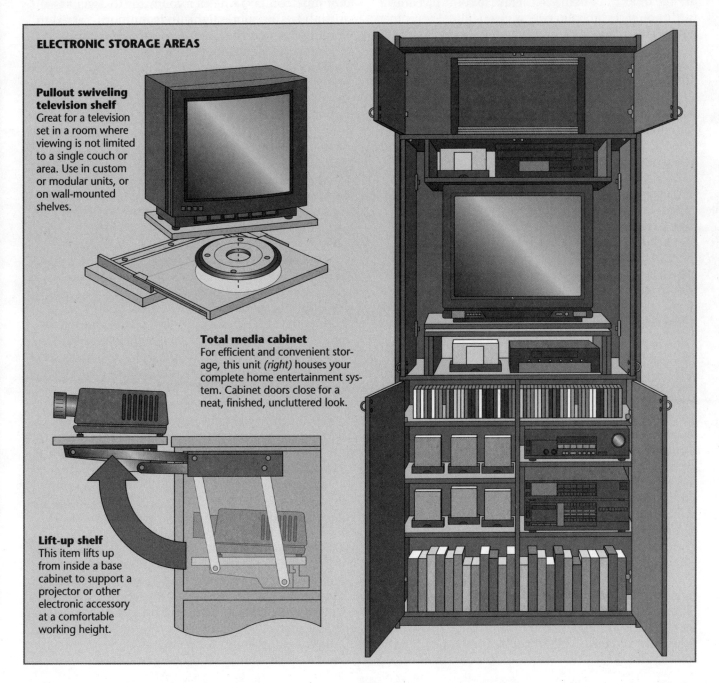

ELECTRONIC STORAGE AREAS

Pullout swiveling television shelf
Great for a television set in a room where viewing is not limited to a single couch or area. Use in custom or modular units, or on wall-mounted shelves.

Total media cabinet
For efficient and convenient storage, this unit *(right)* houses your complete home entertainment system. Cabinet doors close for a neat, finished, uncluttered look.

Lift-up shelf
This item lifts up from inside a base cabinet to support a projector or other electronic accessory at a comfortable working height.

WORKING WITH PROFESSIONALS

Not everyone will have the necessary space or room layouts for ready-made solutions to their storage problems. In the planning, design, and construction of your storage solutions, a number of different professionals can offer helpful services. Concerns such as limited space, lighting and ventilation, construction and installation of storage units, and safety are sure to come to be of primary concern.

No matter which professional you choose, try to get referrals from people who have had similar work done. Or you can turn to the phone book for help. When meeting for the first time, ask the consultant to come prepared with references and photos of previous jobs. For cabinetmakers, visit former clients to check the work firsthand.

Discuss fee structure and billing method beforehand. Some specialists charge by the job, hour, or by the number of items they modify, buy on your behalf, and consult about. You may want a written contract for some jobs in order to minimize misunderstandings later. It should clearly identify the participants and the contracted work—including materials to be used, and the work and payment schedules.

Here's a look at some of the professionals who can help in your pursuit of more effective and functional home storage, and guidelines on how to work with them successfully. Remember that not all design solutions work equally well for each room in the house.

ARCHITECTS
Licensed by the state, architects are trained in all facets of building design and construction. An architect can design a built-in system integrated with the room's style and appearance. Some may hire an interior designer when storage overlaps with furnishing concerns. On a remodel or a new home, an architect may have a hand in designing completely new storage units built right into your rooms.

INTERIOR DESIGNERS
For a large wall system, cabinets, extra-long bookshelves, and other items that tend to dominate a room, your best bet is to see an interior designer. Along with decorators, they specialize in accenting and furnishing rooms and can offer new ideas. Because many designers belong to the American Society of Interior Designers (ASID), a professional organization, they have access to designer showrooms and other resources not available to retailers.

KITCHEN AND BATH DESIGNERS
These specialists concentrate on specifying fixtures, cabinetry, appliances, and materials for the kitchen and bath. Their talents in cabinet design can also prove useful for other rooms in the house.

LIGHTING DESIGNERS
A lighting designer specifies placement of lighting and the fixtures necessary to achieve the level of light required. They can help you plan interior or exterior lighting for a media center, shelving, a home-office wall system, and even lighting for the best working conditions at a child's desk.

RETAIL SPECIALISTS
Showroom personnel, building center staff, and other retailers can help you choose and, in some cases, combine components to maximize storage. Shop around to find someone who is more interested in helping than earning hefty sales commissions.

For retail design help, you should provide a rough floor plan of your rooms. This is often the best way to outfit kitchens with cabinets *(page 37)*. If buying ready-to-assemble component systems, retailers will often provide a finished plan and/or materials list if you buy from them. Most offer installation services.

MEDIA CENTER SPECIALISTS
Cabinetmakers, architects, and interior designers are best for designing a custom media center. Be sure they have experience working with electronics or that they will consult with experts.

CUSTOM WOODCRAFTERS
A number of different tradespeople build shelves, cabinetry, and other furniture.

Nearly all cabinetmakers, whether they're dealers selling manufactured products or local woodshops that build custom cabinets, focus on kitchens and bathrooms. They typically install the units. Woodworkers offer services similar to those offered by small cabinet shops—but they're more likely to handle jobs with a wider, less-specific slant, such as building furniture. Contrast this to custom furniture makers, who work in their own shops and typically handle difficult—and often expensive—projects.

Finish carpenters are hired by contractors or homeowners to install trimwork and cabinetry in a house. Most do the work on site, ruling out complex cabinetmaking (though they do install premade cabinets).

CONTRACTORS
State or local licensing requires that contractors meet minimum training standards and have a specified level of experience—but it doesn't guarantee that they are good at what they do. Usually, a general contractor will oversee a remodeling project, hiring subcontractors to do the work. In this case, the contractor is responsible for the quality of work and materials and for paying the subcontractors.

STORAGE HAZARDS

Well-ordered storage is more than a matter of being neat. Papers, clothes, and coats strewn about is one thing, but tools, firewood, and boxes cluttering walking space can be dangerous. If you're setting your storage space in order, be sure to consider safety, too.

To prevent accidents, discard old paint cans, broken toys, and other useless items. Ensure that storage areas are well lit and the floor is clear. For more safety guidelines, contact fire, health, or other appropriate officials.

TOOLS AND TOXIC SUBSTANCES
Children are inherently curious and often view workshops and garden sheds as places to explore. Trouble is, these same areas house tools and toxic substances. To ensure that no accidents occur when you're not there to supervise, store toxic supplies and sharp tools wisely.

Hang tools with blades and bits high on walls with strong, secure hooks. And keep dangerous chemicals away from easily reached places, such as under sinks; keep kitchen cleaning products away from the pantry. And don't forget to pet-proof your storage spots.

Store tools and toxic substances in drawers and cabinets that have plastic safety latches *(page 53)*, available at baby, department, or hardware stores. The hooked latch attaches to the inside of the door or drawer front and fastens to the inside of the cabinet frame. Once closed, you must unhook the latch from the frame to open the door or drawer—something a young child cannot easily do. But make sure you can open the latch yourself—it's useless if it keeps you from your kitchen, workplace, or other storage areas. The latch should be made of sturdy plastic that won't break or lose its flexibility. Check it regularly to make sure it hasn't worked loose or become misaligned. On less frequently used units, install metal locks.

To keep children from getting into off-limit storage units, install doorknob covers *(right)*. Cabinet locks *(page 53)* keep cupboards, cabinets, or closets locked.

POWER TOOLS AND WIRING
Make sure there are enough electrical circuits in your workshop, kitchen, or any area in which you will use electrical devices; check with an electrician. Power and kitchen tools should be on circuits separate from lighting; tool circuits require at least 20 amps to prevent overload.

New power tool outlets in the work area should be the grounded (three-prong) type. To guard against shock, buy double-insulated power tools and install ground fault circuit interrupter (GFCI) outlets, designed to trip instantly when they detect a leak in current. Use a master switch with a key to keep kids from playing with the tools.

Don't plug too many things into an extension cord, or use extra-long cords with insufficient gauge wires, since the insulation could overheat and ignite. Don't

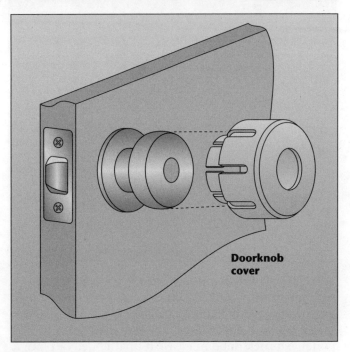

Doorknob cover

string extension cords under rugs or tie them to nails; punctured insulation on wires can result in fire. Periodically inspect extension cords for cracks, fraying, and broken plugs.

FLAMMABLE SUBSTANCES
Don't let sawdust or wood chips pile up in workshops, and keep kitchens clear of discarded paper products.

Storing flammable liquids is a risky practice. Keep gasoline for lawn mowers and other equipment in a can specially designed for gasoline, with a closure valve, vapor vent, and pour spout. Store gasoline or kerosene outside the home in a detached shed or garage. Close flammable bathroom and kitchen cleaner containers tightly after using; keep them high up in a closed closet. Keep all flammable liquids in their original containers, or in metal cans with labels and tight-fitting lids, in a well-ventilated area far from heat sources. For extra security, place them in a special fireproof metal cabinet.

Throw out gas-soaked rags, but make sure you hang them up to dry outside before putting them in the garbage. Store fireplace ashes in a metal container. Clean up any oil drippings.

HEATING EQUIPMENT
Make sure that combustibles are not positioned anywhere near heating equipment such as a furnace, water heater, a chimney, or the oven or stove top. Leave at least three feet of space around all sides of such heating equipment. Install heat-safe tops to counters that are close to your stove *(page 47)*.

Security hasp with padlock

To prevent fire in a storage area, have your heating equipment inspected and professionally cleaned at least once every year. If you use a basement, garage, or shed storage space as a work area, you may want to use a portable heater. But don't leave it unattended or place it where someone can tip it over.

LADDERS AND STAIRCASES

Make sure ladders and staircases are adequate for the loads they will have to bear, and that they are in good condition. Stepping surfaces of kitchen stepladders should be smooth and flat. Never block a ladder or staircase with boxes or overflow storage.

Position a ladder so that its base is offset from the perpendicular by one-quarter of its length; the foot of a 20-foot ladder, for example, should be 5 feet away from the point directly beneath the top of the ladder. Fold-down ladders usually aren't intended for heavy use.

Handrails on staircases should be solidly secured, and the steps clear and well lit with light switches at the top and bottom. A minimum of six and a half feet of headroom all the way up is often required by code.

VALUABLES

The best way to foil burglars is to use a security hasp and a heavy-duty padlock with a solid case and a steel shackle attached to an integral bolt, as shown in the illustration at left. When closed, the hasp covers the screws that attach it to the unit. Hinges mounted to the inside edges of both the frame and door, and fitted with nonremovable hinge pins, are the most secure.

EARTHQUAKE-SECURE STORAGE

If you live in an earthquake region, be sure your storage can withstand a jolt without collapsing or spilling your stored treasures. The goal is to protect your possessions and protect your family *from* your possessions; in an earthquake, most people are hurt by falling objects. You won't be able to completely quake-proof your possessions, but by identifying and minimizing the risks, you can reduce the probability of damage and injury. Here are a few steps you should take:

• Begin by walking through your home and looking for potential hazards. Mentally shake every room to see what could fall.

• Secure anything that is top-heavy. Fasten freestanding bookcases and other storage shelving and cabinets to the wall with L-braces or metal plumber's strapping screwed into wall studs. Tie off everything that is unstable or tall; use rope or wire and eye screws, bolts, or straps. Don't rely on nails for anchoring objects to walls; depend only on threaded fasteners, such as screws, driven into secure wall framing.

• Place heavy items low, breakables in secured spaces, and caustic chemicals in secure cabinets at floor level.

• Prevent objects on shelves from sliding or "walking" during earthquake shaking. Hold-fast putties, hook-and-

loop fasteners, adhesive tapes, and other adhesives will keep items from moving. Restrain all items of electronic equipment by either fastening them directly or tethering them to secured shelves. Place secure barriers—such as a curtain rod or a raised molding—across the fronts of shelves to keep items from falling off.

• Be sure cabinets latch securely. Don't count on magnetic catches; they often shake free. You can retrofit cabinets with heavy spring-loaded hasp or touch latches, or replace the pulls with latches or catches that lock to the cabinet frame. In the garage and other areas where storage doesn't have to be pretty, you can use tight-fitting eye hooks. For more visible cabinets, childproof latches are inexpensive, invisible from outside the cabinet, and easy to use.

• At the very least, install secure catches on the cabinets that hold your precious breakables. To minimize damage, also pay attention to how items are stored within cabinets. You can put cushioning layers of foam or paper between seldom-used heirloom plates and install nonskid shelf padding, available at marine and RV-supply stores.

• Be sure ceiling-mounted storage is secured to joists or beams with threaded fasteners. Check the security of any item that hangs from the ceiling.

A GALLERY OF KITCHEN STORAGE IDEAS

Given the number of daily activities that take place in the kitchen, it's no wonder that it is the busiest room in most homes. From a food preparation area to a dining room to a place where children do their homework, the kitchen is asked to do it all. In order for it to remain clutter-free however, it's important to develop an efficient storage plan and to stick to it.

A wide variety of shelving units, racks, and cabinets are available to keep food, appliances, dishes and cookware and even garbage where you see fit. Many of these items are available commercially or can be made easily in the home workshop.

Whether the idea is to put the things that make your kitchen work on display or to keep them hidden from view, the storage ideas and solutions shown on the pages that follow can help you make the most of one of the most important rooms in your home.

A lazy Susan installed in the corner section of a lower kitchen cabinet provides lots of space for cookware and small appliances. China is stored behind the glass doors of the upper cabinets, while the space between the top of the cabinets and the ceiling provides an opportunity to display pottery or other decorative touches.

The modern kitchen layout shown above features a traditional element as its focal point—an island workstation. There is plenty of room there to store pots, pans, and dishes, as well as in the cabinets along both walls. Abundant countertop space allows for easy food preparation.

The cabinet runs in the L-shaped kitchen at left integrate the major appliances, while an island workstation houses the sink. A chopping block that pulls out from a lower cabinet, along the far counter, is a practical kitchen accessory.

This single-wall setup shows how most of the elements in a kitchen can be arranged along one wall. The sink is sandwiched between the oven and microwave and the cooktop, while upper and lower cabinets run the full length of the wall.

More than a simple workstation, the island in this kitchen dominates the middle of the room. The large countertop and twin sinks provide space for preparation, cleanup, and storage.

For storing dry foods such as flour and sugar, consider installing metal-lined drawers. The corner unit in this custom-designed lower cabinet features five such pivoting drawers. If you have to commission a piece to be built for your kitchen, first read the information on page 43.

Drawers are also a smart place to store fresh produce, as shown at left. Instead of lining the drawers with metal however, simply fit them with plastic or wire baskets. For ease of access, plan to install the drawers near cooking or food preparation areas.

When storing leftover food, or meals that have been prepared for the week in advance, it's smart to use containers with tight-fitting lids. As shown at right, commercial models are available in a variety of shapes and sizes.

To keep a spice bottle collection properly organized, consider dedicating a kitchen cabinet just for this purpose. Housed in a small-size cabinet, the system shown at left features both permanent and swing-out shelving. A door keeps the spices concealed when they are not being used.

A large hutchlike cabinet serves to house the lion's share of this kitchen's cookware, jars, and china while adding a touch of rustic elegance to the room. An open rack over the countertop provides easy access to stacks of dishes.

Convert cabinet space under a kitchen sink or wet bar into a wine rack by removing a door and adding adjustable shelving. Plastic separators on each shelf help sort different types and sizes of bottles.

Today's modern kitchen cabinets come equipped with a bevy of new shelving hardware. Choose units with adjustable shelves to help you organize your dry food storage. The model above uses every inch of available space by attaching racks to the interior of doors and installing thin sliding drawers between the upper and lower units.

Use your imagination to help use counter, wall, and cabinet space for storing the odds and ends that can otherwise cause chaotic clutter. In the kitchen above, a microwave oven is suspended from the bottom of a cabinet, thereby freeing the counterspace below for handy storage baskets. The wall space above the range holds a host of hanging pots and dried herbs.

*Maximizing available
space, the kitchen at right
features an island with
storage that extends from
just below the countertop
to just above the floor.
Keeping with this theme,
the cabinets in the back-
ground extend close
to the ceiling.*

*The kitchen shown below features several clever storage ideas.
The rounded, open shelves at the end of the counter house
photos and decorative items, while the vertical dish rack adds
an attractive visual element to the upper cabinets. The shelf
above the window is a good place for knickknacks.*

With as much of an eye toward decorating as maximizing space, the country flavor of the cabinets shown above adds charm to this kitchen. The upper units house fine china and glassware, while the lower units feature a mix of drawers, base cabinets, and open shelves.

The modern fridge in the kitchen shown at left is flanked by open shelves for storing everything from dry foods to small appliances. The bottom drawers on the lower left are used to store produce; other items can be kept out of sight behind the solid cabinet door on the lower right.

The kitchen pictured below is a fine example of how large appliances can match the decor of a kitchen. The double doors of the fridge are finished in a wood-grained motif to harmonize with the surrounding cabinets. The smaller appliances in the foreground sit on lift-up shelves in the island, and can be quickly stored out of view when not needed.

If your kitchen boasts a lot of appliances, make sure it also has ample storage space. In the kitchen at left, cabinets are built into the island and above the fridge. The food preparation area, in the foreground, has a convenient base unit, while upper and lower cabinets are featured in the microwave area, in the background to the left.

Cabinets are often called upon to house—and conceal—appliances. The clothes dryer in the kitchen at right fits into a lower cabinet; the microwave slips neatly into an upper unit. Be sure to follow building and electrical codes when wiring fixtures behind a cabinet.

The electric mixer in the kitchen shown at left swings up when needed; a lower drawer conveniently holds other baking tools. The lift-up shelving mechanism can hold a host of other appliances including blenders, coffee machines, and toasters.

Storage systems aren't always designed on a grand scale. The simple toaster holder at right fits into the wall above the kitchen table. It is pulled down when the toaster is required and goes back into the wall after mealtime.

There are some items in the kitchen that you'll want stored in plain view, while others are better kept out of sight. In the kitchen shown opposite, an attractive collection of pots placed in the open space below the island adds character to the room. Small appliances are concealed within appliance garages on the main countertop.

Keep kitchen pantries and closets neat and organized by hanging brooms, mops, and dustpans from a wall-mounted wire rack. Install the rack in an out-of-the-way place like the back of a door or the corner of a room.

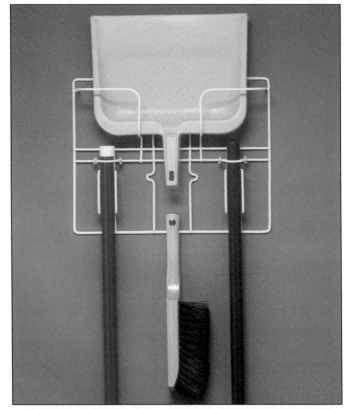

For homes with no dedicated ironing areas, consider installing a fold-away ironing board behind the false drawer front of a kitchen cabinet. The model below fits easily into a normal drawer space and needs only four inches of height clearance. The width can be adjusted to anywhere between 14^{1}/$_{4}$ and 19^{5}/$_{8}$ inches.

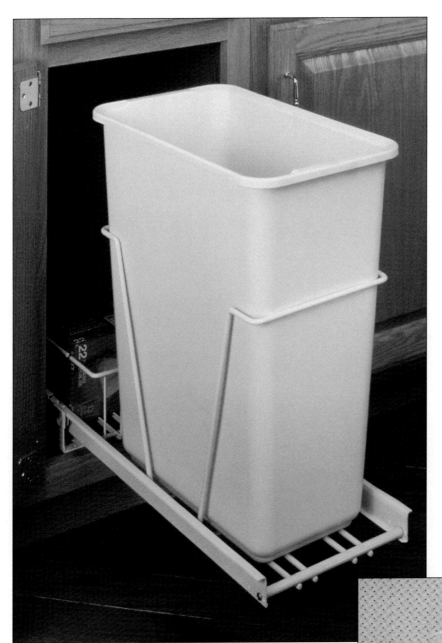

Unsightly garbage cans can be kept hidden from view but still at arm's length by installing a sliding waste container inside your kitchen cabinets. The model at left has a basket in the back of the unit that is perfect for storing a box of extra garbage bags.

The spring-top waste container at right opens to more than 90 degrees with a touch of the hand, allowing for easy disposal of large objects.

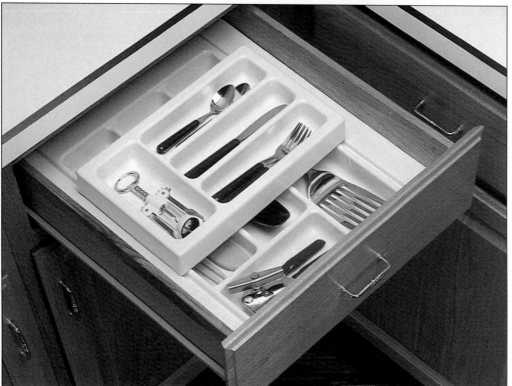

Take advantage of the normally neglected wall space between upper cabinets and kitchen counters by installing a rack system for accessories. The model shown above is brass and holds everything from cookbooks to spices, providing a decorative touch while helping to keep often-used items close at hand.

To make maximum use of your utensil drawer, try a two-tiered tray system like the one shown at left. The upper tray rolls back and forth allowing easy access to the one below.

KITCHEN DESIGN WITH STORAGE IN MIND

A kitchen is much more than a place to cook meals. In this room, you'll help your kids with homework seated at the table, cook holiday feasts, and just sit and chat over coffee and cake with friends. But if your kitchen is small, cramped, and disorganized, it will be difficult to find adequate space to enjoy these and other activities. The solution? Well laid out storage units, such as cabinets, pantry closets, and shelves.

Adding or reorganizing storage space in your kitchen is not only easy—it's smart, and, in the long run, economical. Installing a lazy Susan to win back the space lost in the corner of a bottom cabinet, for example, might allow you to buy and store dry food items in bulk—always a cheaper option. At the very least, it will make access to this space more convenient.

This chapter offers a host of ideas on how to plan for storage in a practical way. From the base map shown on page 34 to the discussion of typical kitchen layouts on page 35, you'll be able to determine what's best for your space.

The information on page 36 will help you plan upper and lower cabinet runs, and decide how to match the two. To familiarize yourself with the myriad cabinet types, shapes, and sizes available on the market today, see the section beginning on page 40. For an overview of some of the basic considerations of cabinetry, such as style, price, and quality, turn to page 43. Finally, page 47 offers a look at countertops.

From corner units with lazy Susans to countertop appliance "garages," modern cabinets maximize space in a kitchen. To learn how you can take advantage of the many different cabinet options, turn to page 40.

MAKING A BASE MAP

A base map of your kitchen, drawn to scale, may be the handiest tool to have in the planning stage. It will give you a good overview of the space you have, and will allow you to experiment with the positions of appliances, cabinets, and other features.

To make a map, use a measuring tape or a folding wooden rule. You may find the folding rule easier to use for short measurements, as it will hold its form when extended, making it easier to measure deep cabinets, for example.

Using a pencil and a plain sheet of paper, sketch your kitchen's layout—be sure to include windows, doors, counters, and fixtures. Then measure each wall at the counter height. Here's an example, using a hypothetical kitchen: Beginning in one corner, measure the distance to the outer edge of the window frame, from there to the opposite edge of the frame, from this edge to the

cabinet, and from one end of the cabinet to the corner. After measuring one wall, total the figures; then take an overall measurement from corner to corner. The two figures should match. Measure the height of each wall in the same manner. Also check corner angles with a carpenter's square.

The next step is to draw your kitchen to scale on graph paper—most kitchen designers use 1/2-inch scale (1/2 inch equals 1 foot). A T-square and triangle will also make your job easier.

The base map shown below, includes both center-lines to the sink plumbing, as well as electrical symbols for outlets, switches, and fixtures. It's also wise to note features that may affect storage, such as bearing walls and joist direction. Use the map, along with the scale cutouts of cabinets and appliances *(page 35)*, to get an overview of your kitchen before you begin work on it.

SAMPLE BASE MAP
Once you've measured room dimensions, draw the map to scale. Include details such as sinks and doors, as shown. Once complete, the base map will help you decide how to best lay out your kitchen for maximum storage and space usage.

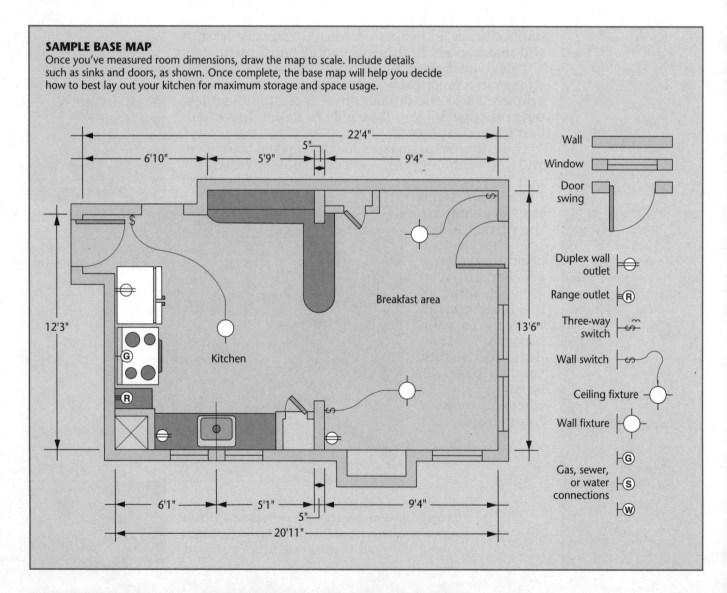

CABINET LAYOUT

When laying out any room, it's often difficult to visualize how the different features will come together. Plotting out the location of kitchen cabinets—considering all the different elements that are present—could be doubly hard. From ranges to dishwashers to cooktops, there are many items you'll have to keep in mind when planning your cabinet layout. As shown below and on the following page, there are a couple of easy methods to help you along your way.

A scale-sized plan: Make scale-sized cutouts of cabinets, ranges, sinks, and other features in the kitchen as shown below. Then sketch a scale outline of your kitchen floor, and experiment with the position of the items you want or need in the room. When you have settled on a layout that makes use of

WORKING TO SCALE

To visualize possible layouts, first trace or photocopy the scale outlines shown at right. Move the cutouts around a sketch of your kitchen floor plan until you're satisfied with the layout. Draw the floor plan to the same scale as the cutouts—½ inch equals 1 foot.

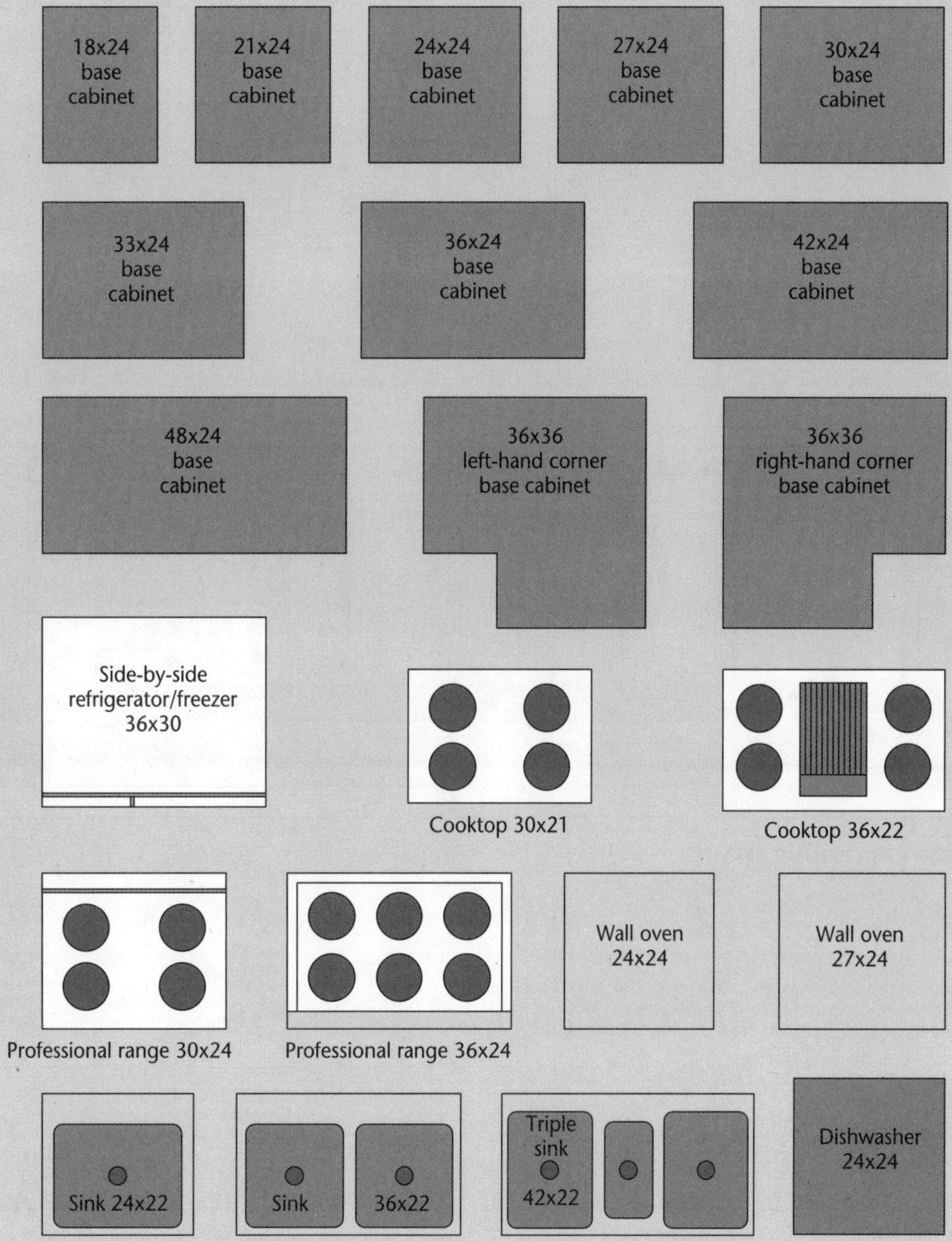

18x24 base cabinet

21x24 base cabinet

24x24 base cabinet

27x24 base cabinet

30x24 base cabinet

33x24 base cabinet

36x24 base cabinet

42x24 base cabinet

48x24 base cabinet

36x36 left-hand corner base cabinet

36x36 right-hand corner base cabinet

Side-by-side refrigerator/freezer 36x30

Cooktop 30x21

Cooktop 36x22

Wall oven 24x24

Wall oven 27x24

Professional range 30x24

Professional range 36x24

Sink 24x22

Sink

36x22

Triple sink 42x22

Dishwasher 24x24

the available space to the best advantage, trace your plan onto the "floor." You can also use this idea to organize storage areas in other rooms in the house.

Dividing cabinet runs: In general, kitchen cabinets fit the spaces between appliances. Therefore, to determine the number of cabinets in a run, measure the distance between the fridge and stove, for example, and, using the cabinet measurements below as a guideline,

divide the remaining space into units. The units are further divided into doors and drawers or, in the case of lower cabinets, both.

The kitchen layout illustrated below shows upper and lower cabinet runs that match—the edges of the doors and the handles are in alignment. For a different pattern, see the various matching examples featured at the bottom of the page.

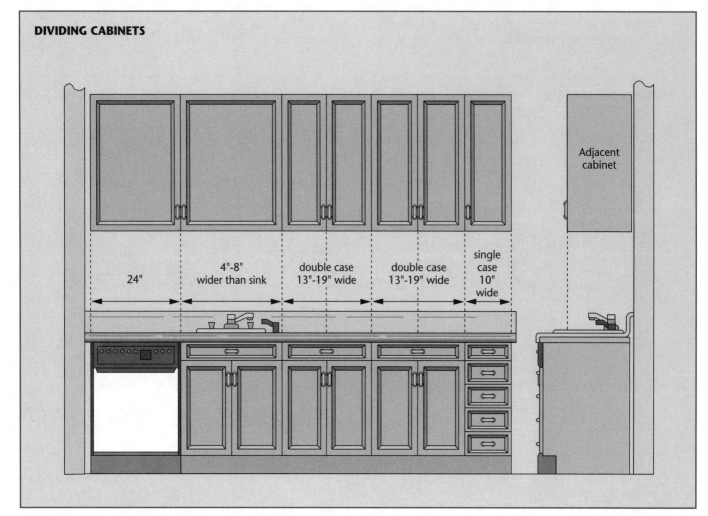

DIVIDING CABINETS

24"

4"-8" wider than sink

double case 13"-19" wide

double case 13"-19" wide

single case 10" wide

Adjacent cabinet

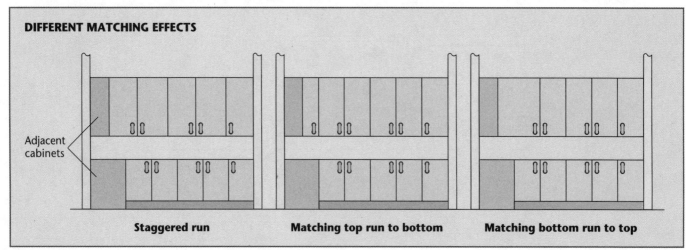

DIFFERENT MATCHING EFFECTS

Adjacent cabinets

Staggered run   **Matching top run to bottom**   **Matching bottom run to top**

FLOOR PLAN FOR UPPER AND LOWER CABINETS

Obviously when laying out a kitchen, matching cabinets for appearance is a major concern *(page 40)*. But more than just esthetics, upper and lower runs must match to accommodate appliances and fixtures. This section will show you how cabinets match up within a typical L-shaped layout.

In the overhead view shown at right, the cabinets in the lower run are indicated by the letter L; those in the upper run are marked with a U. Note how L3, the space allotted for the sink in the lower run, is matched by the window space above. As well, the stove top, L6, is matched by unit U6 which spans the entire cooking area. Remember that the corner units, especially in lower cabinet runs, can be lost storage space because they are hard to access. You might want to consider installing a lazy Susan or rotating pullout shelves.

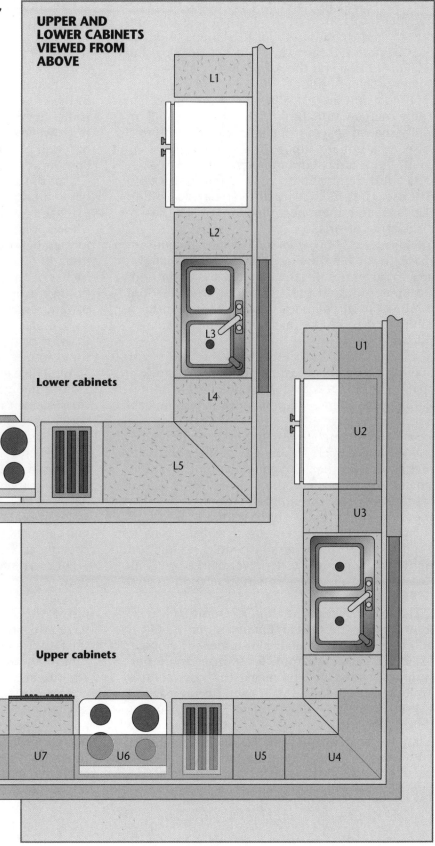

UPPER AND LOWER CABINETS VIEWED FROM ABOVE

Lower cabinets

Upper cabinets

One of the keys to planning a kitchen is to keep the five main work areas in mind—the fridge, the sink, the stove, the countertop for food preparation, and the countertop for serving—and to plan accordingly. The illustrations on the opposite page show a few practical layout options.

Listed below are guidelines for planning each area. These rules are not absolute, and in very small or oddly shaped spaces you might need to compromise. Adjacent areas may share space. Corners don't count—you can't stand in front of them.

As a rule, items should be stored in the area of first use. The one exception? Everyday dishes and flatware: store them near the point of last use—the dishwasher or sink.

Fridge area: Allow at least 15 inches of countertop space on the handle side of the fridge as a landing area for groceries. Ideally, the fridge is at the end of a cabinet run, near the access door, with the door rotating out. If you need to place a fridge inside a cabinet run, consider installing a built-in, side-by-side model.

An over-the-fridge cabinet is a good bet for infrequently used items. Custom pullouts or a stock "pantry pack" are a hit for the tall, narrow spot flanking the fridge. For more information on cabinets, turn to page 40.

Sink area: Figure a minimum of 24 inches of counter space open on one side of the sink and 36 inches on the other. (If you're planning a second, smaller sink elsewhere, those clearances can be less.) It's best to locate the sink and cleanup area between the fridge and the stove or cooktop.

Traditionally, designers place the dishwasher for a right-hander to the left of the sink area and to the right for a lefty. But do whatever makes you comfortable. Consider the location in relation to your serving area.

Plan to store cleaning supplies in the sink area. A large variety of bins and pullouts—both built-ins and retrofits—are available for undersink storage (*page 54*). Tilt-down fronts for sponges and other supplies are available on many sink base cabinets. To learn how to install your own, turn to page 55.

Stove area: You'll need at least 12 inches of countertop space on each side of the stove or cooktop as a landing area for hot pots and casseroles, and to allow for pot handles to be turned to the sides while pots are in use. If the cooktop is on an island or peninsula, the same rule applies.

You should also allow for 15 inches of countertop on one or both sides of a wall oven. Typically, stacked wall ovens are found at the end of a cabinet run; if they're in the middle, allow 15 inches on both sides.

Although we think of a microwave oven as part of the cooking area, many people prefer it near the fridge/freezer or in the serving area. Mount the microwave inside an oven cabinet, on the underside of a wall cabinet, or just below the countertop in a base run or an island.

Plan to store frequently used pots and pans in base pullout drawers mounted on heavy-duty, full-extension drawer guides.

Food preparation area: This auxiliary area is ideally located between the fridge and sink; plan a minimum of 42 inches of countertop, a maximum of 84 inches. Although it may not be a good idea to raise or lower countertop heights (if you have an eye toward resale, that is), the food preparation area is a good place to customize. A marble countertop insert is a great feature for the serious pastry chef, for example.

Appliance garages with tambour or paneled doors are still popular in this area. (Be sure to add electrical outlets in the recess.) If you need a place for spices or staples, consider an open shelf or backsplash rack—both provide a nice accent. For more on food and spice storage, turn to the section beginning on page 62.

Serving area: If you have the room, locate this optional area between the range and the sink if possible; size it between 36 and 84 inches (remember, you can save space here with both cleanup and cooking areas).

For convenience, everyday dishes, glassware, flatware, serving plates, and bowls, as well as napkins and placemats, should be kept in this area. The dishwasher should be nearby; some models even have integral trays that can be placed right into the flatware drawer.

Auxiliary areas: In modern kitchens, there are three additional options that have become so popular they are quickly gaining unofficial status as main kitchen work areas—the breakfast/dining area, the menu planning/office area, and the built-in pantry or wine cellar. Before you solidify your plans—and providing you have the extra space, of course—think about including one or more of these useful areas in your kitchen.

SMART KITCHEN LAYOUTS

The average kitchen will have an area to prepare food, another place to enjoy the meal, and yet another for cleanup. Within this space, the fridge, stove, and sink are all key points in what's commonly known as the kitchen work triangle.

When planning any kitchen, it's best to consider the work triangle that works best for you, then organize your kitchen cabinets around it. Although the reign of the work triangle is being challenged by two-cook layouts, peninsulas, elaborate island work centers, and specialized appliances, it is still a valuable starting point for any kitchen design. For efficiency, you'll want to situate the cabinet holding the baking pans close to the oven, for example.

Keep in mind that the smaller you make the triangle the better—the ideal sum of the three legs is between 12 and 23 feet—as it will cut down on the amount of walking during food preparation time.

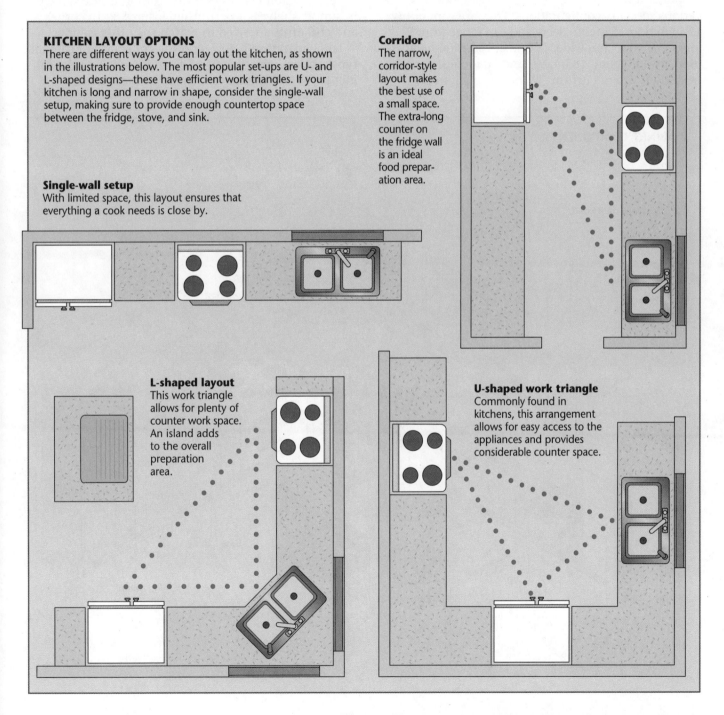

KITCHEN LAYOUT OPTIONS
There are different ways you can lay out the kitchen, as shown in the illustrations below. The most popular set-ups are U- and L-shaped designs—these have efficient work triangles. If your kitchen is long and narrow in shape, consider the single-wall setup, making sure to provide enough countertop space between the fridge, stove, and sink.

Single-wall setup
With limited space, this layout ensures that everything a cook needs is close by.

Corridor
The narrow, corridor-style layout makes the best use of a small space. The extra-long counter on the fridge wall is an ideal food preparation area.

L-shaped layout
This work triangle allows for plenty of counter work space. An island adds to the overall preparation area.

U-shaped work triangle
Commonly found in kitchens, this arrangement allows for easy access to the appliances and provides considerable counter space.

A COLLECTION OF CABINETS

Although kitchen cabinets come in a host of different styles, materials, and colors, a typical kitchen will contain variations of two standard cabinet types: base units that rest on the floor, and wall cabinets that are hung onto the walls. These, along with end and corner units, are used to design upper and lower cabinet runs. Additionally, there are also tall utility units, bases to hold sinks, and matching facades for dishwashers, refrigerators, and other appliances.

Standard wall cabinets come in singles, doubles, and various specialty configurations. They are commonly 12 inches to 15 inches deep, and can range from 9 inches to 60 inches wide. The most common heights used are 15 inches, 18 inches, and 30 inches, but cabinet height can range from 12 inches to 36 inches.

Base cabinets, complete with a toe kick, normally measure $34^1/_2$ inches tall, with another $1^1/_2$ inches tacked on for the counter. They vary from 9 inches to 60 inches wide. Standard depth is 24 inches. A typical base cabinet includes a drawer above a shelf with a door, but there are variations.

Corner units best serve angled and corner spaces. With curved doors, tamboured appliance garages, and lazy Susans, hard-to-reach spots are made more accessible. End cabinets offer handy front and side storage in simple shelves or narrow enclosures. Both corner and end units are sized to match the other cabinets.

The illustration below, and the collection of cabinet types shown opposite, provide an overview of the cabinet types and the role they play in the kitchen.

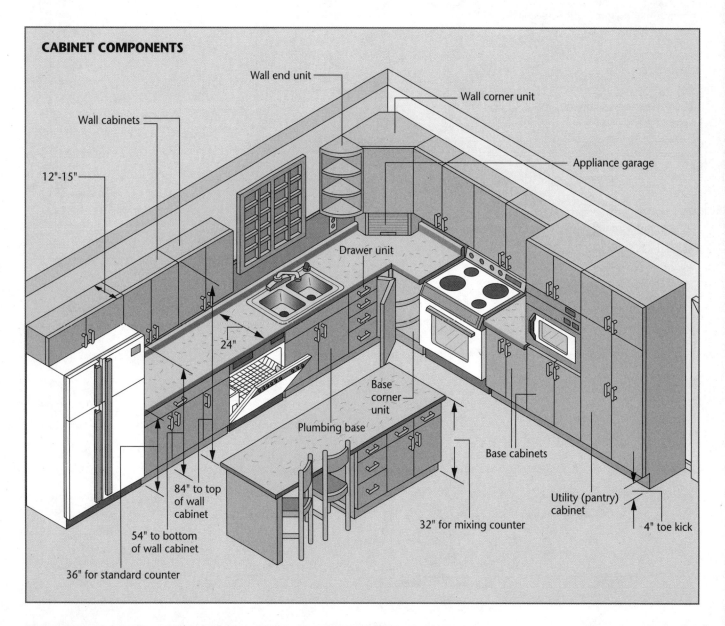

CABINET COMPONENTS

Wall end unit
Wall corner unit
Wall cabinets
Appliance garage
12"-15"
Drawer unit
24"
Base corner unit
Plumbing base
Base cabinets
84" to top of wall cabinet
54" to bottom of wall cabinet
36" for standard counter
32" for mixing counter
Utility (pantry) cabinet
4" toe kick

STANDARD WALL CABINETS

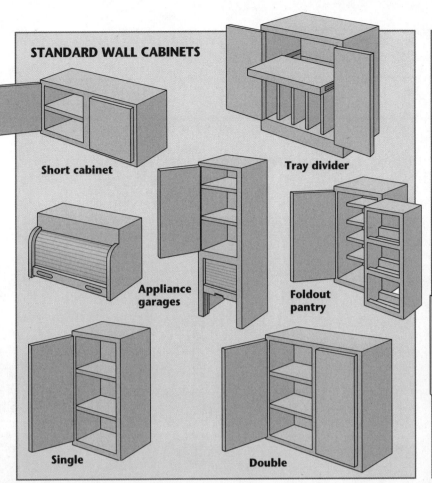

Short cabinet

Tray divider

Appliance garages

Foldout pantry

Single

Double

WALL CORNER UNITS

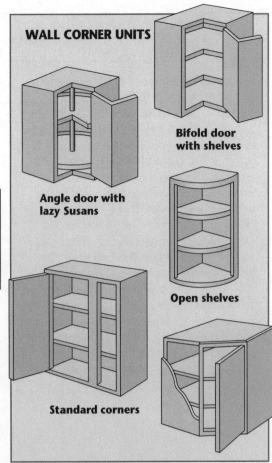

Bifold door with shelves

Angle door with lazy Susans

Open shelves

Standard corners

BASE CABINETS

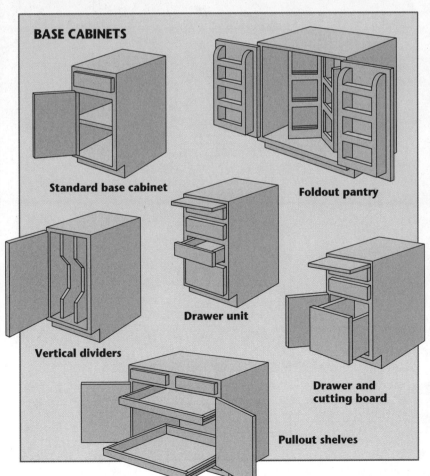

Standard base cabinet

Foldout pantry

Drawer unit

Vertical dividers

Drawer and cutting board

Pullout shelves

BASE CORNER AND ENDS

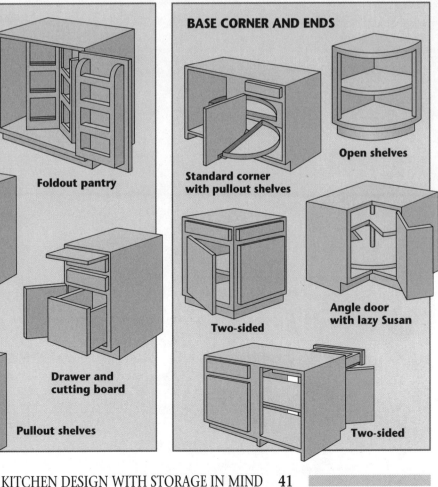

Standard corner with pullout shelves

Open shelves

Two-sided

Angle door with lazy Susan

Two-sided

Dimensions for upper and lower cabinets, as well as those for the countertop and backsplash, are shown at right. Use these as a guideline to help you determine the dimensions for your own kitchen.

Kitchen cabinets can range in size and depth—as long as they match, and no one cabinet is blocking the accessibility to another, or to a work space, there should be no problems.

A quick and easy guide for upper cabinet height is to place the bottom of the lowest cabinet at shoulder height—keep in mind that units over the sink and stove will have to be placed higher, but the tops must still align. Leave enough room at the top of the cabinets for decorative molding or a valance. To learn how to lay out cabinets, turn to page 37. To match the upper and lower runs see page 36.

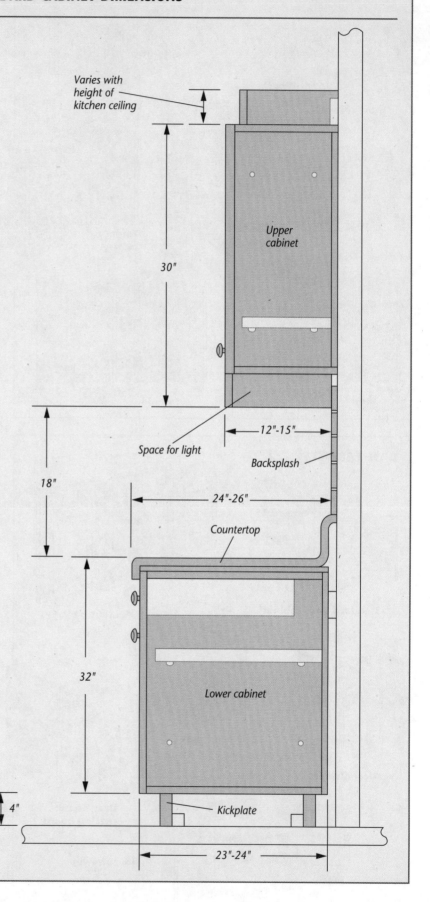

Varies with height of kitchen ceiling

Upper cabinet

30"

12"-15"

Space for light

Backsplash

18"

24"-26"

Countertop

32"

Lower cabinet

4"

Kickplate

23"-24"

THE RIGHT CABINETS FOR YOUR KITCHEN

The theory and planning that's required in kitchen cabinet layout is essential, but there comes a time when pencils, measuring tapes, and sketches are set aside and the process of building or buying your cabinets begins.

Before you commit yourself to a certain style of cabinet—there are many to choose from—you'd be wise to arm yourself with as much information as possible. Cabinets have a greater impact on a kitchen's design than any other element—you don't want to regret your decision in a few years because you were uninformed and chose too quickly.

You will have to choose between traditional or European-style cabinets, and also decide whether you want custom, stock, or custom modular. These units are available at most home centers. It's best to find a knowledgeable salesperson to help you out, and ask questions about durability, compatibility with other units you may already have in the kitchen, ease of installation, and other concerns you may have.

Kitchen cabinet showrooms are the best places to view the many different styles—there are often prominent, well-designed displays of these and other kitchen storage ideas. Ask if the store offers complete design services, or look in the yellow pages for someone who can help.

TRADITIONAL OR EUROPEAN STYLE?
The traditional style, also called faceframe, has long been a common choice of kitchen cabinet designers in North America. Recently, however, the European-style, or frameless, system has been making inroads. This system was developed after the World War II to provide an economical, standardized way to build cabinets. Both are described in more detail below and illustrated on page 44.

Faceframe cabinets: These units have a 1x2 frame that masks the raw edges of the front, or face, of each cabinet box. As well, doors and drawers are fitted to be flush, partially inset with a notch, or completely overlaying the frame.

A major advantage of faceframe cabinets is that you can use thin or low-quality stock for the sides, since the frame will be covering the edge anyway; this reduces the cost considerably. The downside is that the frame takes up space that could otherwise be used inside for storage. The front opening is noticeably smaller, so the drawers and other slide-out accessories must be scaled down to accommodate this. As well, door hinges are easily visible from the front of the cabinet.

Frameless cabinets: European kitchens have traditionally been small, with every inch of space used to

maximum advantage. Because of this, frameless cabinets, which take these relatively cramped working areas into account, became popular. Eager to adopt these space-saving qualities on this side of the Atlantic, North Americans have caught on to this style of cabinetry. These modular units are now as common as faceframe assemblies.

Frameless cabinets have a simple narrow strip which covers raw panel edges that butt against each other. The doors, drawers, and other hardware accessories mount directly to the inside faces of the units; the hinges are almost never seen when the door is closed. As well, not much trim is visible on these cabinets, as doors and drawers are typically mounted no further that $1/4$ inch apart. Drawers, sliding shelves, and other interior components can be almost as big as the frame itself, so very little storage room is lost.

Each component in a frameless cabinet is standardized, so you can plug add-ons right into any of the precise holes drilled on their inside faces. Cabinet names and measurements reflect the metric system which predominates in Europe—"system 32" or "32 millimeter" refer to the distance between all holes, hinge fittings, cabinet joints, and mounts.

CUSTOM, STOCK, OR CUSTOM MODULAR?
Manufactured cabinets are sold in three different ways: custom, stock, or custom modular. The type you decide on will affect the overall cost of your remodeling, the appearance and accessibility of items in the kitchen, and cooking space.

Stock cabinets: These mass-produced standard-size cabinets are the most cost-efficient choice, but the availability of nontypical sizes is limited. However, if you clearly understand the cabinetry needed for your kitchen, they may be ideal.

The direction of door swing, as well as the door style, and finished or unfinished side panels are all choices you have to work with. Add-ons like breadboards, sliding shelves, special corner units, and cabinets for peninsulas or islands—with doors or drawers on both sides, and appropriate toe places, trim, and finishes—are all more options that will allow you to maintain some personal choice in the final look of your stock cabinets.

Custom cabinets: Custom cabinet shops still abound because people enjoy the convenience of having a professional come to their home, measure the space that will be filled with cabinets, ask exactly what the homeowner has in mind, then return with custom-built units ready to install.

These shop workers can match old cabinets, build assemblies to the same dimensions as old family heirlooms, and accommodate complexities that can't be handled with stock or modular cabinets. The only hitch is that this might be an expensive way to outfit your kitchen. Like everything else, it's a good idea to shop around. Get quotes from several different shops before choosing one.

Many cabinetmakers use stock parts, such as door and drawer fronts, from the manufacturers of the stock units, as well as the same high-quality hardware and accessories used in modular systems—all this keeps prices reasonable.

There are also cabinetmakers and specialized shops that take old units and give them a makeover—by refacing them. This is an economical, environmentally conscious alternative to replacing old cabinets entirely. And the results can often be indistinguishable from new cabinets.

Custom modular cabinets: These units fall in between stock and custom-made cabinetry and are sometimes referred to as custom systems. Although they are manufactured, they are of a higher quality

and offer more design flexibility than stock cabinets. Not surprisingly, they cost more, too.

Custom systems come in a wide range of sizes, with many options available within each size. A good modular cabinetmaking shop can do all but truly custom work, using its own components to build a kitchen from finished units. By modifying modular components, you come very close to the results created by custom cabinetry.

There is almost nothing you can't modify on these basic modules. If there is too much unused room in the base of a particular cabinet, why not add another shelf? Maybe you feel that drawers take up too much space or are too confining. Simply remove them and attach a swinging door which opens to reveal a set of inner compartments, for example. You can add appliance garages, pullout pantries, or anything else that suits your storage needs. See page 40 for a selection of different cabinets.

The beauty of these versatile custom systems lies in the fact that you can modify basic dimensions to fit

Traditional and European cabinets

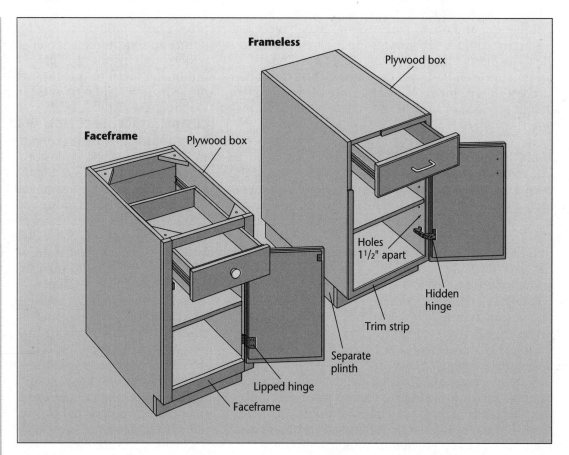

Faceframe vs. frameless
Traditional faceframe cabinets, as shown above left, have a wooden frame that covers the cabinet's front edges. European-style cabinets *(above, right)* eliminate the frame. This results in a simpler, more flexible system which uses the available space more efficiently. Even the door, attached with a hidden hinge instead of a lipped hinge, allows for easier access to the storage area.

practically any kitchen style and size. Because the height, width, and depth can be changed, the cabinets can be adjusted to practically any size—there is no need for wasted space.

Though frameless modular cabinets are sized using the metric system, manufacturers design their units to fit North American appliance standards. Sizes break into about 3-inch increments, with custom dimensions available.

OTHER CONSIDERATIONS

Apart from choosing between traditional and European style, and deciding on custom, stock, or custom modular, there are just a few other points—such as price and finding help—to take into consideration when selecting your kitchen cabinets. The information below and the chart on page 46 should help you in these and other matters.

Units for corner spaces: More options exist for corners than for any other kitchen cabinet space. Units designed specifically for corners make the best use of available space. The simplest corner pieces butt one cabinet up against another, which cuts off easy access to the corner. A better choice would be diagonal units with a larger door, or double-door units which provide full access to the space. You might also want to add lazy Susans or other slide-out accessories (page 41) so items that were previously hard-to-reach are now easily at hand.

Quality check: Determine the quality of your cabinetry by examining the drawers—they are subject to the most wear and tear of any part of the unit. Compare the drawers of several different makes, and you'll likely see that joinery and quality differences are apparent.

If drawer guides and cabinet hinges are not adjustable—you should be able to fine-tune them with the cabinets in place—then you will likely run into problems later. With some frameless units, adjustable mounting hardware lets you relevel the cabinets even after you've installed them. Check that drawer glides allow full extension of drawers, and that doors and drawers are properly aligned.

Service help: Simply deciding on the look and layout of your kitchen cabinets is not enough. Part of the cost of some of these items, most notably custom and custom modular cabinets, includes service and installation help.

A kitchen designer can help you figure out how to make best use of your space. Some retailers will ask you to fill out a survey so that they can zero in on the improvements you need for your kitchen—you might need a specialty area for cooking, or an extra-large dining area for entertaining guests. As well, you may need extra space in the form of pantries for storing bulk food purchases. All these needs should be taken into consideration to help weigh your options.

Go to a showroom which displays many lines of cabinets—you'll get a more complete picture of what is out there, and what you want. Find a designer whose tastes coincide with your own, then together you can choose a look and search for the items that fit nicely into your concept of an ideal kitchen. The designer can also help you find reasonably priced units with high-quality craftsmanship. If you're serious about buying, make arrangements to meet a designer or a cabinetmaker in a showroom. Some places will also carry the other kitchen components you may need, such as counters, sinks, appliances, and fixtures.

Some designers may have contracts to promote a particular cabinet product line, so don't rely on one opinion alone. See a few different people, and ask if they are truly independent contractors. Bring a copy of your base plan map *(page 34)* as well as the floor plan you devised for cabinet placement *(page 37)*. Some designers will prefer to create their own cabinet plan. In fact, some retailers offer a complete kitchen planning service when you purchase their products. This may even include computer printouts and graphics to help customers visualize their finished kitchen.

If budget is a big concern, try shopping in places where design services aren't necessarily tacked onto the price of the cabinets. But remember that with a less expensive price tag comes more personal responsibility—you'll have to be extra keen about the accuracy of each step, and not rely as heavily on an expert's advice.

Pricing units: Many factors influence the final price of kitchen cabinets; prices range from a few hundred dollars for simple layouts, to tens of thousands of dollars for elaborate plans. As a starting point, look at the "Figuring cost" entry in the chart on page 46.

The wide range of prices and styles can make buying cabinets a little tricky. But as long as you have your floor plan sketched out, personal style chosen, and budget considerations in mind, you should have no trouble getting a base price for appropriate standard cabinets. These prices are determined by the style of the doors and drawers, as well as the materials used in the construction of the basic carcass. But remember that each option and add-on will alter the original quoted price.

Make sure that you specifically ask about the prices of these fully loaded units, and don't be led astray by last-minute impulse buying. Even if you're buying manufactured cabinets, get an estimate from a custom shop for comparison. Such a shop can match practically any style or can come up with a pattern or finish not available in a modular or stock line. A cabinetmaker will come to your home to measure your kitchen and give you a price quotation; generally, there is no charge for this.

Evaluating the cabinets: In many showrooms, you can get a general idea of layout and cost by touring the sample kitchens on display. In this regard, a good showroom has an advantage over most custom shops: You can see many of the possibilities set up in one place. You can also get a better idea of the cost of each component by checking the sticker price or asking a salesperson. As with stock and custom modular orders, make sure your plan is specific and clear. This will give you an idea of the number of cabinets you need, and also allow the sales professionals in the showroom to make suggestions.

COMPARING CABINETS

	Stock	Custom	Custom modular
Availability	Lumberyards, home improvement centers, appliance stores, some showrooms.	Shops don't usually have showrooms; most just show pictures of previously completed jobs. Visit the shop and some installations, too.	Check the yellow pages for the names of top-quality manufacturers. These cabinets are mainly showroom items, but you can find some in stock locations and kitchen design centers.
Designer	Some stock cabinet outlets have complete design services. At less specialized stores, you may have to rely on your efforts at design.	You; your architect, builder, or designer; or the maker (but be careful; cabinetmakers aren't necessarily kitchen designers).	The better (and more expensive) the line, the more help you get. Top-of-the-line suppliers design your whole kitchen; you just pick the style and write the check.
Quality	Less expensive product lines often use doors and other hardware of mismatched or lower-quality woods, composite, or thinner laminates that simulate the look of wood.	Depends on your specifications. Assembly methods vary with cabinetmaker; look at door and drawer hardware in a finished sample.	Usually high-quality and durable. Often use factory applied laminates and catalyzed varnishes. Medium-density fiberboard is a good alternative for areas that don't show.
Options	Only options may be door styles, hardware, and which way doors swing—but check the catalog; some lines offer a surprising range.	You can often—but not always—get the same options and European-made hardware that go in custom modular cabinets.	Most lines offer choices galore—including variations in basic sizes and options for corner spaces. Check showrooms and study catalogs.
Figuring cost	Cheapest of the three, but by no means inexpensive. Check home centers for discounts and end-of season sales, but pay attention to quality and craftsmanship.	Range varies depending on materials, finishes, craftsmanship, and added options.	Cost of a basic box will be about equal to that of raw stock, but every modification or upgrade in door and drawer finishes considerably increases overall price.
Waiting period	Generally shorter than for other categories. Warehouse centers can have units ready the same day you order them.	Five weeks or longer, depending on job complexity, material and hardware availability, number of drawers, and finishes.	Five to eight weeks, although some deliveries have been known to take up to six months. It's best to order as soon as you figure out what you need and can afford.
Getting help	Depending on where you buy, the supplier may recommend a contractor for installation. You can otherwise put cabinets in yourself. There is virtually no service available, though.	The cabinetmaker installs and services in most cases. Ask around before contracting out any work.	If you're willing to pay more, you can buy products that include service and installation in the price. Some of these cabinets have lifetime guarantees.
General notes	Be prepared to pay in full up front; there's little recourse if cabinets are damaged during shipment. Be sure the order is absolutely correct and complete.	Make sure the bid you accept is complete, not just a cost-per-foot or cost-per-box charge.	With some manufacturers, any incorrect pieces or shipments will translate to a long waiting period for you. Check beforehand to ensure that you won't be waiting for the right parts to arrive later.

COUNTERTOP TYPES

Few other surfaces in the home are subject to as much wear and tear as the kitchen countertop. Whether it's being used as an unloading area for groceries, a cutting board for mealtime preparation, or a place to stack dishes temporarily, this area is never left bare for very long. When it comes time to choose a counter to top off your kitchen cabinets, you should make your selection carefully. The information in the chart below (and continued on page 48) will help you make the best choice for your situation.

Keep in mind that there is no miracle countertop surface that will be right for every family and every need; each material has distinct advantages and disadvantages you should weigh. You may even want to think about installing a combination of surfaces—such as a smooth stone board for kneading and rolling pie dough, and a heat-resistant ceramic tile near the stove. Consider that some professional chefs prefer stainless steel, marble, or granite. Wood is also a popular choice, but there can be problems with keeping it clean.

Of course, cost is always a major consideration, whether you're choosing cabinet design or a countertop. There's no sense in planning for a granite or stainless steel finish if the most you can afford is plastic laminate or wood. A compromise would be to have a small section of the more expensive material integrated into a countertop made of a more cost-efficient finish.

When choosing a countertop, don't forget the backsplash—the wall surface between the counter and the upper wall cabinets. As the name implies, it guards the wall against moisture that develops as a result of food preparation or cleanup. These surfaces can range from a couple of inches high to a foot or more. Although factory-made laminate countertops come with the backsplash already installed, ceramic tile is a popular material to use if you're making your own.

Don't expect to find all the countertop choices in one place. Check out the showrooms at various dealers, building supply centers, and lumberyards. Designers and architects often have samples of the various materials.

COMPARING COUNTERTOPS

	Advantages	Disadvantages	Cost
Plastic laminate	It's the most popular choice, so it is readily available. Choose from a wide range of colors, textures, and patterns. Laminate is durable, easy to clean, water-resistant, and relatively inexpensive. With the proper tools and know-how, you can install it yourself with no trouble.	Because it's so thin, it's virtually impossible to shape and mold around awkward corners and countertop layouts. It can also be very hard to repair. It's easily scratched, scorched, chipped, and stained. Conventional varieties have a dark backing strip that shows at its seams, and newer laminates designed to avoid this are somewhat brittle and more expensive.	Standard brands range from $1 to $3.50 per square foot, whereas pre-molded, particleboard-backed tops cost $5 to $10 per running foot. Having a custom countertop with a 2" lip and low backsplash can cost from $40 to $100, and even more for solid-color materials.
Ceramic tile	Good-looking, comes in many colors, textures, patterns, and finishes. It's heat-proof, scratch-resistant, and water-resistant if installed properly. You can also get grout to match the surface color. If you're patient, you can install this yourself.	If you don't install with high-quality epoxy grout between the tiles, the grout can stain and develop mildew. Some kitchen designers recommend using less grout space—$3/32$" versus the typical $1/4$"—but this thinner joint is weaker. Grout sealers may not always be effective. Hard, irregular surfaces can also chip glasses and china. As well, high-gloss tiles show every smudge.	Prices can range from 50 cents to over $50 per square foot. It's best to choose nonporous glazed tiles which won't soak up kitchen spills and stains. Cost of installation varies, depending on tile type and the size of the job. But generally, smaller countertops are more expensive, based on per-foot cost, to install.

	Advantages	Disadvantages	Cost
Solid surface	It's durable, water- and heat-resistant, nonporous, and easy to clean. You can shape and install this marble-like material, but be careful, as woodworking tools can cause cracks, particularly around cutouts. It can also be joined or repaired with no visible seams. You can easily sand out any blemishes or scratches. It allows for a variety of sink installations and fittings.	It can be expensive, and requires sturdy support underneath.	Expect to pay between $100 and over $150 per running foot for a 24"-deep counter with a 2" front lip and 4" back-splash, installation price included. The cost is about half if you do it yourself. Costs are higher still for wood inlays and other fancy edge details.
Wood	It's nice-looking, natural, easy to install, and won't chip glasses, dishes, and fine china. It's well suited for old-fashioned, rustic kitchen styles. Ideal as a chopping or cutting board insert.	It's the least durable of all the choices, and harder to keep clean than nonporous materials. It can scorch and scratch, and become dark or black if it is too near a sink or another source of moisture. Seal it with mineral oil, but do both sides or the counter may warp. If using it as an insert, make this removable for easier cleaning and resurfacing. If you use a permanent protective sealer like polyurethane, you won't be able to use it as a cutting surface.	The most popular choice, maple butcher block, can cost from $12 to over $16 per square foot for a $1\frac{1}{2}$"- to $1\frac{3}{4}$"-thick countertop. It will cost more than $50 per running foot, including miters and cutouts, to have it installed. Buy it in 24"-, 30"-, and 36"-wide slabs. You can also get smaller pieces for inserts.
Stainless steel	It's waterproof, heat-resistant, easy on cleanups, seamless, and very durable. You can even get a counter with a sink molded right in. Use it especially near the sink, or any other part of the kitchen where you'll be using a lot of water.	It's not ideal as a cutting surface, since you're likely to damage both the surface and your knife. It's expensive, but you can reduce the cost by using flat sheeting and a wood edge, as shown *(left)*.	For a $\frac{1}{16}$"-thick, 16-gauge countertop, expect to pay upwards of $5.50 per square foot, not including installation costs. With sink and faucet cutouts, and shaping around back-splashes, you're looking at three to six hours of fabrication time, at $45 per hour for an installed 6'- to 10'-long counter. Custom detailing and high-chromium stainless can be as high as $500 per running foot.
Stone	Granite and marble are both beautiful, natural materials. These cool, smooth surfaces are ideal for working with dough or making your own confections and candies. They're heat-proof, water-resistant, durable, and easy to clean.	Very expensive. Some home-owners and designers have turned to stone tiles—including slate and limestone—to cut back on cost. It needs to be professionally cut and polished, and is very hard to install yourself. Oil, alcohol, and food and other acids will stain marble or damage its high-gloss finish, whereas granite is unaffected.	Polished and finished with a square or slightly beveled edge, a custom-cut granite slab will cost more than $60 per square foot, whereas marble will range from $40 to over $70. Decorative edge details and other extras are more expensive. Marble counter inserts can run from $30 to over $45 per square foot. Expect installation to cost at least $75 an hour.

KITCHEN STORAGE IDEAS

While the well-designed kitchen is less likely to fall into disarray, layout alone cannot guarantee neatness. To win the battle against clutter, particularly in this, the busiest room in the home, you will also need to employ some of the storage devices and space savers shown in the following pages.

The first step in evaluating your storage options is to take a detailed inventory of your kitchen. Ask yourself which items require storage and how they could best be stored to maximize space and convenience. Then leaf through this chapter. It contains dozens of practical and creative solutions to your kitchen storage needs.

Appliances, small or large, are the most unwieldy of kitchen items and require some of the most ingenious storage methods. A selection of storage ideas for appliances begins on page 50.

Ideas for stashing the myriad cleaning supplies that make their home around the sink are shown on page 54. For help in coping with cutlery, flatware, and other utensils, turn to page 56. For bottles, dishes, and glassware, see page 58.

A selection of ideas for storing food is highlighted starting on page 62. Linens are tackled on page 67; the section on cooking and serving equipment starts on page 68. Last, but certainly not least, ideas for trash containers are featured on page 71.

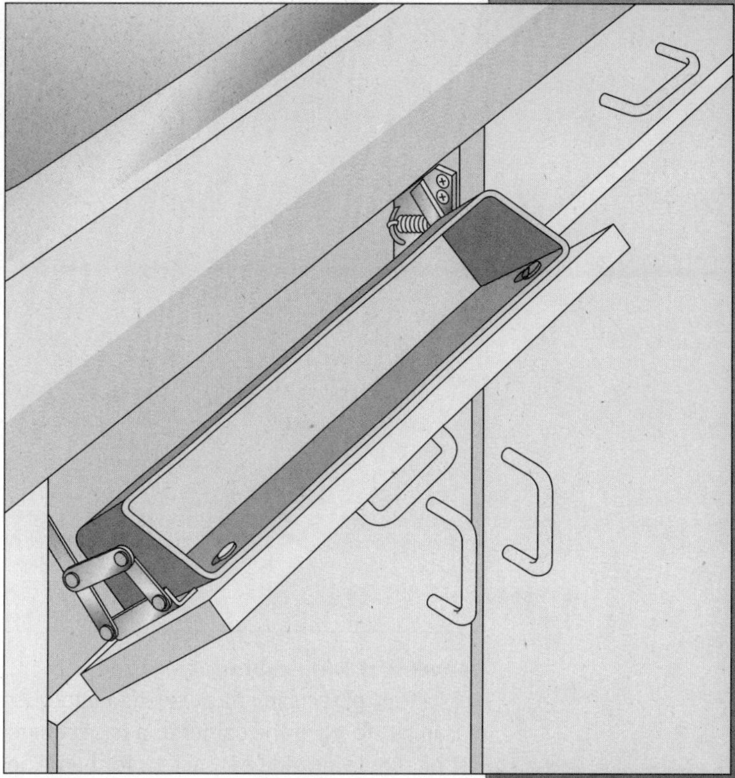

The handy tilt-out tray shown at right is a smart way to store sponges and scouring pads close to the sink but out of sight. For more on installing the tray, turn to page 55.

STORING APPLIANCES

As long as people strive to find more efficient ways of preparing food, new appliances will continue to clutter our kitchens—the sheer number in most kitchens today makes a thoughtful storage strategy a must. The storage ideas featured below and on the following pages will help you get a handle on these modern necessities.

The key to storing appliances successfully is to take into account how often you use them. Toasters, coffee makers, and other kitchen workhorses must be easily accessible. Waffle irons, slow cookers, and the like may receive less frequent use, and can be stored in more out-of-the-way spots. Space-saving ideas for both groups are offered here and on page 52.

A large machine like a top-load washing machine, need not monopolize the kitchen. In fact, by using the novel idea shown at the bottom of page 52 you can gain some additional counter space.

Storing appliances

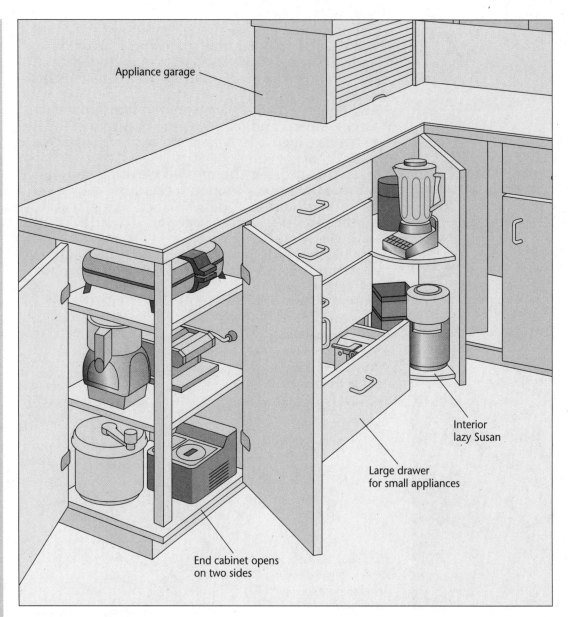

Appliance garage

Interior lazy Susan

Large drawer for small appliances

End cabinet opens on two sides

Convenient base cabinet storage

Appliances, particularly those needed infrequently, can be stored in the corner of a base cabinet—just be sure to provide easy access for handling their large, bulky shapes. An interior corner cabinet with lazy Susan, and an end cabinet with doors that open on two sides, are also good spots. Large, lower drawers can hold really small appliances, such as an electric can opener.

PULLOUTS, SWING-UPS AND SPACE SAVERS

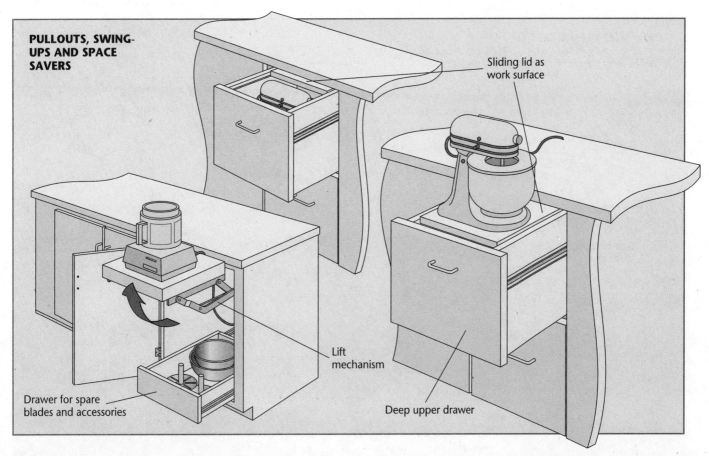

Sliding lid as work surface

Lift mechanism

Drawer for spare blades and accessories

Deep upper drawer

SMALL APPLIANCE STORAGE IDEAS

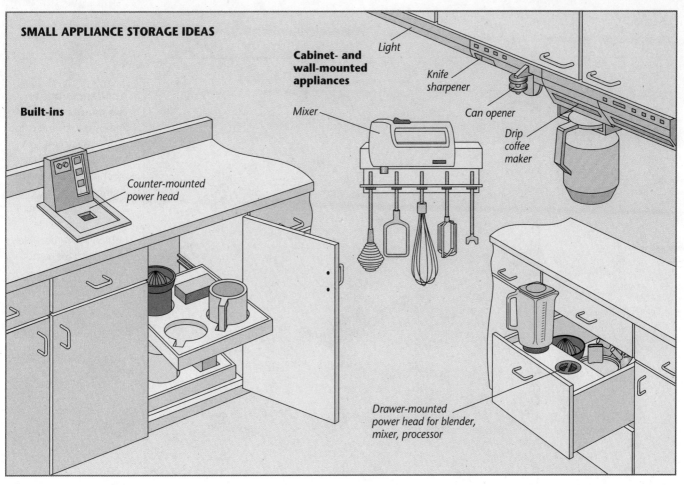

Built-ins

Counter-mounted power head

Cabinet- and wall-mounted appliances

Mixer

Light

Knife sharpener

Can opener

Drip coffee maker

Drawer-mounted power head for blender, mixer, processor

APPLIANCES BEHIND DOORS

Doors that work best for enclosing small appliances are those that stay out of the way when they are open.

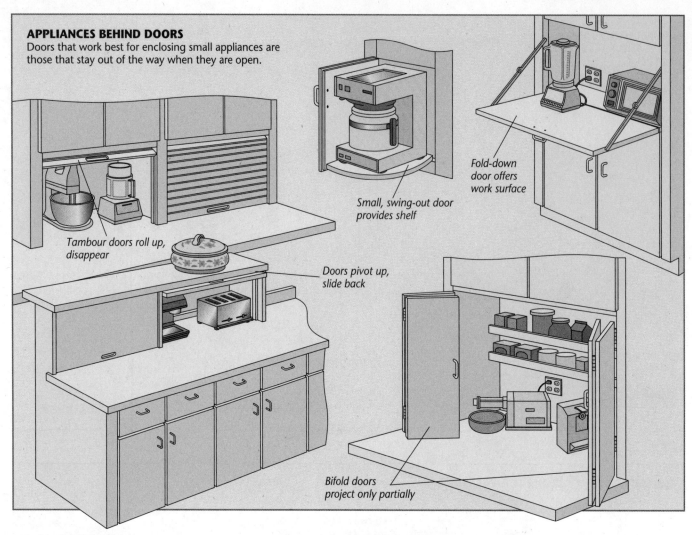

Tambour doors roll up, disappear

Small, swing-out door provides shelf

Fold-down door offers work surface

Doors pivot up, slide back

Bifold doors project only partially

Storing appliances

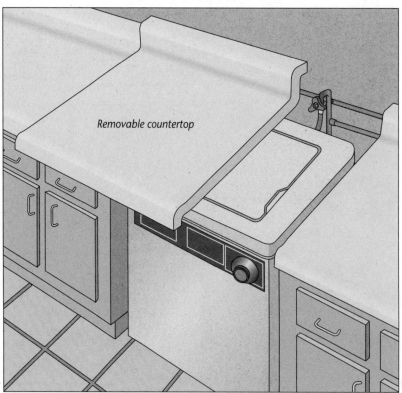

Removable countertop

Appliances under the countertop

Removable countertops allow easy access to a top-load washing machine; they provide counter space when the unit is not in use. For a unified appearance, fashion the removable piece from the same material as the surrounding countertop.

Because it is filled with machines, utensils, appliances, and other tools, the kitchen can be a dangerous place, particularly for young children. More children's lives are lost in home accidents than from all childhood diseases combined. Attention to safety is a must. To make your kitchen a safer place, consider taking the following important precautions:

• Install a smoke detector between the kitchen and living areas. Also mount a Class A-B-C fire extinguisher near the exit, no closer than 6 feet from the range.

• Store flammables away from heat.

• Clean the cooking area frequently; grease buildup can be a fire hazard. Extinguish a grease fire in a pan by placing a lid over the pan and turning off the heat. *Never try to put out a grease fire with water.*

• When cooking, wear trim-fitting clothes and use pot holders designed for the purpose. Loose sleeves and dish towels can catch fire.

• Natural and LP gas are scented to alert you to leaks. In the event of a leak or service interruption, evacuate the house and call your utility company immediately.

Do not turn on electrical switches or appliances if you suspect a leak.

• Use properly grounded outlets with adequate fuses or properly sized circuit breakers. (Ground fault circuit interrupter receptacles are required by many local codes.) Do not overload circuits.

• Unplug appliances immediately after use. Keep them away from water and never touch water while using them.

IF YOU HAVE SMALL CHILDREN

• Keep young children out from underfoot when working in the kitchen.

• Pick up and store anything that might be hazardous to your baby—small, sharp, breakable, or poisonous objects.

• Remove dangerous items from cabinets within your child's reach. Put garbage in a container with a hard-to-open lid or in a low cabinet with a child-resistant latch on that door. Never leave chemical products within children's reach. Never store them in containers that originally held food or beverages. Move liquor to a cabinet with a child-resistant latch or to an out-of-reach spot.

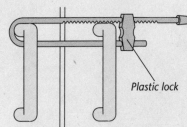

Plastic lock

Keeping doors closed
Where pulls pair up, the simple plastic lock (*above*) secures them together. Spring-loaded latches (*below*) screw easily onto the doors. When shut, the latch hooks to the underside of cabinet rail, allowing the door to open only far enough for adult pressure to release it.

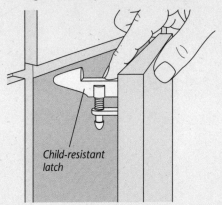

Child-resistant latch

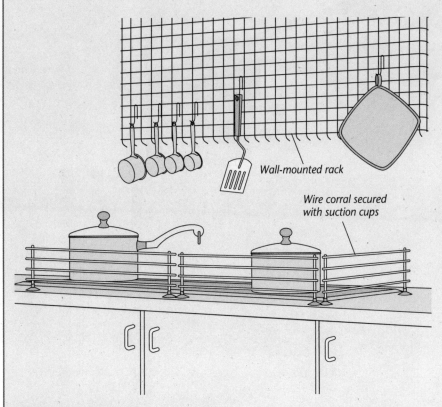

Wall-mounted rack

Wire corral secured with suction cups

Child-safe cooking area
Wire corral stuck to countertop with suction cups, keeps small fingers from reaching pots or burners. Pot handles are turned inward to prevent spills. Wall-mounted rack hangs utensils well out of reach.

STORING CLEANING MATERIALS

For all the activity that goes on in a typical kitchen, it's no wonder that it needs its own store of cleaning supplies to be kept in order. Unfortunately, the unglamorous mop and pail tend to be overlooked when planning for storage, and cleansers and detergents sometimes wind up in a clutter under the sink. This section will give you a few practical tips on providing proper storage for cleaning materials.

As illustrated below, the space under the kitchen sink is a popular spot for storing cleaners, scrub brushes, and paper towels. Having these items close at hand makes it easier to pick up spills, tend to dishes, and wipe down countertops after mealtime. As well, various accessories added to this space, such as door-mounted shelves and racks and pullout bins, help to keep it tidy.

Also around the sink, it's handy to have a place to store sponges and dishcloths when they're not being used. The tilt-out tray shown at the top of page 55 is an ideal way to keep these items close at hand yet out of sight.

As for cleaning tools that are used only once or twice per day, such as mops, brooms, and dustpans, it's smart to find storage that's out of the way but not so far out of the way that they become hard to reach. The end cabinet shown opposite is tall enough to accommodate the long handles of mops and brooms. When the door is closed, the unit blends in with the surrounding cabinets. The broom and mop hangers shown at the bottom of page 55 are easy to install in a utility cabinet or a nearby broom closet.

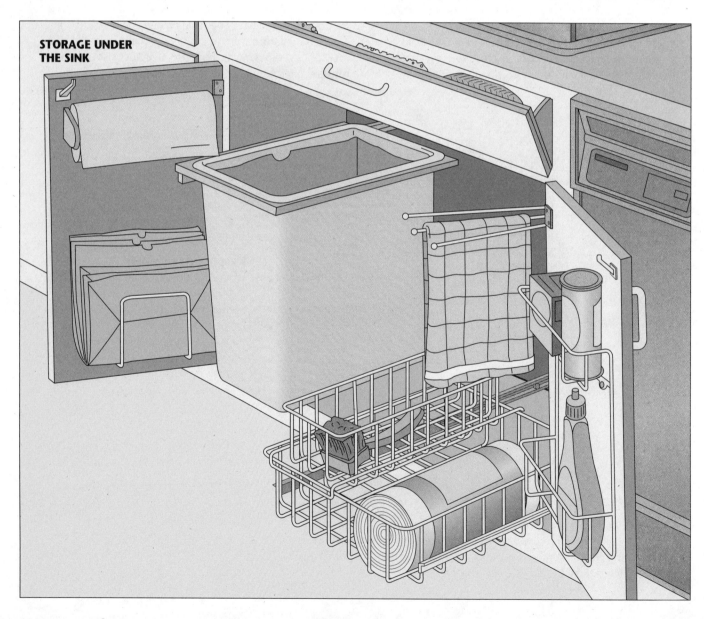

STORAGE UNDER THE SINK

Cleaning up cleaning tools

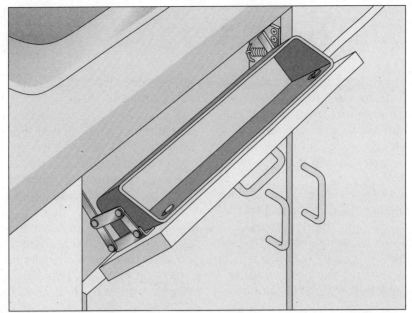

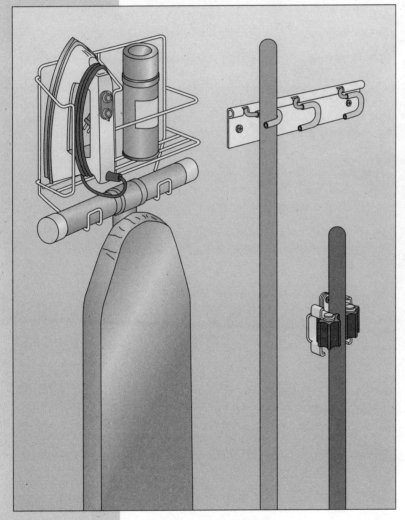

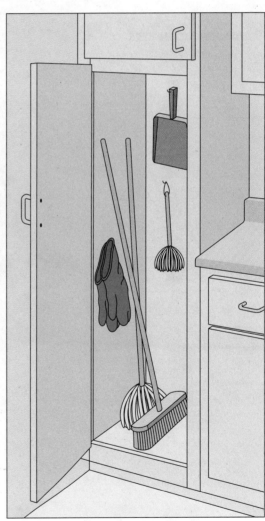

Tilt-out sink storage
This tray makes use of space that would be otherwise wasted. It is handy for scouring pads and sponges. Hinges attached to the tray and cabinet frame allow it to tilt open or closed. When closed, the tray's facade matches the style of the surrounding cabinets.

Mop and broom hangers
Available at home-improvement centers and hardware stores, special hangers hold broom and mop handles, cleaning supplies—even ironing gear. The hangers are screwed to wall studs or cabinet sides.

Mop and broom storage cabinet
Planning for an end unit storage cabinet for cleaning tools will allow you to keep mops and brooms where they are needed most—in the kitchen. After cleanup, simply close the door to conceal the space.

CUTLERY AND FLATWARE STORAGE

Keeping utensils organized goes a long way toward creating a smooth-running kitchen. As any cook will attest to, there's nothing more frustrating than searching for a mislaid utensil right in the middle of preparing a meal. The storage ideas for cutlery and flatware shown on these pages should help ensure that this doesn't happen.

Start by dividing your kitchen drawers so utensils and flatware remain organized—forks with forks, knives with knives. You can add dividers to existing cabinetry or choose new cabinets with dividers already built in, a feature offered by many manufacturers. A selection is shown below. For keeping expensive silverware separated from everyday uten-sils, consider the solid wood box with slots and soft lining also shown.

When it comes to storing knives, plan to place them each in their own dedicated slot, such as in a knife block *(see below)*. This will keep the blades sharp because they won't rattle against each other as they would if randomly thrown into a drawer. Knife blocks are also a good way of preventing accidental nicks and cuts.

Knife blocks can be made to integrate with a surrounding countertop. A few examples of these are shown opposite. To make your own knife holder, all you need are a few basic materials and some skill with power or hand tools. Two plans for easy-to-make holders are shown at the bottom of the opposite page.

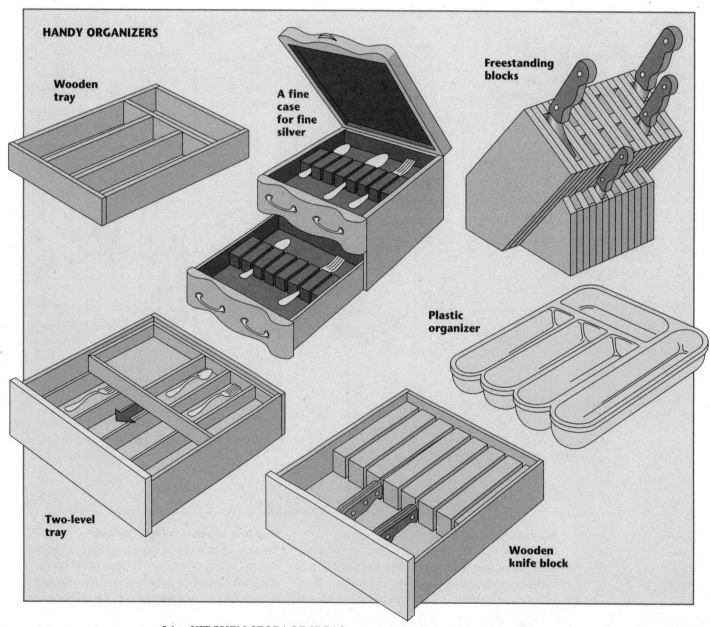

HANDY ORGANIZERS

Wooden tray

A fine case for fine silver

Freestanding blocks

Plastic organizer

Two-level tray

Wooden knife block

COUNTERTOP KNIFE BLOCKS

To minimize countertop clutter and still keep knives where you need them, build a knife block into the counter. Or you can use specially made chopping blocks or modifications to countertops to provide convenient storage. Just be sure blades extend down into unused space, so they can't cut anyone.

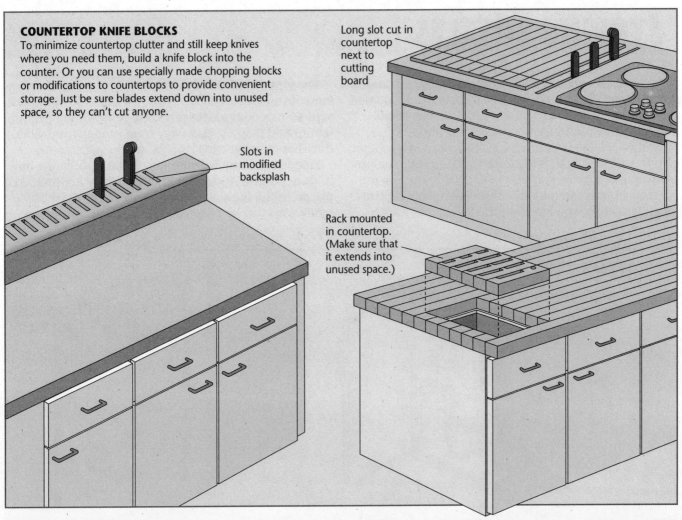

Long slot cut in countertop next to cutting board

Slots in modified backsplash

Rack mounted in countertop. (Make sure that it extends into unused space.)

EASY-TO-MAKE KNIFE HOLDERS

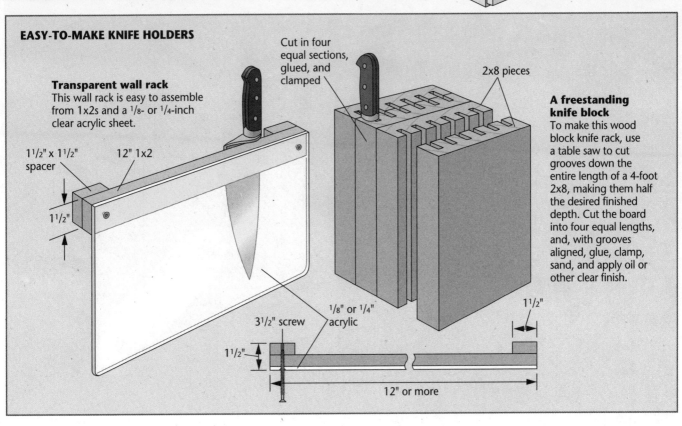

Transparent wall rack
This wall rack is easy to assemble from 1x2s and a 1/8- or 1/4-inch clear acrylic sheet.

1 1/2" x 1 1/2" spacer

12" 1x2

1 1/2"

3 1/2" screw

1/8" or 1/4" acrylic

1 1/2"

12" or more

Cut in four equal sections, glued, and clamped

2x8 pieces

1 1/2"

A freestanding knife block
To make this wood block knife rack, use a table saw to cut grooves down the entire length of a 4-foot 2x8, making them half the desired finished depth. Cut the board into four equal lengths, and, with grooves aligned, glue, clamp, sand, and apply oil or other clear finish.

STORING BOTTLES

Because they are often tall, awkwardly shaped, and breakable, bottles present a real challenge to kitchen storage. The selection of methods shown below will provide some useful ideas to meet your needs.

Commercial drawer inserts, available at some cabinet shops, will keep bottles organized and upright. Shallow shelves also provide easy access to bottles. For horizontal storage, you can purchase stock cubbyhole cabinets or add notched wooden strips to shelves.

The type of product in a bottle will often dictate what kind of storage is suitable. Wine, for example, should be kept on its side at a relatively cool, constant temperature (around 60°F/16°C), and away from sunlight and vibration. For more on wine storage, see the ideas below.

Frequency of use will also play a part in deciding how to store bottles. Products that receive daily use should be placed in the most accessible locations, while those rarely used can be stored a little more out of the way.

BOTTLE DRAWERS AND SHELVES

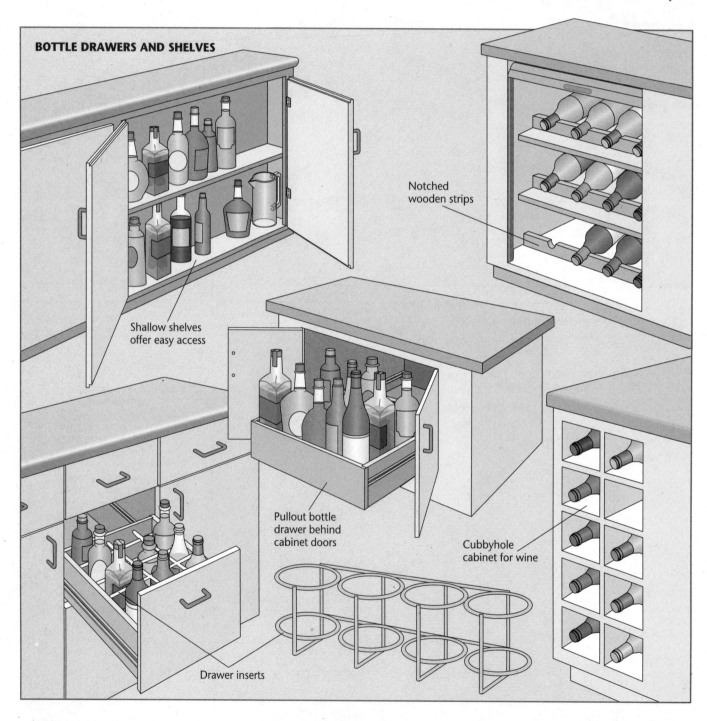

Shallow shelves offer easy access

Notched wooden strips

Pullout bottle drawer behind cabinet doors

Cubbyhole cabinet for wine

Drawer inserts

DISHES AND GLASSWARE STORAGE

A typical kitchen could always stand to have more space to store dishes and glassware. If this is true of your situation, consider the storage options shown on the following pages. And as you do, keep in mind the basic rule of thumb that says shelving should be fitted to its contents, not the other way around.

For greatest convenience, store everyday glasses and dishware in cabinets close to the serving area, dishwasher, and refrigerator. Many people find shelves in upper cabinets to be the best location for dishes, while others prefer base-cabinet drawers. Remember, dishes can chip or crack if drawers are opened and closed too abruptly. A selection of shelving organizers is shown below and on page 60.

For smaller, and less expensive storage solutions, turn to the collection of shelf maximizers shown on page 61. The wooden hangers and racks featured on the bottom of that page offer ways of storing mugs and stemware.

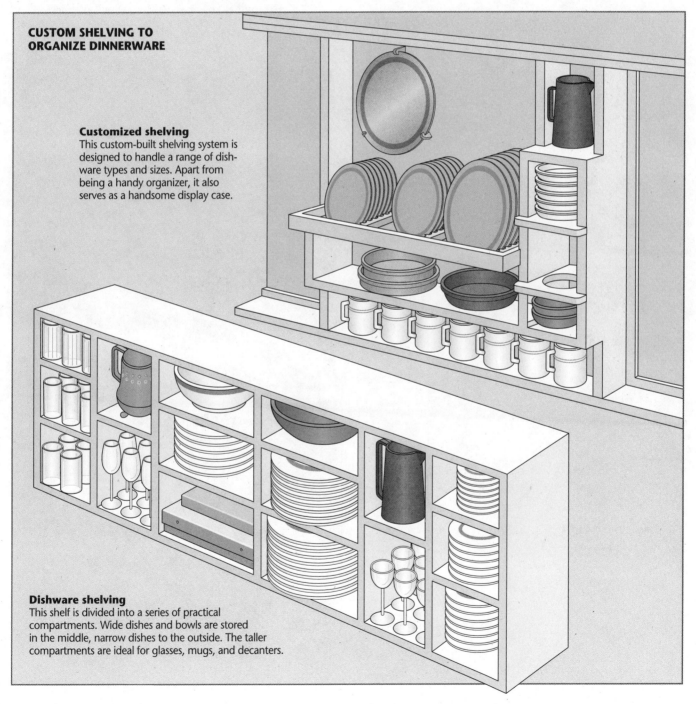

CUSTOM SHELVING TO ORGANIZE DINNERWARE

Customized shelving
This custom-built shelving system is designed to handle a range of dishware types and sizes. Apart from being a handy organizer, it also serves as a handsome display case.

Dishware shelving
This shelf is divided into a series of practical compartments. Wide dishes and bowls are stored in the middle, narrow dishes to the outside. The taller compartments are ideal for glasses, mugs, and decanters.

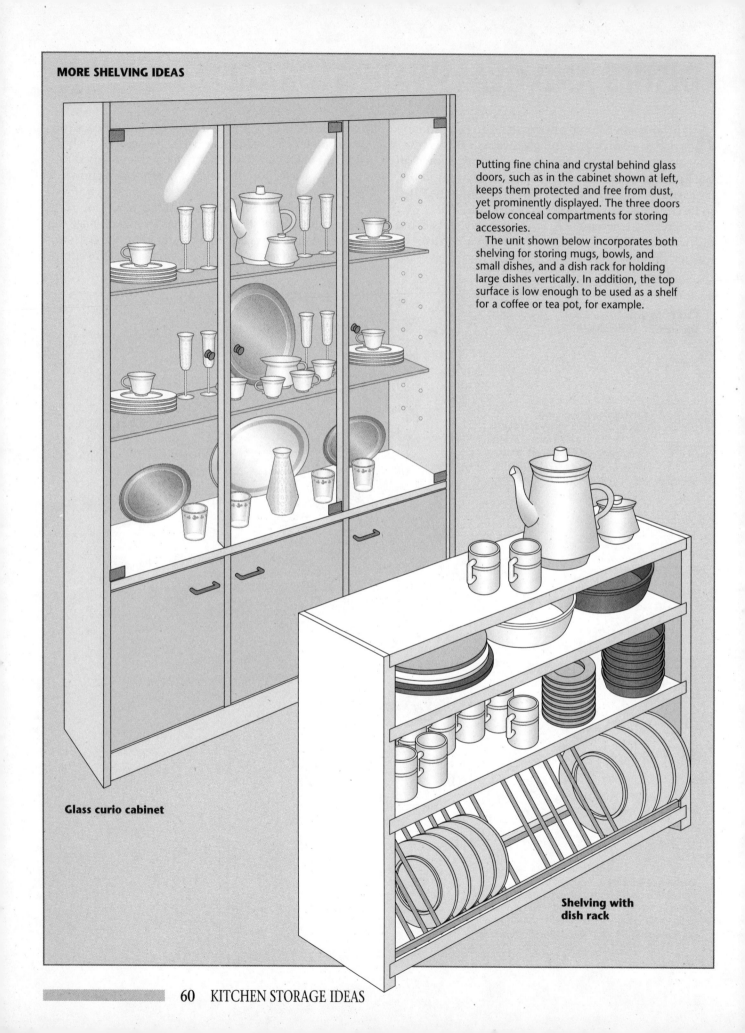

Putting fine china and crystal behind glass doors, such as in the cabinet shown at left, keeps them protected and free from dust, yet prominently displayed. The three doors below conceal compartments for storing accessories.

The unit shown below incorporates both shelving for storing mugs, bowls, and small dishes, and a dish rack for holding large dishes vertically. In addition, the top surface is low enough to be used as a shelf for a coffee or tea pot, for example.

Glass curio cabinet

Shelving with dish rack

SHELF MAXIMIZERS

There are numerous products available for extending the capacity of standard shelves. These organizers can double or triple usable space, protect dishes, and make access easier.

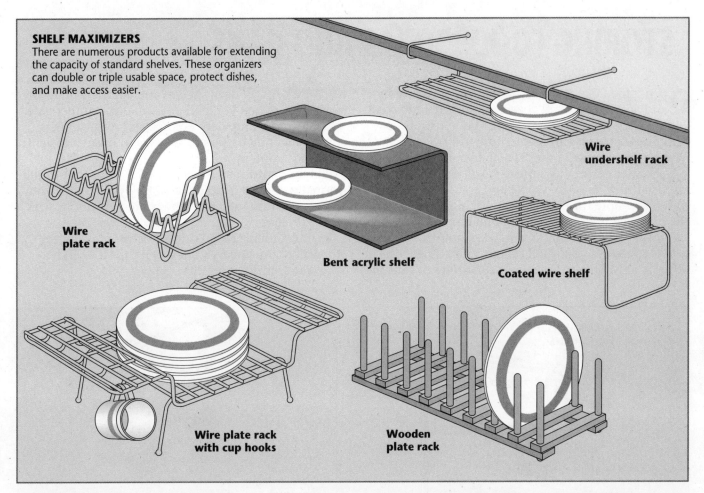

Wire plate rack

Bent acrylic shelf

Wire undershelf rack

Coated wire shelf

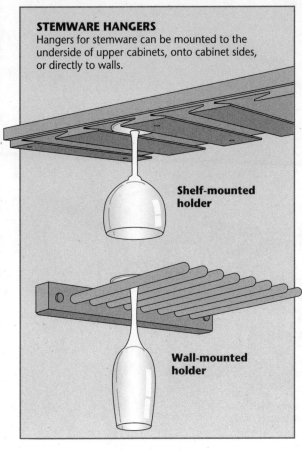

Wire plate rack with cup hooks

Wooden plate rack

STEMWARE HANGERS

Hangers for stemware can be mounted to the underside of upper cabinets, onto cabinet sides, or directly to walls.

Shelf-mounted holder

Wall-mounted holder

MUG RACKS

Mugs can take up considerable cabinet space. Instead of setting them on shelves, hang mugs from inexpensive wall- or door-mounted racks. Among your options are a "scissor" rack, a Shaker-style peg rack, or a freestanding mug tree.

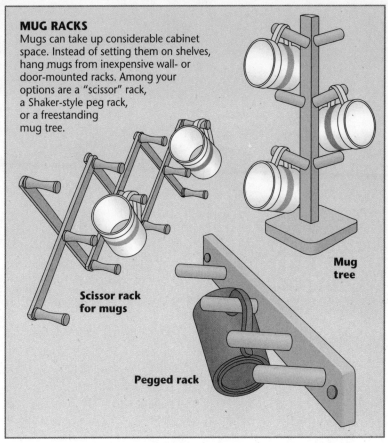

Scissor rack for mugs

Mug tree

Pegged rack

STORING FOOD: BOXES AND CANS

Open a food cupboard in most American kitchens and you'll likely find dozens of canned and boxed goods filling the shelves. There is a good reason for this: These products are staples for most cuisines and, when stored properly, they last almost indefinitely.

No matter where you store these goods, it's important that they be easily visible and accessible. Few things are more frustrating than reaching blindly into the back of a high cupboard and pulling out can after can until you've found the one you want. One solution is to reserve your high cabinets for a single line of boxed goods. You can keep bulk quantities of cans in

reach by slanting deep shelves and adding a lip to the front edge. When you pull one can out, another automatically rolls into view. For deeper lower cabinets, consider adding baskets or drawers to make it easier to access the contents.

Pullout pantries take advantage of space that would normally be hard to reach, enabling you to slide your shelves out into full view. They come in various sizes to fit tall, narrow cabinets or short, lower units.

Finally, durable metal utility shelves are an ideal storage option when you have a lot to store and appearance is not a priority.

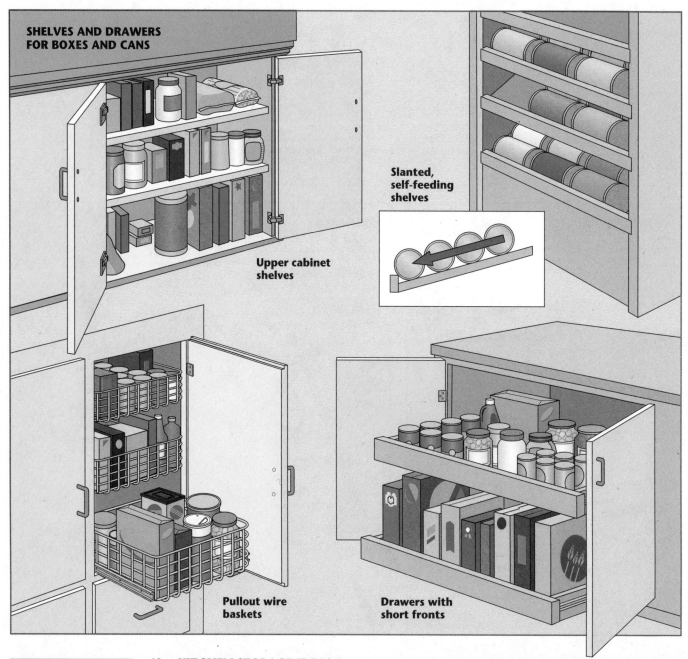

SHELVES AND DRAWERS FOR BOXES AND CANS

Upper cabinet shelves

Slanted, self-feeding shelves

Pullout wire baskets

Drawers with short fronts

PULLOUT PANTRIES

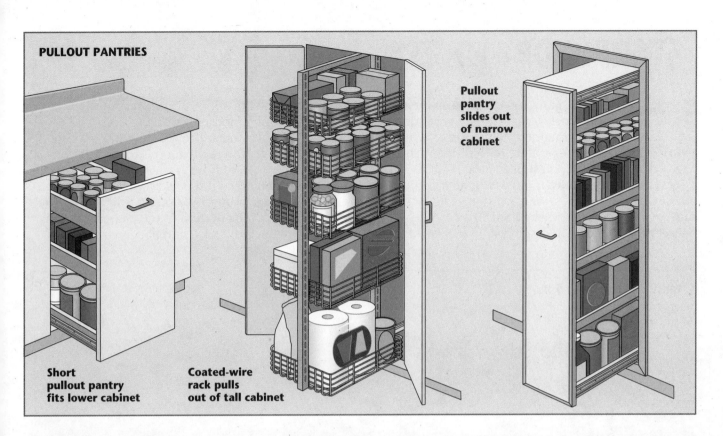

Pullout pantry slides out of narrow cabinet

Short pullout pantry fits lower cabinet

Coated-wire rack pulls out of tall cabinet

SHELVING UNITS

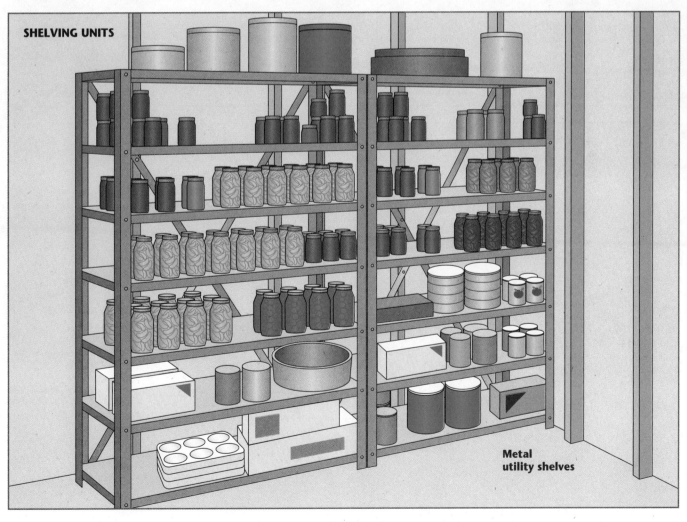

Metal utility shelves

STORING DRY FOOD

Staples, such as rice, pasta, and flour, keep for a long time given the proper storage. In fact, most dry foods last about a year (although the rising agent in self-rising flour may degenerate in that time). This page offers a few dry-food storage ideas.

As shown below, drawers lined with metal or plastic provide convenient, easy-to-reach storage for flour, sugar, and a host of other dry foods. You can choose between stock drawer liners or custom fabricated units.

To reduce the threat of insects spreading among grains and similar foods, it's smart to keep a lid on your storage containers. The best method is to use sealed containers where the food is protected from moisture and isolated from errant bugs.

From wooden bread boxes to acrylic canisters, containers can range from store-bought units to recycled jars. As shown at the bottom of the page, some can be stacked while others are hung beneath shelving.

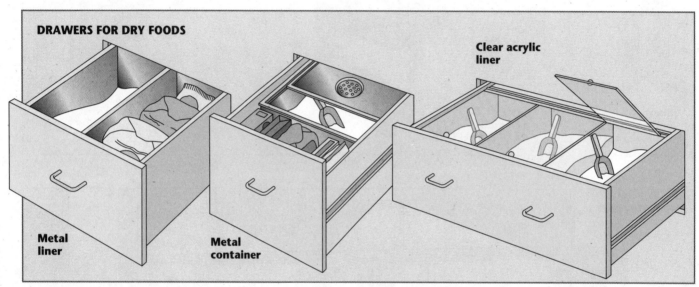

DRAWERS FOR DRY FOODS

Clear acrylic liner

Metal liner

Metal container

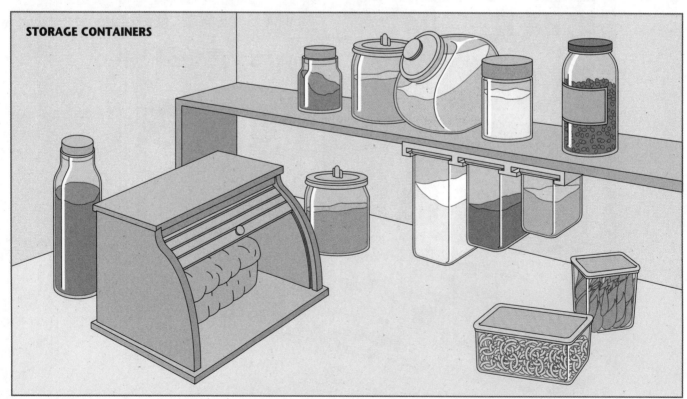

STORAGE CONTAINERS

STORAGE FOR SPICES

There's an endless supply of spices available to the average cook these days. Although this variety no doubt helps add flavor to most domestic menus, it can also create a bit of a storage problem in and around the food preparation area. Since spice containers come in many different shapes and sizes, they can clutter up counter and pantry space almost overnight. The ideas featured on these two pages should help you organize your oregano and tidy up your thyme.

The swing-out shelves shown below are an ideal way to make double use of a space. You can store the spices on the cabinet shelves or place them on the back of the doors. For pullout storage, consider installing angled dividers, such as those shown at right, in a drawer near the cooking area. Alternatively, a vertically designed drawer with shelves can be installed beside the stove. An example of this is shown at the bottom of page 66.

For a few ideas of spice racks that can be incorporated into your food preparation area, see the selection of built-in units at the top of page 66. Freestanding, portable units are shown at the bottom of that page.

Whichever system you choose, remember that spices keep best if they are stored away from direct heat, moisture, and light. Tightly closed containers help prevent loss of flavor.

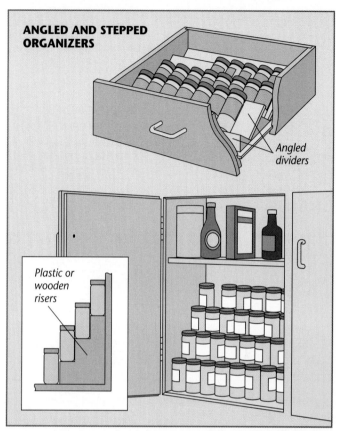

ANGLED AND STEPPED ORGANIZERS

Angled dividers

Plastic or wooden risers

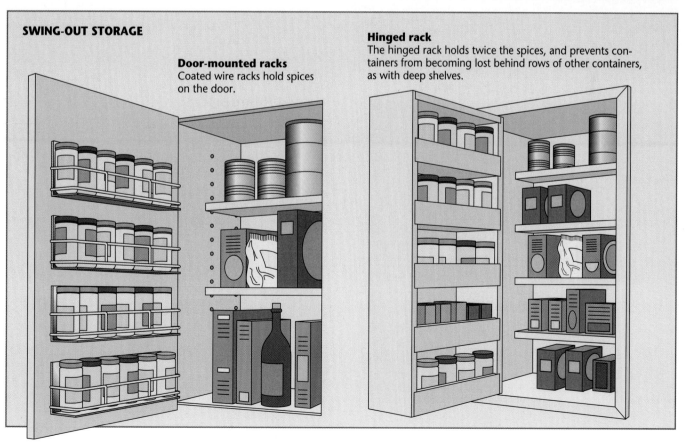

SWING-OUT STORAGE

Door-mounted racks
Coated wire racks hold spices on the door.

Hinged rack
The hinged rack holds twice the spices, and prevents containers from becoming lost behind rows of other containers, as with deep shelves.

BUILT-IN SPICE RACKS

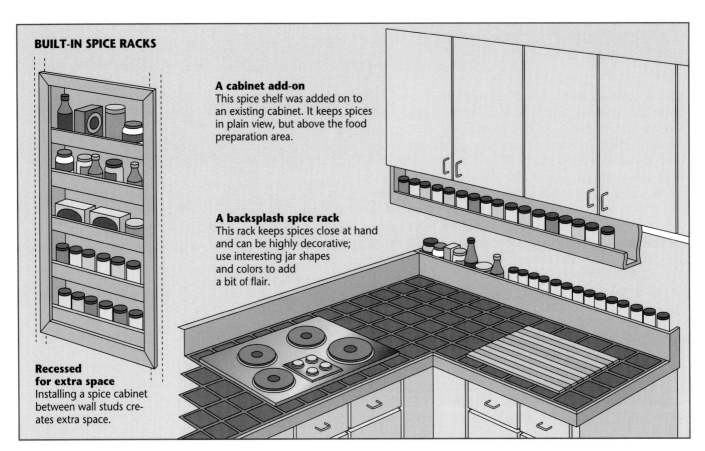

A cabinet add-on
This spice shelf was added on to an existing cabinet. It keeps spices in plain view, but above the food preparation area.

A backsplash spice rack
This rack keeps spices close at hand and can be highly decorative; use interesting jar shapes and colors to add a bit of flair.

Recessed for extra space
Installing a spice cabinet between wall studs creates extra space.

PULLOUT STORAGE FOR SPICES

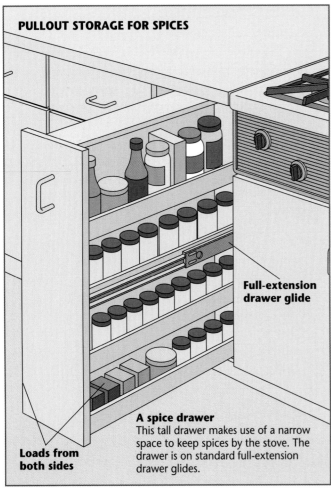

Full-extension drawer glide

Loads from both sides

A spice drawer
This tall drawer makes use of a narrow space to keep spices by the stove. The drawer is on standard full-extension drawer glides.

FREESTANDING SPICE RACKS

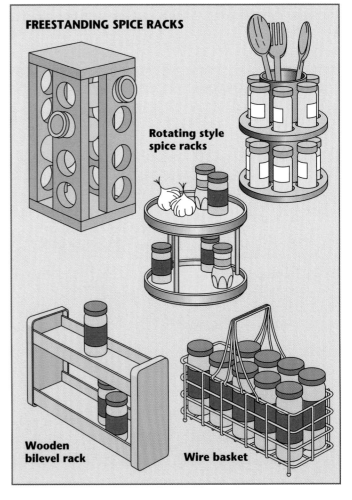

Rotating style spice racks

Wooden bilevel rack

Wire basket

STORING LINENS

The primary goal when storing linens is to keep them free of wrinkles and dust. In the case of napkins and placemats, this can be accomplished relatively easily using shallow drawers or shelves, or wire trays and baskets. Because of their size, tablecloths pose a greater challenge. Ideally, they should be hung from dowels or slats in a cabinet or closet. If you don't have the space needed to hang tablecloths, roll them around large mailing tubes and place them in a drawer. A variety of linen storage ideas is shown below.

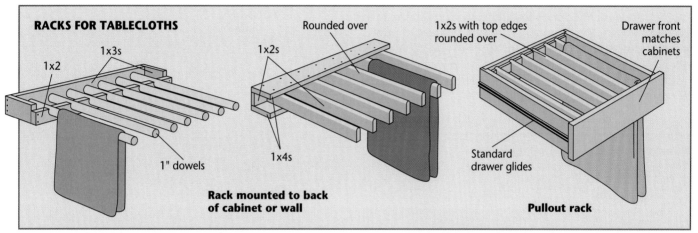

RACKS FOR TABLECLOTHS

1x2

1x3s

1" dowels

Rack mounted to back of cabinet or wall

Rounded over

1x2s

1x4s

1x2s with top edges rounded over

Drawer front matches cabinets

Standard drawer glides

Pullout rack

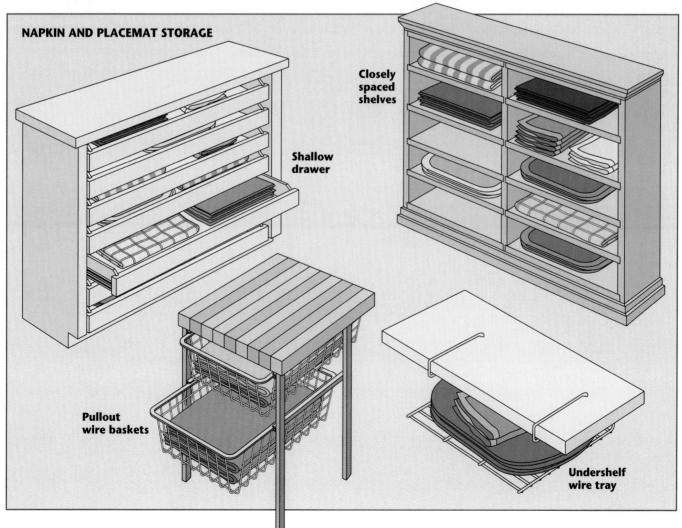

NAPKIN AND PLACEMAT STORAGE

Shallow drawer

Closely spaced shelves

Pullout wire baskets

Undershelf wire tray

STORING POTS AND PANS

When it's time to cook, the last thing you want is to spend 10 minutes searching through a jumbled mass of pots for the one you want. This page offers some ideas to help save you from that frustration.

Ideal storage for pots and pans involves having them well organized and near the cooktop and oven. They are typically stored in base cabinets. Choose shallower cabinets for easier access or install heavy-duty drawers or pullout trays in deeper units. Perforated hardboard provides yet another storage option. Mounted on cabinet doors, or sliding between 1-by-2 glides screwed to the top and bottom of the cabinet interior, it offers a ready-made pot and pan rack—just add hooks.

SHELVES AND DRAWERS FOR POTS AND PANS

Shallow drawer behind doors

Rubber rollers protect door finish

Stack to save space

Drawer glides

Shelves in shallow cabinet

Open, shallow drawers

Oversized drawers

PERFORATED HARDBOARD OPTIONS

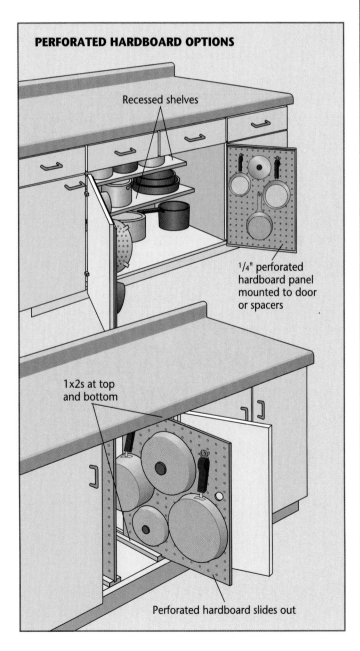

Recessed shelves

1/4" perforated hardboard panel mounted to door or spacers

1x2s at top and bottom

Perforated hardboard slides out

OVERHEAD STORAGE

By hanging them on wall or ceiling racks, pots and pans can become important decorative elements in the kitchen. This method of storage has an added benefit: It allows you to take advantage of overhead space that would normally go unused.

   The type of rack you choose will depend partly on your kitchen design. Suspended from ceiling hooks, hanging pan racks can create a dramatic focal point in the kitchen. The ideal location is generally above a counter near the stove or over a nearby island unit where pots and pans won't interfere with kitchen traffic. Wall-mounted units are a slightly easier option. One note of caution about racks: Because of the weight they will bear, you must be careful to hang them according to manufacturer's instructions.

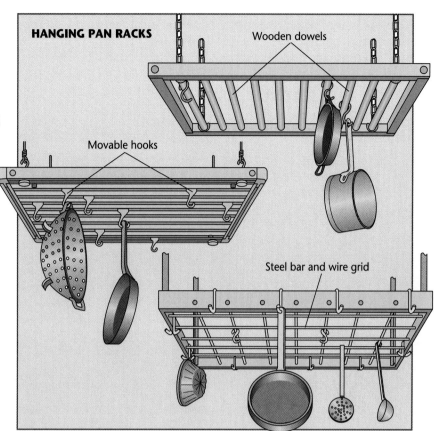

HANGING PAN RACKS

Wooden dowels

Movable hooks

Steel bar and wire grid

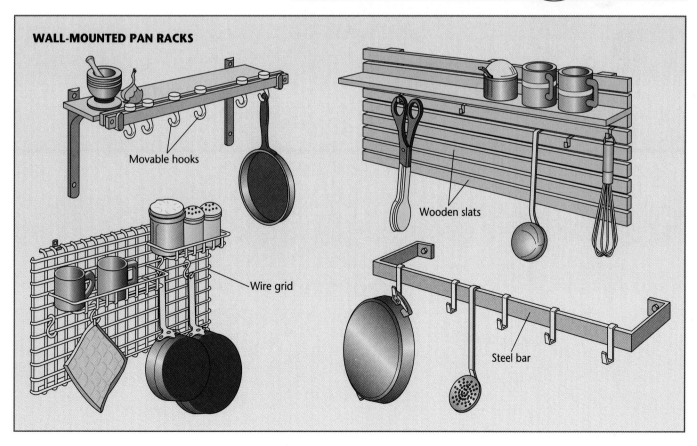

WALL-MOUNTED PAN RACKS

Movable hooks

Wire grid

Wooden slats

Steel bar

STORING BAKING PANS AND SERVING TRAYS

Unless you're the most avid of bakers or host frequent dinner parties, you probably won't use your baking pans and serving trays on a daily basis. For this reason, you'll want to store these items in relatively out-of-the-way kitchen cabinets. To contend with their large and irregularly shaped sizes, consider the selection of lower cabinet storage options shown below.

Vertical dividers allow for tidy storage while keeping each item in view. And with a slot for pan or tray, you can remove the one you want without disturbing the others. Many dividers can be fashioned out of wood, while others are commercially available. Check local kitchenware suppliers for cabinet inserts and dividers specially designed for storing trays and other serving equipment.

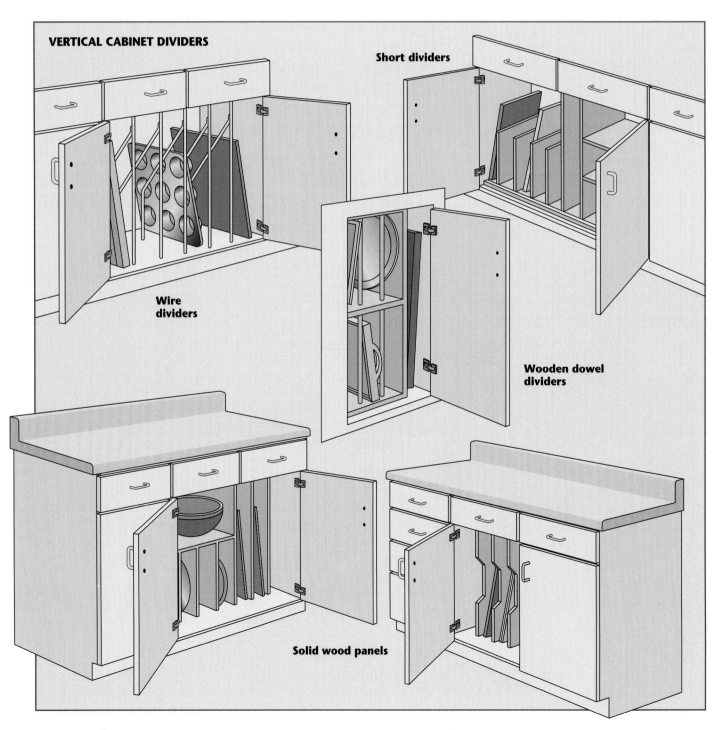

VERTICAL CABINET DIVIDERS

Short dividers

Wire dividers

Wooden dowel dividers

Solid wood panels

A SELECTION OF TRASH CONTAINERS

Dealing with waste in an orderly and efficient manner is essential to maintaining a sanitary kitchen. Obviously, the goal of all homeowners is to avoid messy, overflowing wastebaskets and the unwanted odors that come with them. Choosing from the selection of garbage cans shown at right and below will help you get a handle on garbage before it becomes a problem.

In most kitchens, the garbage can is located in the cabinet under the sink. Before you opt for this spot, take quick stock of the waste production points in your kitchen—such as the can opener, food preparation counter, and chopping block. If the sink is not central to these, you may want to choose a more convenient place.

When choosing your trash container, look carefully at the options. Built-in receptacles come in many designs and can be customized to suit your needs. Mid-sized rubber containers hold a lot of trash, and like the pedal-operated model, can be left out anywhere in the kitchen. Door-mounted containers offer one important benefit: they stay hidden when not in use. No matter what model you choose, make sure it is heavy-duty—your kitchen trash container will work harder than any other in the home.

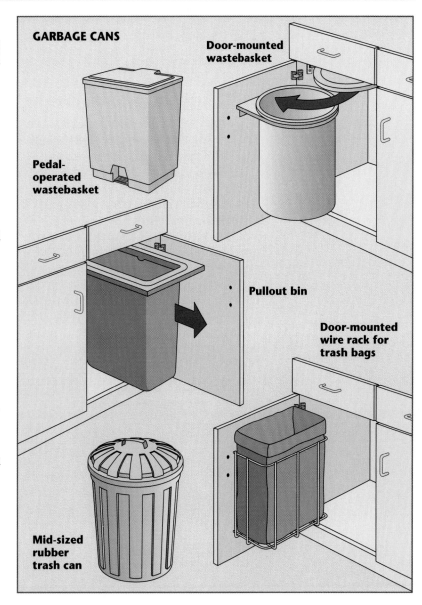

GARBAGE CANS

Door-mounted wastebasket

Pedal-operated wastebasket

Pullout bin

Door-mounted wire rack for trash bags

Mid-sized rubber trash can

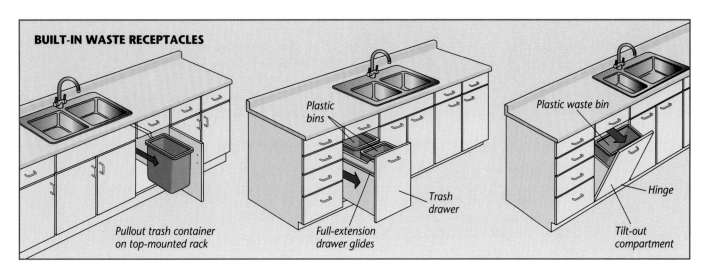

BUILT-IN WASTE RECEPTACLES

Pullout trash container on top-mounted rack

Plastic bins

Full-extension drawer glides

Trash drawer

Plastic waste bin

Hinge

Tilt-out compartment

BEDROOM AND BATHROOM STORAGE OPTIONS

Bedrooms and bathrooms are a particularly challenging storage problem. Since they hold many of life's necessities, their storage spaces have to do more than look good—they have to work well too. The challenge of making these areas functional as well as attractive can be made easier with a little planning and some attention to detail.

The centerpiece of any bedroom, and by extension its greatest space-gobbler, is the bed. For master bedrooms and kids' rooms, consider acquiring beds that do double-duty with underbed linen or clothes drawers. In other rooms, a Murphy bed or pullout sofa can accommodate guests and be stowed in a jiffy once they're gone.

Bathrooms are often the smallest rooms in a home, but they have to handle, and sometimes hide, the paraphernalia that accompanies daily living. A bathroom vanity can house everything from cosmetics to cleaning supplies, and a medicine cabinet can store the odds and ends that often clutter a sink top. Small closets and shelves, as well as smartly placed racks and hooks, can also take advantage of otherwise wasted wall space above toilets, in corners, and behind doors.

In the next few pages, the photos of different storage ideas, and the commercial units that make them possible, will give you an idea of how to handle some of the many storage concerns in the bedroom and bathroom—and help make your space look great in the process.

Small, built-in nooks make for an ideal space to store blankets and other bedroom and bathroom linens. They keep life's daily necessities close at hand while adding a nice touch of color to a room.

Turn your home library, sewing room, or office into an instant guest room by adding an attractive and practical Murphy bed. Library shelves remain undisturbed with the bed in the down position (above), while painted trompe l'oeil books put up a studious front when the bed is closed (inset).

Handy underbed drawer units help free up precious closet and dresser space. Use them to store bed linens and extra pillows as well as night clothes and thick socks for cooler evenings.

There's no denying that bedroom closets are among the hardest areas to keep tidy in a home. Fortunately, closet organizers are available to make sorting your shoes and clothes easier. The lightweight model shown at left hangs from the closet rod and has separate compartments for shoes, pants and sweaters, and suits and dresses.

Built-in closet organizers not only offer plenty of compartments for storing shoes and clothing, but they also add to the bedroom's overall decor. The solid wood unit shown above features fixed shelving for holding hats, sweaters, and keepsakes; drawers and a pair of pullout shelf units handle underwear and shoes respectively. Slacks and skirts are hung on an adjoining closet rod.

Organize your closet with an efficient yet inexpensive wire rack system. Upper and lower hanging racks are just right for shirts and pants, while a wall-mounted rack features tie hangers, shoe racks, and baskets for small items.

Off the beaten track and safe from accidents, guest bedrooms are often an ideal place to display precious collectibles. The built-in wall unit in the bedroom at right features a large four-shelf centerpiece sandwiched between a set of book shelves.

Turn extra space into work space by converting a bedroom nook into a peaceful home office or study area. A couple of built-in shelves and tables or desks are all it takes to make the small corner of a room (below) ideal for reading, writing, or even running a small business.

Just the thing for a guest bedroom or family room, a beautiful built-in cabinet like the one above converts easily into an entertainment center. The upper compartment can house a television and videocassette recorder, while the lower compartment can store records, videos, or even compact discs. Simply close the doors when the unit is not being used.

BEDROOM AND BATHROOM STORAGE OPTIONS   **75**

Handy, mobile, and safe: a rolling underbed cart is perfect for storing small toys and games out of sight but easily within a youngster's reach.

In the room shown above, the shelf-and-bureau unit serves double duty as a storage facility and as a room divider to separate the room into two distinct living and sleeping areas—one for a newborn and the other for an older child.

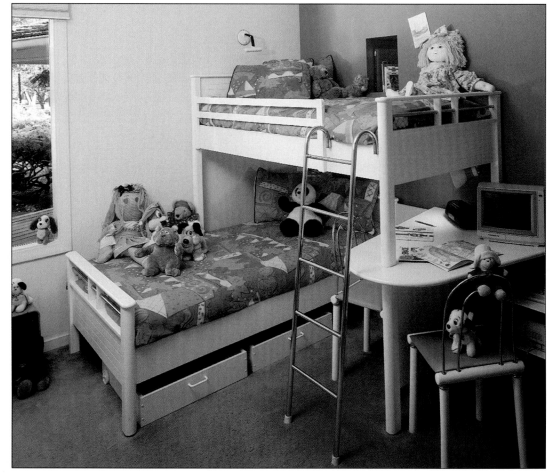

For rooms shared by two school-age children, consider bunk beds with underbed storage and an attached desk for studying. The drawers beneath the bed can hold clothing, toys, or school supplies, while the attached desk allows access from both sides.

Control the chaos in a teenager's bedroom with a versatile closet organizer. Upper and lower hanging bars, multiple shelving compartments and a set of drawers store clean clothes and sports gear; a wire basket for dirty laundry tucks away neatly below. Use the top shelves to house books and board games.

Consider hiding overstuffed storage areas in a kid's room in novel, decorative ways. In the bedroom at right, drawers and shelves are concealed behind a colorful set of wooden doors that are easy for kids to open and close. A rollout toy box fits snugly below one of the units. Dolls and other collectibles, placed on top of the unit, add to the ambience.

Conserve space in your bedroom by building a dressing area outside your bathroom. The built-in units at left have drawer and shelf space for clothing, cubbyholes for footwear, and even a makeup counter. Make sure the shower area is properly ventilated to prevent moisture from invading the clothing space.

Inexpensive and easy to install, plastic-coated wire racks are sturdy and resistant to bathroom moisture. A wall-mounted unit is ideal for storing perfume bottles, decorative soaps, and other assorted knickknacks. Hang one on the back of the bathroom door to hold towels and washcloths.

Keep the sides of bathtubs safe and free from the clutter of soaps, shampoos, washcloths, and razors by storing them in a handy wire basket. You can mount one to the bathroom wall, or simply choose one like the model below which hangs from a showerhead.

Reflected in a bank of mirrors, the wall of cabinets at left provides ample room for storage while separating the bathroom from the adjoining bedroom. Twin vanities with washbasins make preparing for a day at work—or a night on the town—a lot easier.

BEDROOM STORAGE

I f there is one room in the home that is meant to provide a respite at the end of a long, hard day, it's the bedroom. The key to keeping this personal oasis inviting is to organize it. This means finding room to store a wide range of items, from bed linens and bathrobes to books and boots—not an easy task.

This chapter will give you a few ideas on how to handle the storage problems a typical bedroom may pose. Of course, every situation is slightly different, so it's always best to begin by looking at your space as a whole and asking yourself how you will store things in a practical and accessible manner.

A good starting place is around the bed itself *(page 81)*. Headboards, nightstands, and foot-of-the-bed chests keep belongings close at hand but out of the way. Underbed drawers *(page 85)* free up space normally taken up by dressers. Turn to page 86 for a few options on storing beneath the bed.

If your goal is to utilize every precious square inch of closet space, try some of the helpful ideas on page 87. And for a few suggestions on the simple accessories that can make life a bit easier—such as shoe and tie racks, multipurpose hangers, and suspendible closet rods, turn to page 89. Shelf installation tips can be found on page 92.

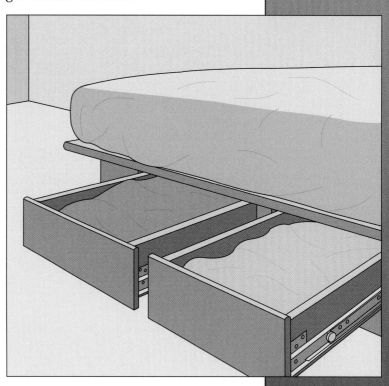

Commonly known as a captain's bed, this drawer-in-frame design is just as practical on land as at sea. Turn to page 85 for more on underbed storage.

SAVVY BEDROOMS

All the amenities that make the bedroom a restful and relaxing place to be—books and magazines for bedside reading, a television and perhaps a stereo system for entertainment, extra pillows and quilts for comfort—can quickly add up to a major space problem unless some thought goes into storage possibilities. Luckily, most bedrooms are equipped with closets, nightstands, dressers with drawer space, and, in some cases, hollow headboards and foot-of-the-bed chests.

This section will highlight some of these common storage areas, as well as introduce a few ideas that you may not have considered. You can build an underbed storage system, for example, or purchase low-profile containers designed to fit under the bed; both are shown on page 86. To save floor space, consider a commercially available hideaway bed *(page 73)*. And if you're looking for a few tips on how to make better use of your closet space, turn to page 87.

Storage around the bed

Choosing a variety of components

Your bed can dominate the floor space of a room like no other piece of furniture in the home. For this reason, the bedroom can be a tricky place to organize a storage strategy. Fortunately, there are furniture pieces associated with a typical bed setup that can handle the bulk of your storage concerns.

As illustrated below, the headboard and foot-of-the-bed chest are practically situated to handle reading materials and bed linens respectively. The nightstand is an ideal place for socks and pajamas, for example. If you're planning on building any or all three of these pieces, their dimensions are given on page 82. Alter their dimensions to fit your needs.

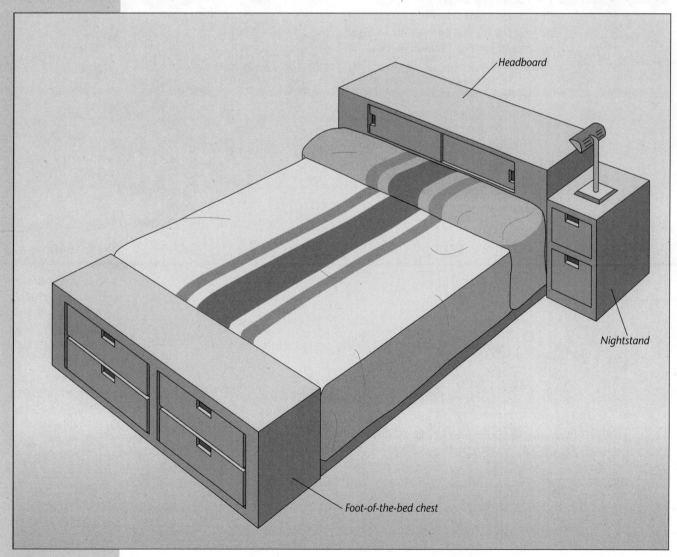

Headboard

Nightstand

Foot-of-the-bed chest

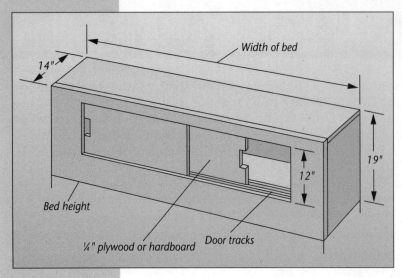

The headboard

The simple unit at left has a storage compartment with handy sliding doors to hide clutter. The portion of the headboard above the mattress should be approximately 19" high and 14" deep; the width and overall height of the headboard will be determined by the size of your bed. Sheets, blankets, pillows, and bedspreads alter measurements, so it's wise to measure when these are in place.

Build the headboard from 3/4" plywood and 1-by solid lumber. Use 1/4" plywood or hardboard for sliding doors, and install plastic, wood, or metal door tracks.

The nightstand

Two storage compartments are stacked inside this compact unit. The top one is a cubbyhole with a hinged, drop-down door in front; below it is a roomy drawer.

The nightstand shown here is approximately 12" wide, 14" deep, and 26" high; you can adjust these dimensions to suit your own needs.

Build the unit from 3/4" plywood and 1-by solid lumber. Buy a ready-made drawer—or build your own—and install it on standard drawer sides.

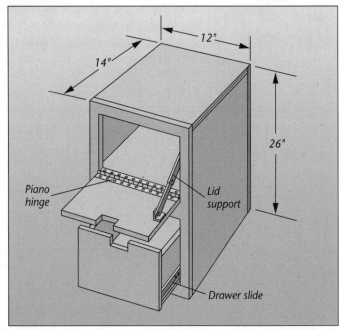

The foot-of-the-bed chest

A low chest of drawers at the foot of a full-size bed has nearly the same storage capacity as a standard bureau, without the bulk.

Make the chest's frame from 3/4" plywood and 1-by solid lumber; then install four custom-made drawers on standard slides. Make the chest the same height and width as your bed and approximately 16" deep.

Headboards for storage

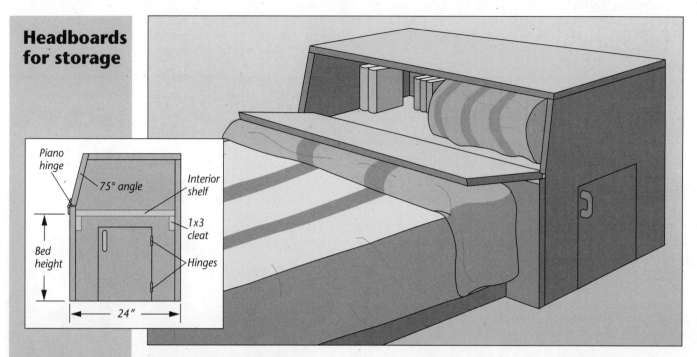

Piano hinge

75° angle

Interior shelf

1x3 cleat

Bed height

Hinges

24"

Easy-to-build headboard

With two storage levels, this headboard has plenty of space for bulky comforters, or even sports equipment. The unit is 24" deep, with the headboard 12 " higher, and a little wider, than the bed. The backrest/door slants at a 75° angle. Build the headboard drop lid from 3/4" plywood. Before assembly, cut a door out of each sidepiece. To assemble the pieces, nail 1x3 cleats to the inside of the headboard to hold the interior shelf, and attach the drop panel with a piano hinge. Attach the side doors with hinges and add door pulls and magnetic catches.

Contemporary storage idea

This Swedish-style queen-size bed features built-in nightstands and an integral headboard. It's a good example of an economical and attractive approach to bedroom storage.

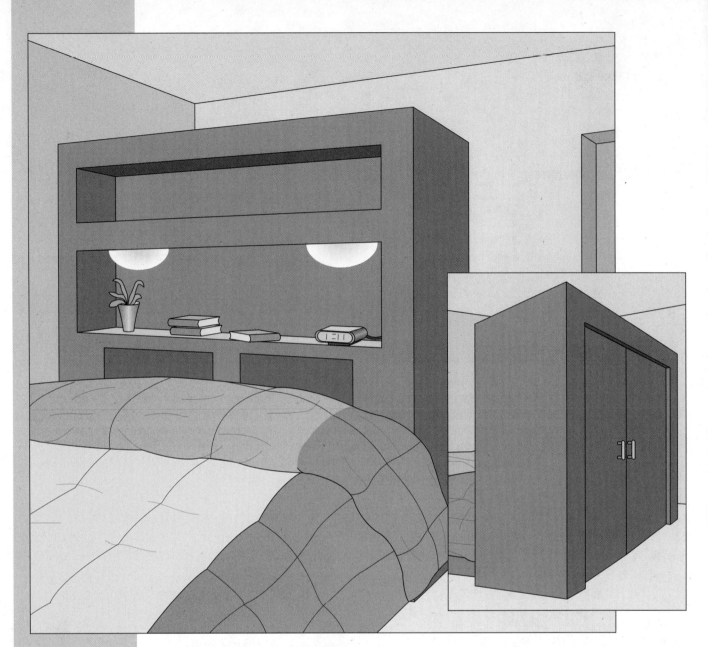

Combining storage with design
The massive headboard of this bed partitions the room into sleeping and dressing areas. On the sleeping side, almost hidden behind pillows, cabinet doors cover niches for bedside necessities; above them, an alcove accommodates such items as reading lamps, books, a clock radio, and plants. On the opposite side, the headboard has a dozen drawers, topped with a mirrored space for toiletries and a jewelry box, all concealed behind pullout doors.

 ASK A PRO

WHAT'S A MURPHY BED?
The original Murphy bed was created in 1905. Designed to swing up into a closet when not in use, it was a great idea—and still is—for freeing up floor space in a room that doubled as a daytime den or family room, for example. Today's models are often made to swing up into a recess in the wall or into a custom-made cabinet instead of a permanent closet.

Countersprings at the head of the bed allow for easy lifting and lowering. Legs at the foot hinge down for needed support and stability. Some units come with integrated shelving and drawers to further increase your storage.

Storage under your bed

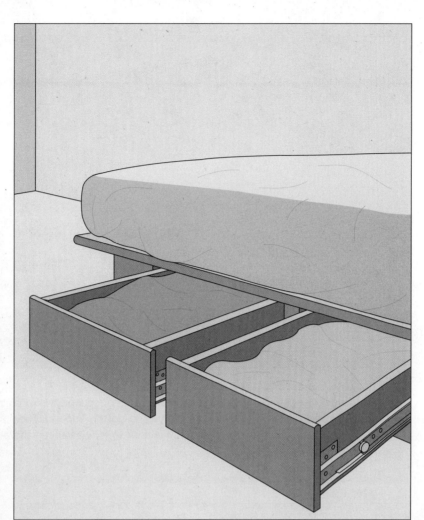

Bed-frame drawers
Drawers designed to fit in the bed frame below the mattress are a practical place to store clothes or bed linens. These drawers, such as the pair shown at left, are available in various widths and depths. Heavy-duty metal slides let the drawers open and close smoothly.

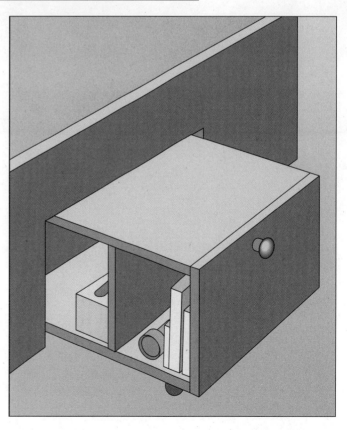

Custom bed roll-around cart
Designing a new bed? Consider leaving space for a handy roll-around cart with storage compartments, like the one shown here. Tucked away, this unit blends in with the rest of the underbed cabinetry. When it is pulled out, the cart doubles as a nightstand or table for breakfast in bed.

Underbed storage

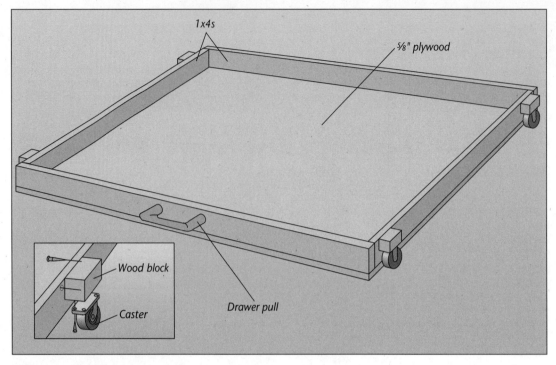

1x4s

⅝" plywood

Wood block

Caster

Drawer pull

Roller drawers beneath your bed

Even a standard metal bed frame can accommodate under-bed storage. To build a simple drawer, fasten 1x4 strips to the edges of a ⅝" plywood bottom *(above)*. Then add the wood blocks and casters (remember to allow an inch or so for clearance—more for thick carpeting) and attach a drawer pull.

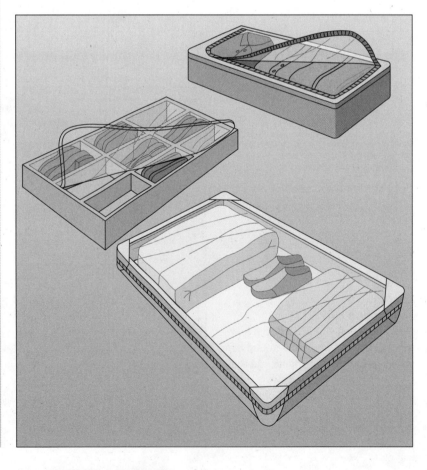

Commercial containers

Trays and chests made expressly for under-bed storage are commercially available in plastic, wood, or cardboard. Many have dividers; most have lids or see-through vinyl covers. These inexpensive storage aids are perfect for shoes, out-of-season clothing, and bed linens. Look for them in the notions section of department stores or in mail-order catalogs.

CLOSETS

A closet is the most important storage area in any bedroom. For this reason, it's essential that it is kept organized and tidy—maximizing space is key. In a typical bedroom, you will either have a roomy, walk-in closet, or a wide but shallow wall type. Both have their advantages. In general, people with large wardrobes prefer a walk-in closet simply because it holds more. But with good space planning and double-decker closet rods, for example, a wall closet can often accommodate the same amount of clothing. Shelves, drawers, pullout bins, and racks, such as those featured on the following pages, can make either of these closet types more space-efficient and organized.

If necessary, consider ways to enlarge your present closet, or think about where you can build a new one. On the following pages, you'll find suggestions for temporary or movable closets, as well as instructions for constructing your own built-ins or free-standing models.

Whether you choose just to add racks and hooks to your present closet, or you decide to install a complete closet system with shelves, drawers, and rods, you're sure to be pleased with the extra storage.

PLANNING CLOSET SPACE

Knowing the general dimensions of items in the basic clothing categories can help you plan just how much room to allow for each article. The illustration below gives measurements based on standards established by American Institute of Architects. But check your own clothing against these measurements; you may have less bulky jackets, longer hemlines, or smaller shoes.

A CLOSET SYSTEM

Shelves are probably the most versatile components in a closet system. They accommodate items in a wide variety of shapes and sizes (from 10-gallon hats to handkerchiefs). As well, they keep stored items visible and are relatively easy to install. And if you use an adjustable system of tracks and clips, or tracks and brackets, you'll find that shelves are easily positioned at various levels.

If you're planning to make shelves out of natural wood, fir and pine are good choices; 3/4-inch plywood is best for shelves deeper than 12 inches. Particleboard, though inexpensive, sags under weight. For shelves longer than 4 feet (3 feet if you do decide to use particleboard), be sure to add a midspan support. This will provide structural integrity for storing heavier loads such as books and magazines.

For added interest—and convenience—use vertical dividers to form clusters of cubbyholes, or convert some of your shelves to pullouts by adding standard drawer slides and lipped edges made from 1x3s. Both cubbyholes and pullout shelves are shown in the illustration below.

Adding a commercially available modular drawer system to your closet can free up floor space by eliminating the need for a bulky dresser. Constructing your own set of drawers may give you greater flexibility. The frame is built to accommodate drawers made to fit your specific dimensions. For visible storage, try a system of vinyl-coated wire bins that glide in and out on their own framework.

In updated closets, the primary space-waster—the traditional single closet rod—has given way to multiple rods, with heights determined by the type of clothing. But you needn't make any major structural changes to accommodate a multilevel rod system. Simply buy an adjustable suspension bar, or make one of your own from a metal bar or wood dowel. The bar can be held in place with steel rings, S-hooks, and some lightweight chain, as shown below.

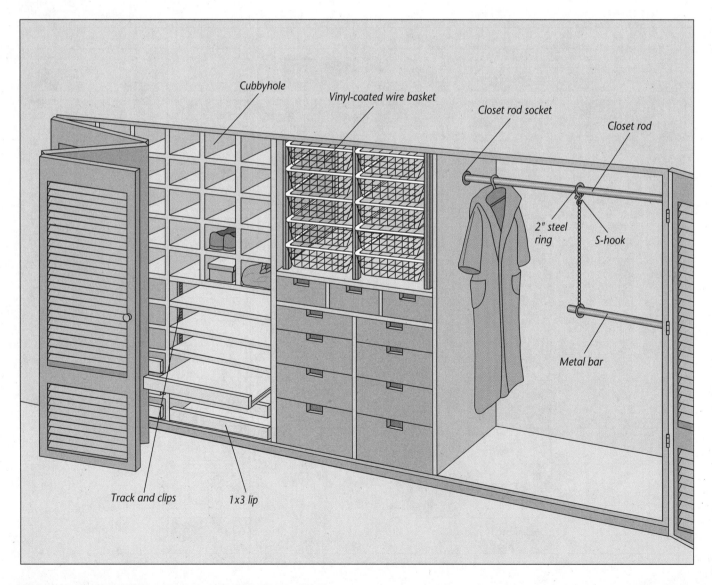

Cubbyhole

Vinyl-coated wire basket

Closet rod socket

Closet rod

2" steel ring

S-hook

Metal bar

Track and clips

1x3 lip

One way of gaining a bit more space is to use multiple-garment hangers. These can hold several shirts or pants in the same space as a single hanger. Some use clips to hold clothing *(right)*. Others resemble more conventional clothes hangers but with several horizontal hanging bars *(far right)*. Specialized versions for ties, belts, and other accessories are available. Since these hangers use vertical rather than horizontal space, they should be hung from a reasonably high closet rod.

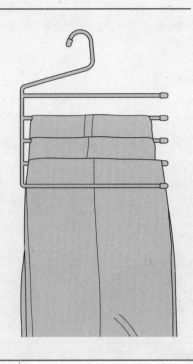

Organizing your accessories

Shaping up your shoes

The three commercially available racks shown here can hold between 9 and 18 pairs of shoes in traditional and less traditional ways. The floor rack *(bottom)* is best placed in a closet. The door rack *(right)* is made to hook on the back of a closet door. The pole rack *(far right)* is pressure-fitted between the floor and ceiling. It's best placed in an unused corner of a room. Epoxy coating on the rack protects it from the humidity commonly associated with shoes. Vinyl models are also available.

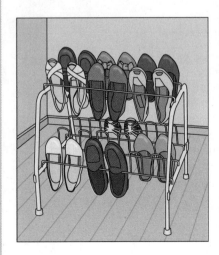

Wall hang-ups

One or more wall-mounted storage accessories hung in or near a closet can handle a variety of storage concerns. The simple wood rack shown *(below, right)* is ideal for hats or umbrellas. The plastic-coated wire basket *(below, left)* is fine for handbags and gloves, for example. Such accessories are screwed to the wall; some plastic models come with adhesive backing.

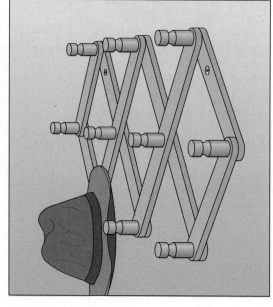

Disappearing tie rack

When in the open position, this "ladder" rack swings up for easy access to as many as four dozen ties slipped over its four wooden dowels. To store, simply swing it back down and slide it into the closet. The rack runs on standard drawer slides. Design: The Minimal Space.

DUAL-FUNCTION STORAGE

This Swedish-designed wardrobe, which rotates on a base, serves two purposes—it is both a full-length mirror and a multishelved storage unit. Its design eliminates doors, a plus in a small space. Such dual-purpose storage ideas can provide innovative solutions to space problems. Just make sure the combination is a workable one. A seat that doubles as a storage box for shoes would be good. But storing videos in a chest that doubles as a TV stand will become annoying if you have to move the TV to get the tapes.

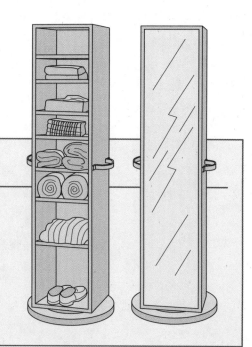

Building clothes storage

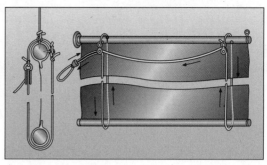

A quick muslin closet

Hung from a ceiling, this lightweight corner closet provides temporary storage in a minimum of space. Cut a piece of heavy muslin or duck canvas into two pieces the desired height and width of the closet. Wooden closet rods, cut into four pieces, slip into hems sewn at the top and bottom of each muslin piece. Drill holes in the upper rods for eye screws. Use cord and screw eyes to fasten the fabric panels to ceiling joists. One end of each upper rod fits into a socket screwed or bolted to the wall; secure the rods with finishing nails.

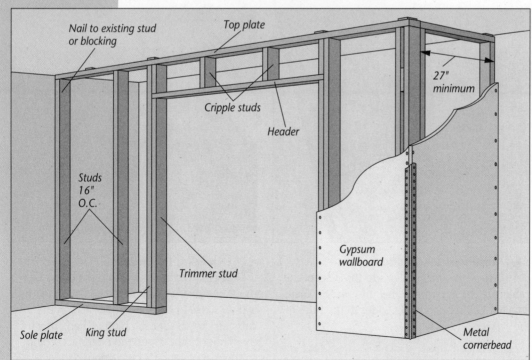

Building a closet

To add a permanent closet to a room, make a frame out of 2x4s, as shown, spacing the studs 16" on center. Add header and trimmer studs to the doorway (have the rough opening measurements on hand before you begin). Size the walls 1/4" less than the ceiling height. Shim between the top plate and ceiling joists and nail the sole plate to the floor. Nail end studs to the existing wall studs. Add gypsum wallboard and paint.

Assembling a commercial shelving unit

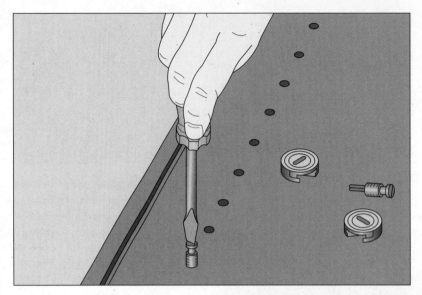

1 Fixing cam studs

Although design and assembly methods differ, many ready-to-assemble shelf systems feature predrilled holes spaced every 32 millimeters, the European style. Simply choose the height of each shelf in the unit and screw the cam studs that support the shelves into the holes *(left)*. Keep turning until they are fully seated.

2 ▶ Attaching the shelves

Place the cam locks into the appropriate holes on the bottom corners of the shelves, then slip the shelves onto the cam studs. With a screwdriver, turn the cam locks *(right)*, fastening the shelves in place.

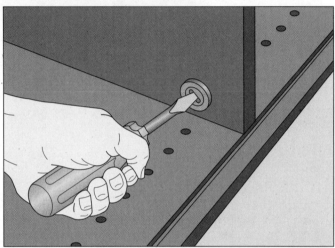

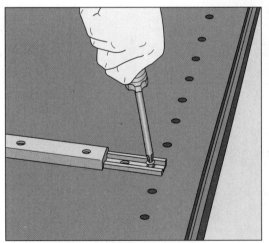

3 Adding drawer slides

Screw the drawer slides to the sides of the cabinet at the appropriate height *(above)*. Then, attach the other part of the slides to the sides of the drawers.

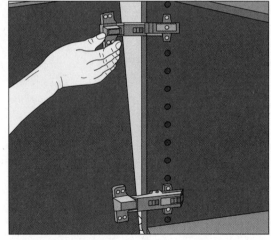

4 Hanging the doors

First attach the hinges to the doors. The mounting plate, which detaches from the hinge, is then screwed into the proper hole in the cabinet; do this for each hinge. Then, attach the hinges to the mounting plates according to the manufacturer's instructions.

STORING IN CHILDREN'S ROOMS

No other room in the home is as important to a child as a bedroom. It's there that he or she will spend time sleeping, playing, studying, and dreaming—basically, growing up. Not surprisingly, a child's bedroom is also a place where clutter can quickly run rampant. Fortunately, a few practical storage ideas will go a long way to solving your storage problems.

It seems that there is always a great need for more storage areas in a kid's room. Closet and floor space are constantly at a premium and, as the child grows, the need grows too. When planning these rooms, remember that although physical size and layout probably won't change, the way you use the space certainly can. As you'll see in this chapter, there's a world of untapped storage space.

Starting on page 94, you'll learn how to choose furniture that grows with your youngster—rolling cabinets which hold an infant's extra diapers can later double as a night table. Beginning on page 96, you'll find ideas for beds with drawers, shelves, and closets built into their base. Page 100 illustrates how to best organize closets, and beginning on page 101, you'll see how desks, bookshelves, and toy boxes can also double as storage units and playthings.

Elevated beds make ideal use of floor space–they free up areas otherwise occupied by dressers, desks, and coat racks. This crib allows room below for clothes, toys, and other items. See the section beginning on page 96 for more on space-saving beds.

PLANNING FOR CHILDREN'S STORAGE

Since your child's bedroom is likely to be the place where he or she spends a great deal of time over the years, it is important that this room meet the changing needs of a growing youth. Efficient storage plays a key role in how well a bedroom works and should be a goal when you plan its layout.

Consider your budget, physical layout, and the age of the child. Stacking drawers, a rolling cart, and wall-hung shelves can all be suited to a youngster's changing needs. The illustrations below show various room setups for children from infancy through to adolescence.

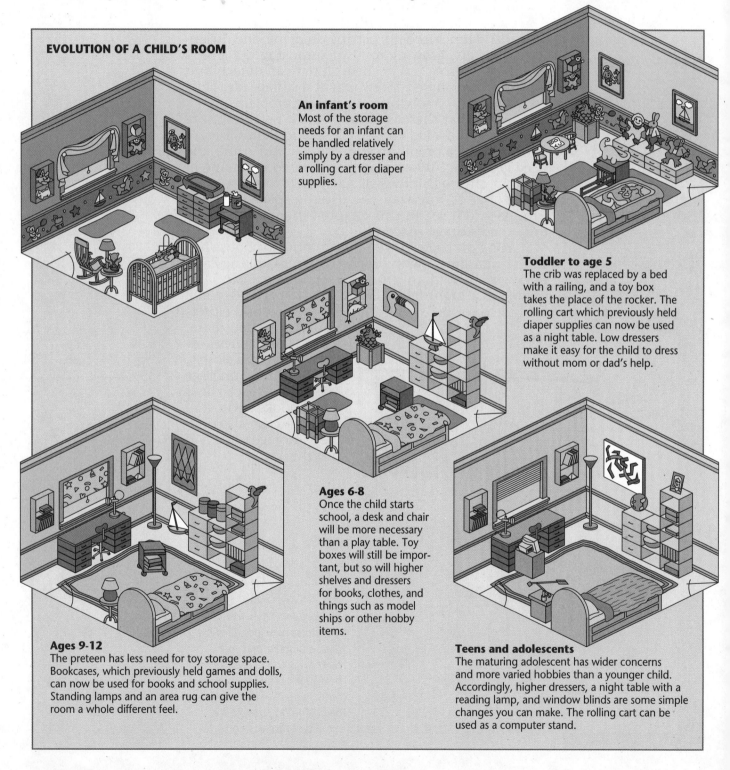

EVOLUTION OF A CHILD'S ROOM

An infant's room
Most of the storage needs for an infant can be handled relatively simply by a dresser and a rolling cart for diaper supplies.

Toddler to age 5
The crib was replaced by a bed with a railing, and a toy box takes the place of the rocker. The rolling cart which previously held diaper supplies can now be used as a night table. Low dressers make it easy for the child to dress without mom or dad's help.

Ages 6-8
Once the child starts school, a desk and chair will be more necessary than a play table. Toy boxes will still be important, but so will higher shelves and dressers for books, clothes, and things such as model ships or other hobby items.

Ages 9-12
The preteen has less need for toy storage space. Bookcases, which previously held games and dolls, can now be used for books and school supplies. Standing lamps and an area rug can give the room a whole different feel.

Teens and adolescents
The maturing adolescent has wider concerns and more varied hobbies than a younger child. Accordingly, higher dressers, a night table with a reading lamp, and window blinds are some simple changes you can make. The rolling cart can be used as a computer stand.

Although your storage space and related furnishings should be appropriate for the age of your children—there is no need for a computer desk if you only have a toddler, for example—you should always plan with an eye to the future. It is far too costly and time-consuming to buy, build, or completely replace items as the children get older.

As much as possible, plan to use storage that is adaptable and can grow along with a youngster's needs. For example, a toy chest, great for storing games and toys until the preteen years, can be easily converted to book and computer disc storage.

The chart and illustration below provide some important measurements to consider when planning for storage in a child's room. By following them, you'll make it easier for your youngster to develop the habit of putting everything in its place. This will surely make your life easier as well.

A ROOM FIT TO LIVE IN

Children enjoy their rooms a lot more when they can sit comfortably at the table or desk, and when many of their possessions are at eye level or within easy reach. This chart, containing average measurements, will help you create a safe, livable environment for your child, from toddler to teen.

Age	Height	Eye level	High reach	Table height	Chair height
3	37	33	41	15	8
5	39-47	35-43	43-52	18	10
7	44-52	40-48	49-59	19	11
9	47-57	43-53	53-65	21	12
12	53-64	49-60	61-73	23	13
15	61-71	57-66	70-82	26	15

SIZES FOR KIDS' STORAGE

Remember that as your children's minds and interests mature, so will their physical size. Shelves that were low enough to accommodate toddlers will be inconvenient for teens. Because of this, you should always keep in mind the fact that every few years, depending on how quickly your child grows, you will have to readjust things such as shelf and dresser height, tables and chairs, and even the height of toy boxes.

The chart above will give you an idea of how high to place shelves and other storage units, and what height tables and chairs to buy so that your children never have any trouble stacking and retrieving books, toys, collectibles, and clothes.

The illustration below depicts bookcase and shelf adaptations as your child ages. Place regularly used items so that kids don't have to strain or reach too far to get them; less-used objects can be stored on higher shelves. And as the years pass, you will have to build more, and higher, storage areas. This is much simpler and easier than planning a whole new room layout, and far less expensive than buying bigger pieces of furniture every few years as your child grows.

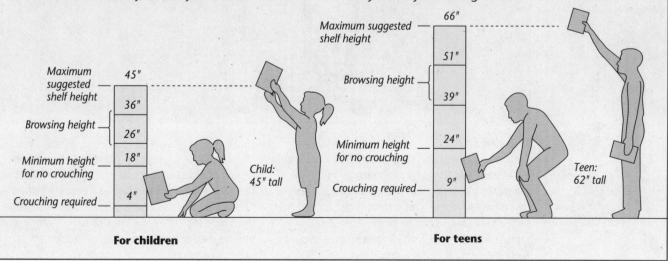

For children

For teens

SPACE-SAVING BEDS

Because children's rooms are often relatively small, they have a way of bulging at the seams with paraphernalia. One great way to gain more space for storage and activities is to monopolize less space with the bed, usually the largest piece of furniture in the room. Where space is tight, you might want to consider a bed that is designed to use space more efficiently than the conventional type.

For extreme space efficiency, investigate a Murphy bed, which is designed to disappear into a cabinet or wall cavity. Bear in mind that, although a wall bed will open up considerable floor space, it isn't very convenient. Raising and lowering it can become a real hassle and, with small children, may prove dangerous. If you choose one of these, be sure it is easy and safe to use.

Perhaps the most familiar alternative is the bunk bed, ideal for saving space in a room for two children or a child who has frequent overnight guests. You can also buy a loft-style bed that resembles a bunk bed but has a convertible couch/bed on the bottom or a desk and bookcases in the lower area.

Another way to make room for two twin beds is to employ trundle beds, where a second bed slides or rolls out from under the primary one as needed. Some trundles are freestanding units on casters, while others sit on attached frames. Many manufacturers make beds—even bunk beds—with trundle units that can be added later. Where drawer or cabinet storage is more important than a second bed, a captain's bed or chest bed is a good way to make use of the space under the mattress.

One other option, particularly in a room that has a high ceiling, is a built-in loft at one end or corner of the room. By building a platform that is high enough to walk under but low enough to allow kneeling above, you can add significantly to a room's floor space and create a cozy sleeping or play nook.

Lofts and a few of your options in beds are shown here and on the following pages.

Ideas for space-saving beds

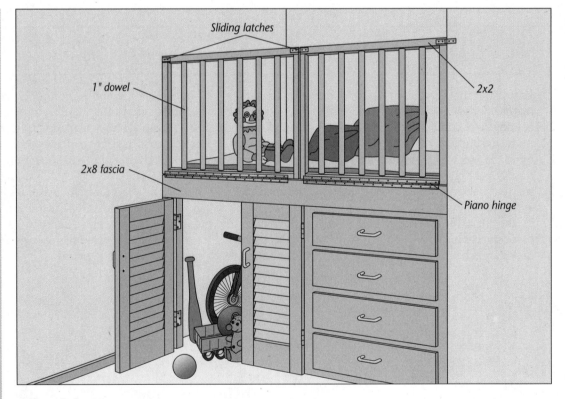

Crib and closet

Maximize space in an infant's room by incorporating storage solutions in a crib's design. In the example shown above, a miniature closet is used to store toys while the drawers hold clothes and diapers.

The crib's frame can be made from 2x6s attached to the wall with joist hangers. It should be between 51¾ and 53 inches long and 27⅜ and 28⅝ inches wide. No more than two fingers should fit between the crib and mattress. The space between the slats should not exceed 2⅜ inches. The latching mechanisms or locks that release the drop side should be well out of baby's reach and require dual action for release, or at least 10 pounds of force.

Five-in-one bed

This cabin bed is an assembly of a twin-sized loft bed, a desk for homework, a closet for clothes, and a built-in shelving unit for school books. The shelf edges double as ladder rungs for easy access to the bed. Elevated beds should be limited to children six years of age or older. They should have guard rails on two sides with the top of the mattress at least 5 inches below the rails. The gap between the lower edge of a guard rail and the bed frame should be no greater than 3½ inches.

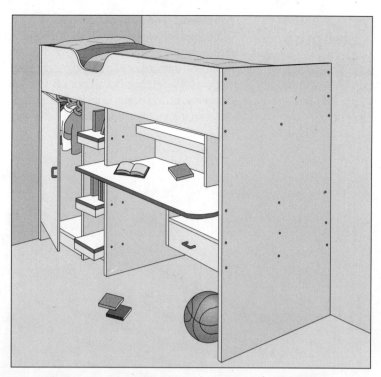

Handsome chest bed

This chest bed is no higher than a standard twin, so it isn't necessary to add protective rails. The unit offers easily accessible drawers for toys and clothes, plus a deep hidden bin—perfect for storing sheets, blankets, and other linens—that rolls out on casters. It is made from 3/4" plywood with 1/4" tempered hardboard for bin and drawer bottoms.

2-by solid wood

3/4" plywood

Trundle bed

A second bed in a child's bedroom is often a luxury that the existing space won't allow. In this case, consider a trundle bed such as the one shown at right.

Based on many of the same space-saving beds shown in this section, a trundle has a twin-size bed that rests on an elevated frame. Concealed below is a second twin guest bed that can be pulled out at the last minute to accommodate a visiting sleep-over friend, for example.

Some trundles include drawers which are sandwiched between the two beds. While some models run on tracks attached to the inside of the frame, others ride in and out on casters. Both are easily operated by young children.

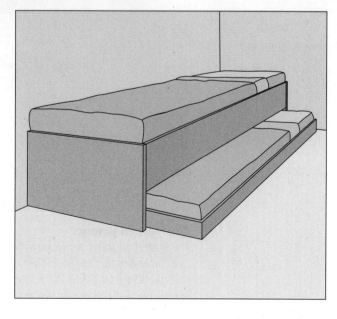

Sleeping lofts

Framework for a corner-post loft

Loft beds sit on elevated platforms designed to hold their weight. The size and spacing of the framing members varies according to the overall span of platform. Always check local codes before building. Obviously, ceiling height is an important factor; allow a minimum headroom of 4'6" above the bed, and about 6'6" for standing room below to accommodate a growing child. The bed itself is about one foot high, so ceilings should be at least 12'. The corner-post loft *(shown below)* is supported by two ledger strips and a corner post. As shown, the corner post should be made of 4x4 lumber.

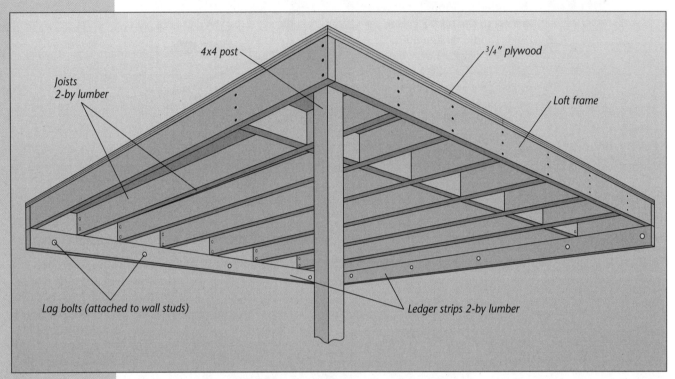

Joists 2-by lumber

4x4 post

³/₄" plywood

Loft frame

Lag bolts (attached to wall studs)

Ledger strips 2-by lumber

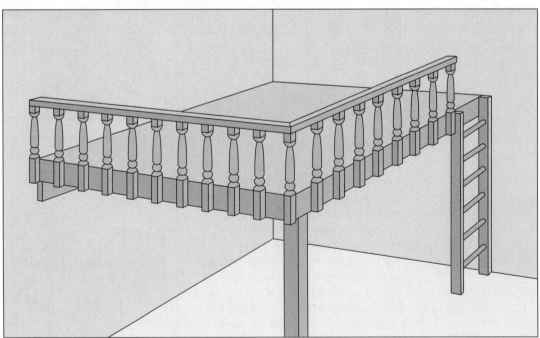

The finished product

The illustration above shows how the finished frame of a corner-post loft can look. Decorative safety railings and a solid ladder at the corner add to the overall function and beauty of the unit. Your child can use the area underneath for work, play, or clothes storage. A cabinet on coasters or a desk with rolling bins *(page 103),* for example, can be easily kept in this space.

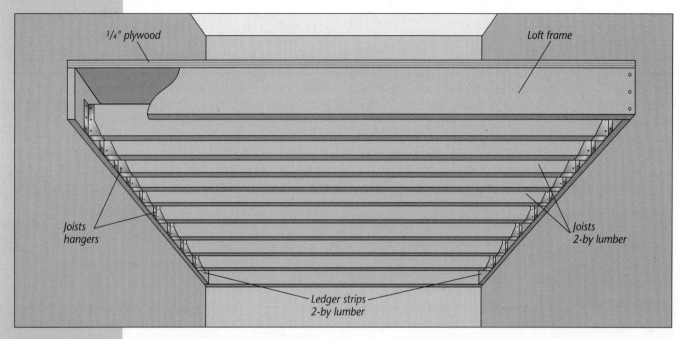

¾" plywood

Loft frame

Joists
hangers

Joists
2-by lumber

Ledger strips
2-by lumber

Framework for a bridge loft

The bridge loft, which fits at the end of a room, is supported by ledger strips lag-bolted to two opposing walls. Use joist hangers to connect the joists directly to the strips.

The finished product

To finish the loft, add plywood flooring (see below) and then a finished floor. The railing can be covered with wallboard and painted to match existing walls. Alternatively, use finish-grade lumber for the railing and add a protective coating or stain (page 189).

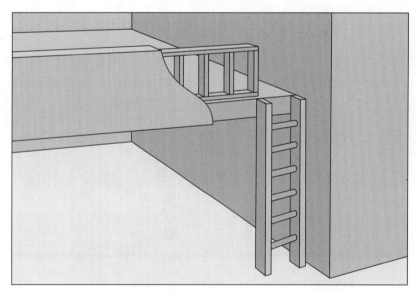

ASK A PRO

BUILDING STURDY LOFT BEDS

Remember that lofts are essentially new floors—so build and support them accordingly. Frames and 4x4 corner supports should be made of structural dimension lumber, and the floor should be ¾" plywood; the ladder should be made of 2-by lumber.

Metal framing connectors, in particular, make for much stronger joints than nails. Joist hangers, angle irons, post caps, post anchors, and others strengthen joints and make it easier to join wood. They also prevent splits in the end of your stock. You can buy them at most home centers. In some cases, there are large holes for through bolts or lag screws, as well as smaller holes for nails. Use whichever fastener you want.

The ledgers that support the frame can be the same size, or slightly larger, than the joists. Remember that a loft bed is meant for sleeping, not heavy storage—don't load it up with too many toys or other items.

CLOSETS

Not every youngster's room will have enough space for large wall units, deep dressers, or tall armoires. But there should at least be enough closet room to hold most toys and clothes. The organizational challenge lies in making the most of this space and making it easy for children to keep tidy.

You might want to add racks and shelves, to maximize closet space. You can either buy ready-made units, such as the metal rack shown below (right), or build your own, such as the wooden cubbyhole shelving system illustrated below (left).

It's a good idea to include adjustable shelves and wire bins so that your child can get a quick overview of his or her belongings simply by opening the closet door. Storage devices that are in plain view and are easy to reach encourage neatness.

Making clothes accessible

Low racks and shelves

A practical strategy for a child's closet is to have both upper and lower storage. In the closet illustrated below, items that are not being used are boxed and placed on the higher shelf. Likewise, out-of-season clothing is hung on the upper rod. Seasonal clothes are hung within reach on hook-on rod extensions. Shoes are in their own cubbyholes and boxes holding toys are placed on the lower shelf—easy to get at and easily put away.

DUAL-PURPOSE RACK

Specialty racks are particularly handy in a child's room where closet space is at a premium. Install a rack on a wall near the door to the room, or in the closet itself. Position the unit within arm's reach of the child so that hanging or folding clothes—not simply tossing them on the floor—becomes second nature.

The model shown below is made of metal and can be screwed directly to wall studs. The stem portion of the rack helps support the shelf. Caps, coats, schoolbags, or shoes can be hung from the 10 arms on the stem. Place sweaters, T-shirts, or even sporting gear, such as a baseball mitt, on the four horizontal bars that form the shelf.

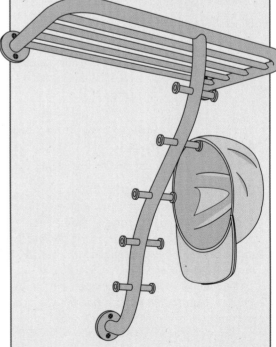

FUN STORAGE

Apart from being a place to sleep, your child's bedroom will likely be a play area, study space, and a place to enjoy arts and crafts. With all these activities going on—often behind closed doors—it's important that the room be recognizable at the end of the day. Unfortunately, parents can't always expect their children to understand basic, adult concepts of order. There are a few steps you can take, however, to encourage tidiness in your child's room. This section will provide a few examples.

Study area: A well-designed area helps kids develop strong study habits. Place bookshelves and wall units within easy reach and sight, and make sure the desk has plenty of drawer space—this will reduce desktop clutter and cause fewer distractions from the subject at hand.

Toys: Many of the diversions a child will enjoy in the bedroom will take place on the floor. Some toys require a smooth and level surface, such as building blocks and model trains; others, like board games and cards, are best suited for a soft carpet. A hardwood floor with a few carefully placed throw rugs is an ideal solution. Teaching the child to pick up toys at the end of the day will ensure a clutter-free and safe floor.

Hobby spaces: Encourage creativity by planning a space suited for hobbies and arts and crafts. If painting is your child's passion, buy or build an easel, stock it with washable paints, brushes, and sketch paper, and set it up in an open, bright area. The floor beneath the easel can be protected with a plastic sheet. Painting supplies can be stored in a commercial container *(page 149)*.

Making storage fun

Vertical bin rack
If you want to add order and color to a child's room, consider the bin storage unit shown at left. Made entirely of 2-by lumber, it is large enough to hold 16 plastic bins. Choose bins in four or five different colors for visual variety and label each to make storage easier. Children can reach bins on the lower levels while parents can handle those up high. NOTE: For safety, screw anchor bolts through the back uprights of the unit and into the wall studs. This will keep the unit from toppling in the event it becomes top-heavy.

Playthings as storage

Making storage fun

While it's fine for a child's storage and shelving units to be functional and efficient, you may want to add some character to them while you're at it. You can make or buy items such as those shown at right. The colorful cubes and high-rise hutch serve as play things as much as storage units. The open-ended cubes have bright, stimulating colors and can be stacked one on top of the other or in a row. The facade of the high-rise is really two doors that open to reveal shelving. Both cubes and hutch can be made out of plywood and finished with paint.

Relaxation and storage

Daybed storage

Besides their bedrooms, children often need a place to relax and enjoy some quiet time playing alone or reading. A daybed, such as the one nestled in the nook shown above, is the perfect solution. The bed frame features several drawers in which to store puzzles, games, and even clothes. An overhead shelf is a good spot for books and magazines. Positioning a daybed near a window allows for plenty of natural light and gives a child a view to the outside. Decorate the bed with sheets, blankets, and pillows so it's ready for a daytime nap or comfortable enough to accommodate a child's sleep-over friend.

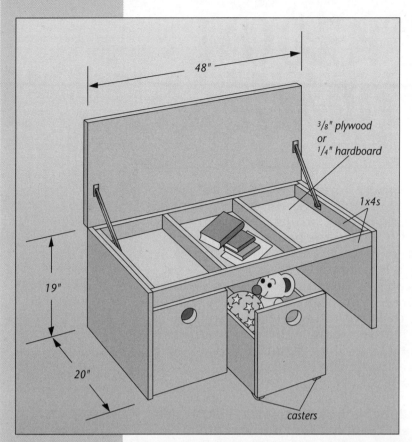

Desk with rolling bins

If you're trying to expand the storage capacity of your child's study area, consider a desk that is as much a storage space as it is a functional unit of furniture. With a lid that doubles as a drawing desk and rolling bins that slide under the desktop, this unit makes the most of its space. The "drawers" can be used as toy bins, or to hold art supplies or school work. You can build this desk using $3/4$" plywood for the sides, back, and lid; use $3/8$" plywood or $1/4$" hardboard for the inside of the desk. The tray frame is constructed from pine 1x4s. Assemble this 19" high, 20" deep, 48" wide desk with glue and finishing nails or woodscrews, then attach the swing-up lid with a piano hinge. Add spring-loaded safety lid supports at each end. NOTE: Lid supports are sold in various strengths. Make sure those you choose are strong enough to hold the lid upright when it is open. Make bins from plywood and add casters to their bottoms. Finish the unit and bins with enamel in bright colors.

Image labels: 48"; $3/8$" plywood or $1/4$" hardboard; 1x4s; 19"; 20"; casters

Versatility with modules

Storage modules, though practical storage devices in their own right, can be combined to form desks, platform beds, and even wall systems. Purchase ready-made wood, particleboard, or plastic units at home hardware stores, or build your own using $3/4$" plywood. A good-sized unit can measure 16" square. For compatibility, rectangular units should be 16"x16"x32". Hinged doors and simple drawers add a finished touch to the unit; use wood molding or veneer tape to hide plywood edges. Finish the modules with enamel. If you plan on stacking modules, bolt them to the wall, floor, or each other.

BATHROOM STORAGE

With all the things stored in a typical bathroom, you would think that it was the biggest room in the house and not the smallest. From blow-dryers to books to bath towels, the bathroom is expected to store a vast array of items and, not surprisingly, it often ends up in a bit of a mess.

While the first step to clearing up bathroom clutter is to get rid of items you don't need, that will still leave the considerable task of organizing a room that's visited by each family member three to four times each day. The practical tips offered in this chapter should help you keep on top of things.

If more space is what you need, consider adding an extra cabinet *(opposite)*. Ideas for using organizers to make existing cabinets more efficient are illustrated on page 106. Less complex, but no less effective, shelves and racks *(page 107)* offer space for books, magazines, and small plants.

Whether they are clean or dirty, towels can be the hardest items to manage in a bathroom. For a few ideas on how to hang them, turn to page 109. And instead of letting soiled towels and other dirty laundry pile up on the floor, it's best to put them in a clothes hamper right away. A few examples of hampers are provided on page 111.

Finally, to get a handle on small appliance storage such as for shavers, blow-dryers, and curling irons, turn to page 112.

Adding a recessed cabinet makes for efficient and attractive storage. Installation instructions are provided opposite.

CAPABLE CABINETS

Cabinets are the most important storage units in any bathroom. At once, they have to be big enough to hold the wide range of items normally found in a bathroom—soaps, cleaners, and cosmetics—but not so big that they dominate what is usually the smallest room in the house.

Rather than installing a completely new cabinet system, adding or modifying a unit can significantly improve your storage space. Recessing a cabinet into your bathroom's wall, for example, creates room without taking up additional floor space. To learn how to do this, as well as how to fashion a drawer to fit under a sink, see the information featured below.

If you're looking for a way to reduce clutter in existing cabinets, consider the organizers and pullouts shown on page 106. Devices such as lazy Susans maximize the entire depth of a cabinet and still keep items close at hand.

Improving cabinet space

Wrapping drawers around sinks
Due to the curve of the sink underneath a bathroom cabinet, storage space is either lost or cluttered. One simple solution to this problem is to build drawers that wrap around the sink and its plumbing, such as the one shown at right. Each drawer has a curved back, cut from 18-gauge sheet metal and fastened to the side and bottom with sheet-metal screws. Design: Bill Ridenour

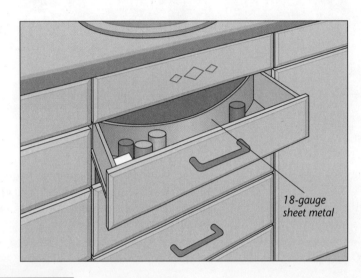

18-gauge sheet metal

16" O.C.
1/2" plywood spacer
Header (double 2x4s)
1/4" plywood back
Magnetic catch
1x6
3/4" plywood door
2x4 sill
Adjustable glass shelves
Remove stud and fire blocks
8"
30 1/4"
Mitered trim

A built-in cabinet
Recessing a cabinet between studs can provide needed storage without taking up too much precious bathroom space. In most cases, you'll have to remove one part of one middle stud and reframe the opening as shown.

First, locate the studs in the area and check for wiring or plumbing. Mark the inside edges of the studs you'll keep; also, mark top and bottom lines at the height you want the cabinet, adding 3½" at the top and 1½" at the bottom for the new header and sill.

Cut an opening in the wall along these lines. Cut the middle stud squarely and carefully pry it away from the wall covering on the other side. Toenail the header inside the opening and then add a sill.

Build the cabinet from 1x6 lumber, making it ¼" less in height and width than the size of the opening. Nail on a ¼" plywood back. Drill holes for shelf pegs or pins, add doors, and finish. Position the cabinet in the opening and shim it plumb and level; nail it to the framing. Replace any wall covering that was cut away to install the header and sill, attach the trim, and then add the shelves.

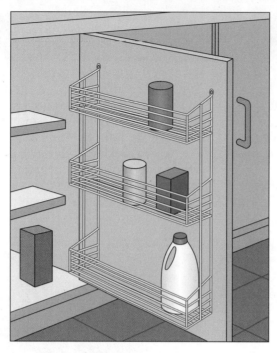

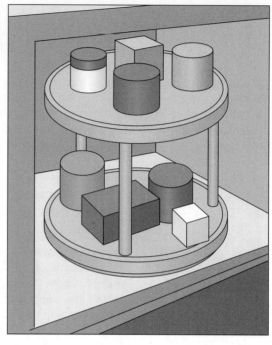

A bonanza of backdoor space

To take greater advantage of cabinet space in a bathroom, plan to make use of the doors. A vinyl-coated wire storage rack mounted to the inside of a cabinet door *(above)* can help you organize soaps, shampoos, and other cosmetics, as well as bathroom cleaning supplies.

Not-so-lazy Susans

These hard-working storage-go-rounds help keep bathroom paraphernalia from finding its way into the far reaches of your cabinetry. Single-level or tiered, a lazy Susan rotates so that everything you store is visible and accessible *(above)*. Be sure to measure your cabinet carefully—allowing for drain-pipe clearance, if necessary—before you build or buy one of these organizers.

Problem-solving pullouts

There's no need to grope around in your bathroom cabinets in search of that extra tube of toothpaste or the bubble bath you got last Christmas. With pullouts like the ones shown at left, bath supplies glide right out for easy access. Available in plastic, wood, and regular or vinyl-coated wire, pull-outs can be installed on full-extension drawer slides or on their own special framework.

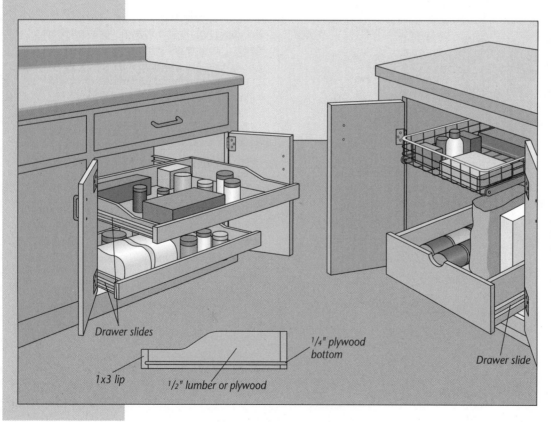

Drawer slides

1x3 lip   ½" lumber or plywood   ¼" plywood bottom

Drawer slide

SHELVES AND RACKS

Given all the permanent fixtures in a modern bathroom—toilet, bathtub, and sink—it's a wonder that there is any room left over—apart from the cabinets and closets—for books, magazines, and extra linens. Of course there is, but the trick is to introduce storage units that make use of seemingly lost space.

This section will provide a few practical ideas for building shelves that fit above toilets and doors (see below) and magazine racks that can be added to a wall (page 108). Most of these units have simple designs and can be easily built by a do-it-yourselfer using standard lumber.

If you choose to purchase a shelving unit, consider an over-the-toilet unit like the one on the bottom of page 108 to take advantage of space that would otherwise be wasted.

Finding forgotten spaces

Storing towels overhead
The idea for this storage system originated aboard passenger trains when rail travel was popular and it was necessary to maximize every inch of compartment space. Today, in a crowded bathroom, it helps keep extra towels out of the way, yet easy to access.

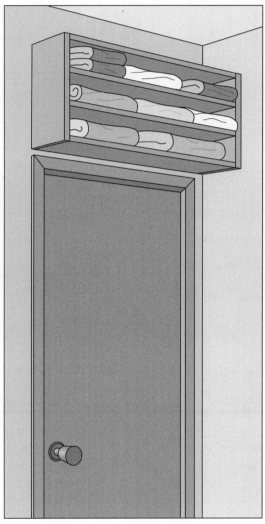

Minilibrary for private browsing
Many people appreciate the privacy bathrooms afford for reading in solitude. Here, a selection offers food for thought, but hospitality and decorative flair as well. The shelves rest on ledger strips screwed into studs on opposing walls.

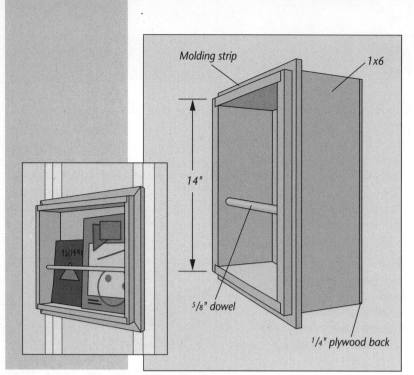

Molding strip

1x6

14"

5/8" dowel

1/4" plywood back

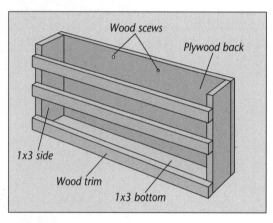

A recessed rack

This rack for reading matter is a simple box that is recessed into the wall, fitting snugly between two studs. Since wall studs are usually 16 or 24 inches apart (center to center), the miniature library will probably need to to be 14$\frac{1}{2}$" or 22$\frac{1}{2}$" wide; 14" is a convenient height. Locate the studs, measure and mark and remove your wallboard to accommodate the box. Use pine 1x4s or 1x6s for the box frame. Before assembling the frame, drill shallow holes in the side pieces to hold a $\frac{5}{8}$" dowel. Assemble the frame and add a $\frac{1}{4}$" plywood back. Slide the unit into the wall cutout, and side-nail the box into both wall studs. Add molding strips for a finished look.

Putting magazines in reach

Wood scews

Plywood back

1x3 side

Wood trim

1x3 bottom

Building a simple wall rack

This simple wall rack is easy to build. Cut two side-pieces and a bottom piece from pine or fir 1x3s, and cut a back from $\frac{1}{4}$" or $\frac{3}{8}$" plywood. Assemble the pieces, then nail $\frac{1}{4}$" thick strips of wood trim across the front to keep magazines and books in place. Finally, drive two wood screws through the back of the rack and into the wall studs. Apply a paint, varnish, or polyurethane finish. The unit illustrated is approximately 12" high and 20" wide, but these dimensions can be adjusted to suit your needs and wall space.

A movable solution

A freestanding commercial shelving unit, such as the one shown at right, fits around and above your toilet. Lightweight and easy to install, you can put books or magazines on its shelves or add some ambience to the bathroom by adding a plant or two.

TIDYING UP TOWELS

Keeping on top of a towel collection is one of the main concerns in any bathroom—but it needn't become a problem. With some of the towel racks shown in this section, both commercial and home-made, you'll find it easy to stack, store, or hang towels in easy-to-reach places that don't take up too much of a bathroom's limited space.

A basic knowledge of woodworking and tool know-how *(page 169)* is all that's required to build the sort of towel racks shown below and at the top of page 110.

Once built, the racks need to be protected against the humidity common to bathrooms. High-quality paints, polyurethanes, and varnishes offer the best protection. All three of these can be found at your local hardware or paint store.

Rather than building your own, you can buy towel racks to suit your decor. Everything from lacquered brass to wood can be purchased at home centers or through mail-order catalogs. A selection of a few popular models is shown at the bottom of page 110.

Hanging towels close at hand

Two towel racks
To make the rustic rack shown *(right, top)*, screw a length of 2x2 redwood to two 2x3 end blocks; attach the rail to the blocks with 3¹/₂" long lag screws. Use 5¹/₂" long lag screws to fix the rack to the wall. (It's best to locate the wall studs before you cut the rail length.)

The more elaborate, two-rung rack *(right, bottom)*, uses 1¹/₂" wooden rods held in place by decorative supports; cut the supports from 2x12 stock. Drill shallow holes to support the rods and screw the rack to wall studs.

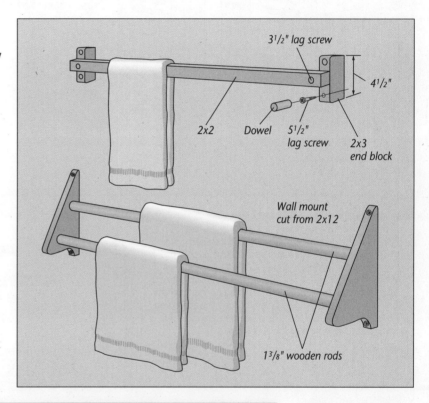

3¹/₂" lag screw

4¹/₂"

2x2   Dowel   5¹/₂" lag screw   2x3 end block

Wall mount cut from 2x12

1³/₈" wooden rods

A recessed towel bar
Located just below and slightly to the side of your bathroom sink, this 1x2 bar allows you to grab a towel without having to grope for it. It uses space that is often overlooked close to the sink. Make the pocket 2¹/₂" deep and finish its surfaces to match the cabinet facing. The bar itself is inset ¹/₂" from the cabinet front.
Architect: Henry Wood

2x2 bar

Inset ¹/₂"

2¹/₂" deep

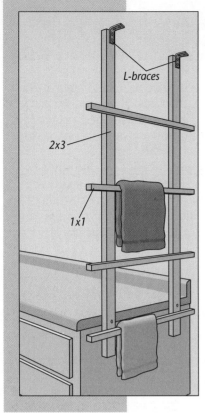

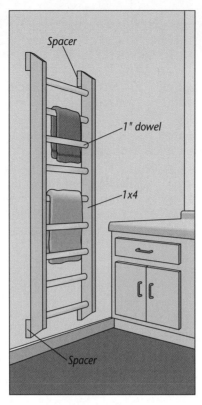

The lowdown on ladders

Floor-to-ceiling towel ladders make the most of narrow spaces. They're also very easy to build.

Simply nail 1x1 strips to the front edges of parallel 2x3 uprights. Or recess 1" dowels into matching holes in two parallel 1x4 uprights; glue the dowels in place and clamp them securely until dry. Fasten your ladder to the floor and/or ceiling with L-braces or attach it to the spacer blocks you've screwed into wall studs.

Redwood is an excellent material for towel holders because it's moisture-resistant. Hardwoods are also good, but are somewhat more expensive. Protect the wood with a polyurethane finish or penetrating resin.

A RANGE OF RACKS

If you'd rather buy a towel rack than build one, you'll find a large selection of commercial models, such as those shown here. Standard bars and rings, sold individually or as components in matching accessory sets, are available in a wide variety of materials—from brass to chrome, from oak to plastic. Another option is a wall rack with wooden pegs or brass hooks. If you have the floor space, consider a freestanding rack that can handle hanging and folded towels.

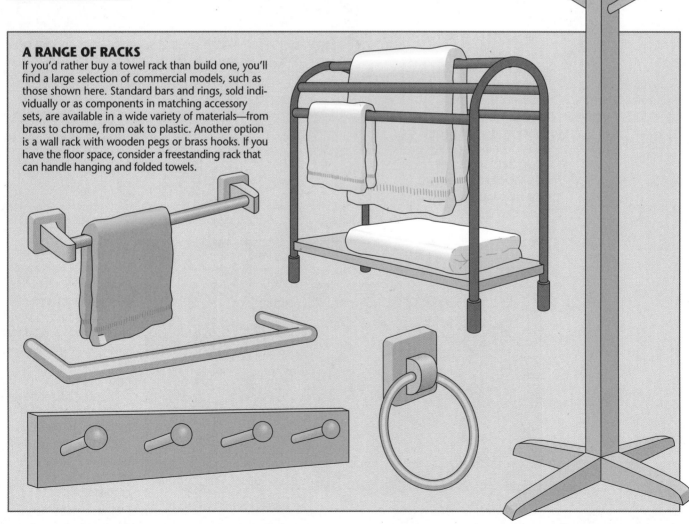

HANDY HAMPERS

No matter how hard you try, laundry always seems to end up in a pile on the bathroom floor. To help control this domestic phenomenon, consider installing one of the clothes hampers shown below.

While it's tempting to get a large model, don't buy more hamper than you'll need or the laundry may accumulate for weeks at a time. As well, too large a laundry basket can be unwieldy to move easily when laundry day comes.

Built-in hampers keep laundry concealed behind closed doors and are easy to access come wash time. The model shown simply hooks onto the back of a pull-down cabinet door and can be carted away when it is full.

Portable floor models are small enough to fit in a corner of the bathroom and light enough to be toted to the washing machine when full. Two examples are shown at the bottom of the page.

Built-in units

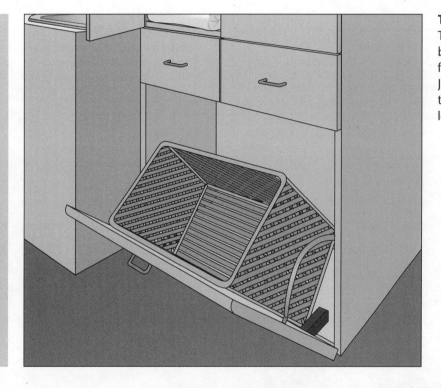

Tilting clothes bins
This vinyl-coated basket attaches to a flip-down cabinet door. Just lift the basket out to carry the laundry load to the washer.

Portable hampers

Smart floor models
The natural rattan clothes hamper *(right)* fits into a corner, taking up the minimum of bathroom floor space. The foldable hamper *(far right)* is not only light, its cotton bag can be easily removed for cleaning.

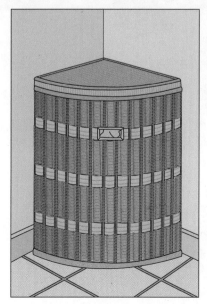

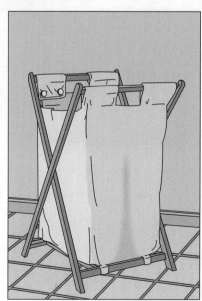

BATHROOM APPLIANCES AND ACCESSORIES

Year after year, we seem to add more and more electric gadgets and other accessories to our already crowded bathroom countertops and closet shelves. The list seems endless: electric toothbrushes, water jets, blow-dryers, curling irons, and shavers to name but a few. Eventually, not only do we have to find room for these items, but we have to store them in a manageable way.

Shown below are some easy ideas for keeping small appliances organized. You can choose to put them in wire baskets or, for those with hanging loops, suspend them on hooks underneath shelving. A dual-purpose sink-top shelf is also shown. For a simple tip on keeping power cords neatly coiled and undamaged, see the top of the opposite page.

Other paraphernalia, like toothbrushes and bathroom tissue, can be kept in smart and easy-to-reach holders. As shown *(opposite)* there is a wide range of commercial and homemade models to choose from for both.

PUTTING APPLIANCES IN THEIR PLACE
Storage aids not designed specifically for small appliances can be easily pressed into service: consider shower caddies (they can be hung on an open wall as well as in the shower), wall-mounted vinyl pouches (sold as closet organizers), and under-shelf baskets of vinyl-coated wire.

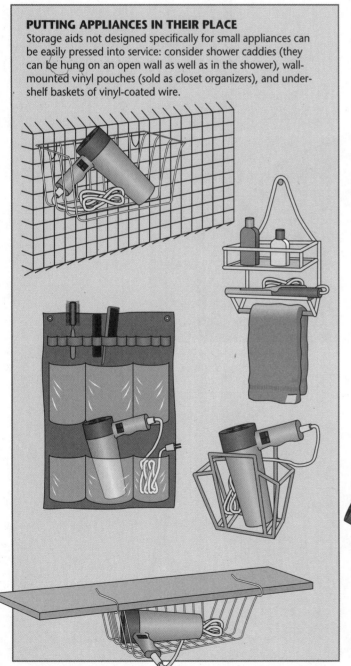

SOME IMPROVISED SOLUTIONS
If your small grooming appliances have hanging loops, then simple hooks or pegs are all you'll need for storage. Put together a rack from redwood backing strip and some brass hooks or hardwood-dowel pegs; or simply screw cup hooks to the underside of a bathroom shelf. Rather than hanging your appliances, consider a narrow shelf with carefully measured holes drilled through it to form holsters for your curling iron, your shaver, or the nozzle of your blow-dryer. For several large or heavy appliances, try a wider shelf running the length of the sink counter and 6" to 8" above it; support the shelf with wood blocks spaced to form counter-level cubbyholes for cosmetics and grooming aids.

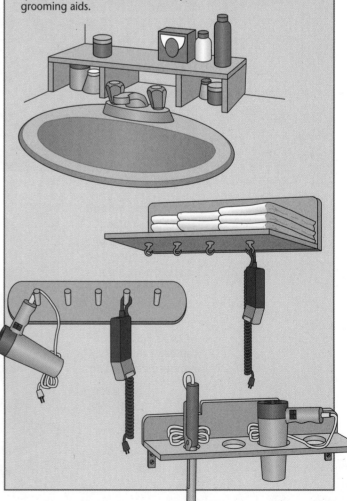

ASK A PRO

HOW CAN I COIL ELECTRIC CORDS SAFELY?

Appliance cords become easily tangled if they are not stored out of the way. Wrapping the power cord around an appliance can damage the cord, eventually causing it to break. Instead, coil the cord into a small, loosely held loop; then stuff the coil into an empty bathroom tissue tube. This will help keep the appliance safe, neat, and handy.

Another hint: Never coil power cords around objects, such as around an elbow and a palm. This produces a neat loop the first time, but eventually causes the electrical cord to twist and break. Always loop power cords loosely, and carefully.

TISSUE HOLDERS TO BUY OR BUILD

Tissue holders come in a wide range of styles and materials—from traditional steel or ceramic holders with spring-loaded inserts, to high-tech plastic models in bright colors, to costly antique reproductions in solid brass. But tissue holders are also easy to make, and the handsome wooden ones shown here are fine examples. Remember that a new roll of tissue is about 5 inches in diameter, so the insert's center must be at least 2¾" from the wall. Mounting tissue holders may require some patience. Some end pieces are easier to mount if they are first bridged by a backing piece that is then attached directly to the wall. Try to anchor holders to wall studs; if that isn't feasible, use expanding anchors or toggle bolts.

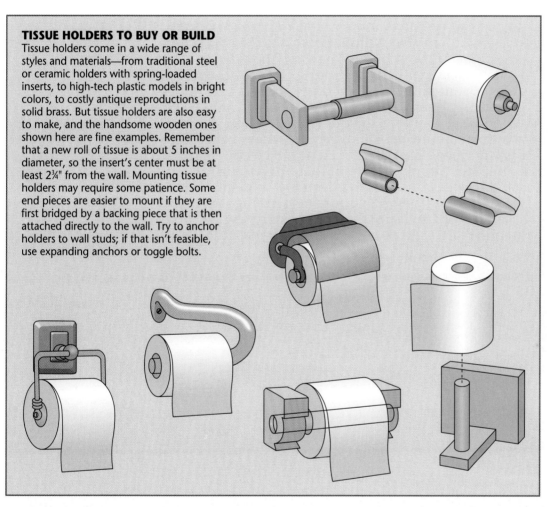

BRUSH UP YOUR DENTAL DETAILS

Choose one of many commercially available toothbrush holders—free-standing or wall mounted, with tumbler or without—or make one of your own from a scrap block of oak. Begin with a 9" long 2x4. Drill eight ⁵/₈" diameter holes into one edge, each 3" deep. Smooth the entire holder with fine sandpaper. Finish the wood with two coats of clear polyurethane to protect it from the humid bathroom climate—and from dripping toothbrushes.

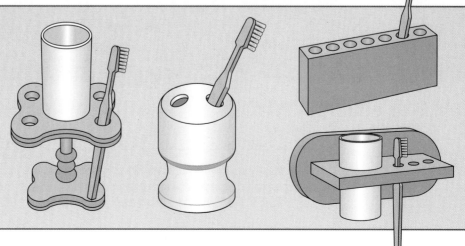

COMMERCIAL STORAGE OPTIONS

From tool boxes and storage bins to wine racks and closets, there are an almost infinite variety of commercial products to help you organize the tools, equipment, and household goods that would otherwise clutter up your home. The ideas shown in the following pages are just a beginning. A trip through the aisles of your local hardware store or home renovation center may help you discover some other simple and economical solutions to your storage needs.

Many commercial storage systems are made up of easy-to-assemble units that can be mixed and matched as needed. Simply combine these units with boxes, stacking crates, and bins to suit your own requirements.

When purchasing a commercial storage product, take note of any weight restrictions suggested by the manufacturer, and be careful how you stack the items.

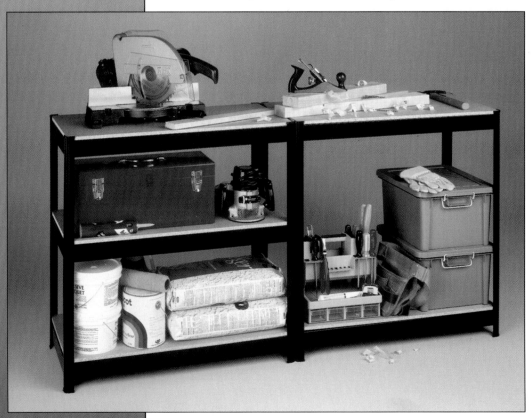

In small basements and garages, where space is always at a premium, a sturdy rack with shelves for storing tools and a built-in wooden work surface can prove invaluable.

Plastic crates and bins are ideal for storing items like paint cans, cleaning products, and automotive accessories. They are stackable, fit nicely between larger shelving units, and are easy to clean. If portability is important, choose a model with casters.

The attractive storage boxes at right can take care of the overflow from cupboards and closets. The boxes feature lids and have handles to facilitate carrying.

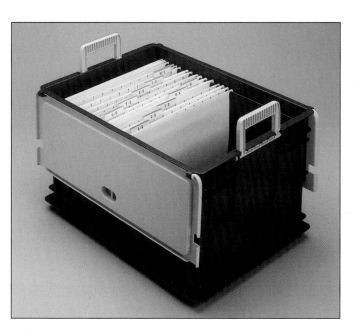

Cardboard file boxes are susceptible to moisture damage and can be hard to get at when you need them most. Plastic crates, specifically designed to hold files, protect the documents inside and can be stacked to save space. A lid helps keep out dust.

More attractive than metal units, wood shelving kits like the one above are efficient and easy to assemble. The multiple shelf holes allow you to chose your own compartment size, and the heavy-duty bolt fasteners are more durable than screws or nails. Before buying these types of units, check for warped, knotty, or split boards.

The rack at left holds up to four dozen bottles. Cradled in the front and back supports, the bottles are stored horizontally to prevent them from falling over and to keep the corks from drying out.

Plastic-coated wire shelving units help turn a messy laundry area into a neat, well-organized, and safe space. The large loose wire baskets are ideal for hauling laundry to and from the appliances, and the basket drawer system is great for sorting clean clothes. Use the upper shelves and baskets to store cleaners and detergents out of the reach of small children.

This recessed closet contains a folding ironing board and shelves to hold an iron and accessories. An attractive, finished wood door conceals the contents when they're not in use. Make sure the closet is equipped with a safety switch to cut the power to the light and the electrical outlet when the door is closed.

A lack of shelf space means that many laundry rooms end up with a lot of unwanted clutter. The freestanding rack at left solves that problem. It's also light enough to be moved to wherever it is needed.

Boot bins allow you to stow wet and muddy footwear in one place and keep your entrance floors clean and clutter-free. In the model shown at right, the lower area has a drainage shelf to catch snow, water, or mud, while the upper half is perfect for storing socks, mittens, and other loose items. Flip down the top and you have a handy bench.

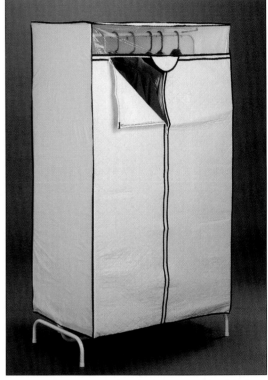

Keep out-of-season clothing stored safely from moths and moisture with portable garment racks, like the freestanding model shown above. To save floor space, some racks can be hung from ceiling joists or rafters. For easy mobility, choose one with casters. Make sure the model you choose has a heavy-duty zipper.

This metal garment rack is light enough to move easily, while the sturdy metal braces prevent the unit from swaying.

Store bicycles on wall-mounted racks to save floor space and to protect them from falling over. The model shown at left includes a small shelf to hold cycling accessories. If you need to store several bikes, consider hanging them vertically by the front tire. Whatever system you choose, remember to secure the rack to wall studs or solid surfaces. Brick or concrete walls require anchors or special self-tapping screws.

Organize your home's athletic goods with simple but sturdy wall-hung sports racks. Made of epoxy-coated heavy-gauge wire, the rack below consists of a series of hooks, hangers, and baskets to hold objects of all shapes and sizes.

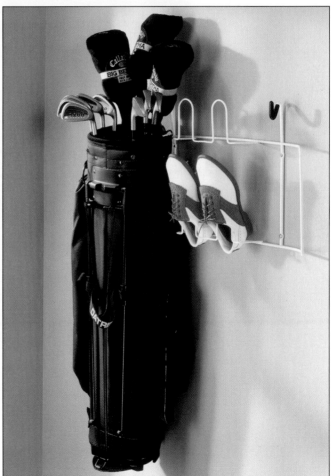

Don't risk damaging expensive golf clubs by propping them up against a wall or in the corner of a room. The plastic-coated wire rack shown above keeps your golf bag stored securely. It even provides a shoe rack to help dry your golf shoes.

Designed to fit snugly in the corner of a room, the sturdy metal shelving system at left has large compartments to hold a garageful of tools, supplies, and hardware. The center section features a large lower unit to store taller objects.

Design your own storage organizing system with durable, versatile, and easy-to-hang melamine cabinets. The model at right features units with reversible doors, a pegboard tool rack, and a laminated work surface.

Storing the supplies that keep a home running smoothly and looking clean can be a challenging task. Choose a shelving system like the one at left to hold paint cans, industrial cleaners, and anything else that clutters your basement or garage. Its hard rubber surface is durable, resistant to scratches, and easy to clean.

Backyard storage sheds are ideal for handling the overflow from over-stuffed basements and garages. They are particularly helpful for storing seasonal tools, supplies, and sporting goods like lawn mowers, gardening equipment, barbecues, and even bicycles. Consider installing a small shelving unit to handle your backyard odds and ends. Choose a shed that fits with the colors and decor of your yard and set it on patio stones, brick, or a concrete slab to avoid water damage.

Simple to hang just about anywhere, this wire rack is useful for neatly storing gardening tools and accessories that often end up taking up valuable space in a garage.

With its large, deep-set shelves, the plastic storage booth shown at right houses up to 17 cubic feet of tools and supplies without taking up a lot of room in a garage or basement. Waterproof and easy to clean, the unit also features a lockable door.

GARAGE, ATTIC, AND BASEMENT

There are basically two steps in the home storage process: identifying the best areas around the home for storing various items, and then deciding what goes where. This is especially important when considering long-term storage. Rarely needed items should be stowed in less-accessible areas, leaving seasonal and often-used items in more easily reached areas. But what is the ideal spot for firewood? And where can you put your wine collection? This chapter provides information about storing a variety of items to help make some of your decisions easier.

Remember that the storage space and the items you intend to store must suit one another. Drawers or bins are best for smaller articles, whereas larger ones are more suited to deep, open shelves, or cupboards built to fit. Hang long-handled tools from racks or prop them against the wall. And, as much as possible, plan to store overhead or high on walls to free up floor space for other activities.

This chapter will also give you a few ideas for designing storage units you can build yourself, such as food cellars *(page 126)*, wine racks *(page 128)*, and firewood bins *(page 134)*. Most of these units are built using common materials and simple construction methods. Turn to the *Tools and Techniques* chapter, which begins on page 169, for some helpful tips.

The space under the basement stairs is perfect for storing firewood: There's good air circulation, no possibility of dangerously high wood stacks, and no space taken up in the home. See page 134 for more on storing wood.

BOOKS, DOCUMENTS, AND PHOTOS

There comes a time when everyone must struggle with the dilemma of how to store magazines, books, photographs, and various personal documents. These are the items that accumulate fastest around the home and that require the greatest care to store. To avoid damaging paper products in storage, you must protect them vigilantly from light, moisture, heat, insects, and poor ventilation.

Librarians recommend temperatures between 60°F (16°C) and 75°F (24°C) and humidity between 50% and 60% for storing most papers. If you use good-quality storage units that permit air circulation, you can safely keep documents in a dry and insulated attic or basement. Unless you control the temperature and humidity *(page 124)*, hot attics and damp basements are unsuitable for photograph and paper storage.

When using cardboard boxes to store paper items, don't fasten the lids or flaps—air must flow freely. Pack books and magazines loosely, and check occasionally for signs of dampness or mold. Metal units or units lined with metal will protect paper from insects and rodents. Cardboard and metal boxes block out light.

Store books and magazines on shelves in an area that is dry and temperature-stable; cold spaces are acceptable as long as they're kept dry. Keep shelves away from an uninsulated wall; set them against furring strips fastened to the wall or place polyethylene sheeting between the wall and shelves. If your books will be exposed to a lot of light, especially fluorescent or direct daylight, equip the shelves with doors or curtains. You can store magazines in slipcover cases or binders, available from publishers or office suppliers.

ASK A PRO

WHAT IS THE BEST WAY TO STORE VIDEOCASSETTES?

Videocassettes should be stored upright in their cases in a cool, dry spot. To avoid accidental erasure, keep the cassettes away from magnetic fields produced by equipment such as speakers and telephones.

Storing files

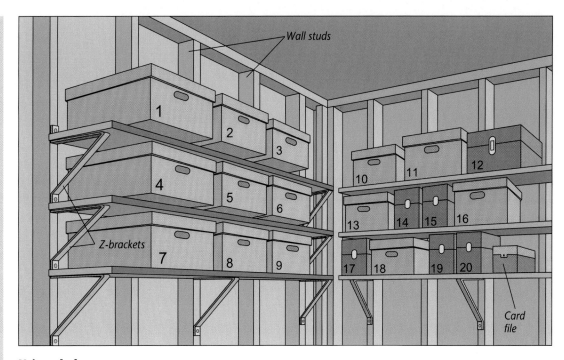

Using shelves

An organized collection of cardboard or metal containers for household records, receipts, documents, and correspondence will meet the storage needs of most homeowners. Use individual filing boxes or cartons to handle large items, and canceled check organizers with filing inserts, slipcover letter files, and binding cases for documents. Store bits and pieces of paper in metal and cardboard card files, available in many sizes.

Arrange your box system on 1x12 shelves supported by Z-brackets or individual shelf brackets fastened to wall studs. To keep track of what's where, you can number each box to match a corresponding index card which lists the contents of the box.

Knee wall

Using file cabinets

A metal file cabinet, with one to five stacked drawers, is a very efficient and safe way to store important documents and photo negatives. To save space, recess the cabinet under stairs *(above, left)* or into a knee wall in the attic *(above, right)* so that only the drawer fronts are exposed. A light above the cabinets makes finding files easier. File cabinets are expensive, but to reduce the cost you can buy used equipment; look up "Office Furniture and Equipment—Used" in the Yellow Pages.

For maps, oversize documents, and art paper, use wood or steel flat files like the one shown below.

PRESERVING PHOTOS

Although photographic films and papers are more stable and long-lasting today than they were in the past, your photo memories can still fade or discolor if exposed to excessive light, heat, or moisture. Keep them in covered boxes, cupboards, or flat file drawers *(below, left)*. Storage conditions for photo materials must be dry; place a packet of silica gel in each container to help absorb moisture.

Store color slides in boxed projector trays or special clear plastic 8 1/2 x11-inch sheets. Keep black-and-white and color negatives in protective file sheets *(below, right)*; you can then organize the sheets in three-ring binders which you can keep in a drawer or box. Separate prints with pieces of paper or enclose them in individual rag-paper envelopes, then lay them in flat file drawers or boxes.

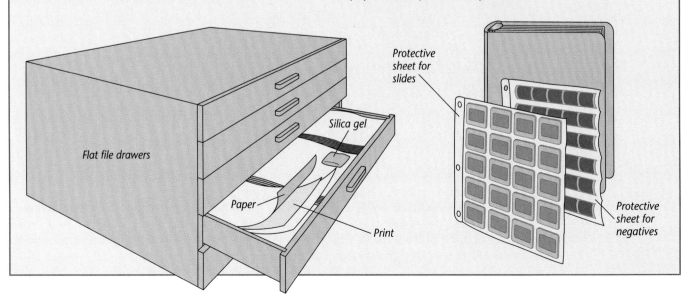

Flat file drawers

Silica gel

Paper

Print

Protective sheet for slides

Protective sheet for negatives

FOOD AND WINE

If you're looking for the right spot to store food or wine, you need not look any further than your basement or crawl space. In the summer, these areas stay naturally cooler than any other place in the house. If your basement is heated, consider partitioning off a section to act as a cold-insulated food or wine cellar.

FOOD

There are two ways to store household food: in the pantry, or other room-temperature storage, for canned goods and nonperishables; and cool root cellar storage for fruits, vegetables, staples, and preserves.

You can store cans and jars just about anywhere that's convenient in the garage or basement—except near a furnace, water heater, or other heat source. Place items on orderly shelves, inside an unused utility closet, or behind cabinet doors. Insect eggs or larvae may be present in dried foods, even if they can't be seen. Be sure to keep dried goods in rigid containers to confine any insects that may develop.

To create a food cellar in a basement, insulate a small area along a cool basement wall, *(page 126)*. Partition off an area adjacent to a shaded north or east wall and away from heating ducts and pipes. If possible, choose a site with an outside opening—a window is convenient—to provide air flow. Cool ground temperatures and, when the weather is cool, the outside air will keep cellar temperatures low; the insulation will keep out heated air from the surrounding basement. In a hot climate, the area will be hard to keep cool in the summer. You can consider installing an air conditioner with a thermostat, although this will tend to dry the air. To keep the room moist, set out large pans of water, or spread peat moss or sawdust and dampen it periodically. Wood slats laid on top will keep your feet dry.

An old-fashioned root cellar with a cool dirt floor is another food storage option. Traditionally, root cellars were dug below the house, into the ground outside, or into a hillside. A modern-day crawl space may be just the place to locate your root cellar.

ASK A PRO

WHERE CAN I KEEP FOOD OR WINE COOL IF I DON'T HAVE A BASEMENT?
Search the house for an area that stays naturally cool; the north side of the house is shadiest, therefore the coolest. If possible, choose a spot that can be vented to a naturally cool crawl space or outside area.

Root crops (except potatoes) require moist, cool storage conditions. Other crops, including potatoes, winter squash, and pumpkins, prefer warmer, drier surroundings (50° to 60°F; 10° to 16°C). Don't store fruits and vegetables right next to each other: Apples and pears can cause root vegetables to sprout and some vegetables will cause fruits to take on an earthy odor. Consult your local university agricultural extension service for more information about proper food storage guidelines. Protect storage areas against rodents and other animals by keeping the areas clean and screening all openings to the outside.

WINE

If you plan to make wine collecting a serious hobby, you'll have to create an organized and stable environment for your collection. By purchasing young wines or sale wines in bulk, and letting them mature in your own cellar, you'll save the appreciable markup that dealers tack on each year that the wines age on their shelves. Moreover, many fine wines disappear from the market long before they're mature. Keep in mind that there are four factors for successful wine storage: peace and quiet, absence of light, bottle positioning, and temperature stability.

For the optimum aging of wine, it's best to keep the storage area between 50° and 60°F (10° and 16°C); 58°F (14°C) is generally regarded as ideal. Some experts, however, wouldn't pale at the idea of storing wines at room temperature—65° to 70°F (18° to 21°C). Temperature stability is more critical than precise temperature: Wine can tolerate slow temperature changes over a period of weeks, but avoid rapid or extreme fluctuations, as they will cause damage.

To control temperature fluctuations or to keep the wine cool, create an insulated wine cellar in your basement. Follow the guidelines for a food cellar *(page 126)*.

You must protect wine from vibration and light, as well. Avoid storing it near sources of vibration such as stairways, washers, and dryers. Sturdy wine racks will help; in earthquake country, bolt racks to fixed walls.

Direct sunlight and other sources of ultraviolet light may harm wines, so make your cellar lightproof. But don't forget good artificial light for those times when you're hunting for that special bottle or hosting a wine-tasting party.

Always store the bottles on their side. This ensures that the wine keeps the cork moist, preventing air or airborne organisms from entering and spoiling the wine. Keep a complete log of your stock, including stored locations, and label each slot in your rack to ensure you don't mix up the Beaujolais with the Zinfandel.

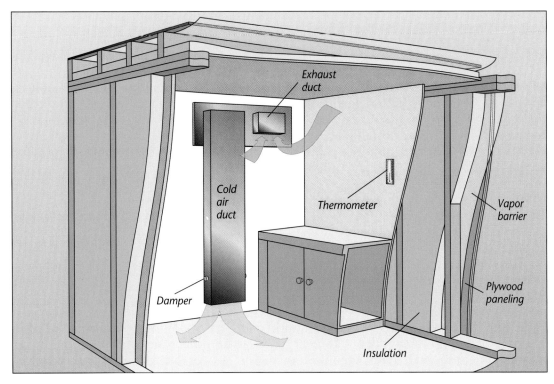

Creating a food cellar

Once you've chosen a spot for your cellar, insulate the ceiling, new interior walls, the door and, unless the climate is cool year-round, the exterior wall above ground level. As shown above, install a cold air duct with a damper to bring cool air in and a duct with a sliding vent to exhaust warm air to the outside. You can also install a fan in the exhaust duct to blow warm air out. You can control the temperature of the room by opening and closing the damper or by turning the fan on and off.

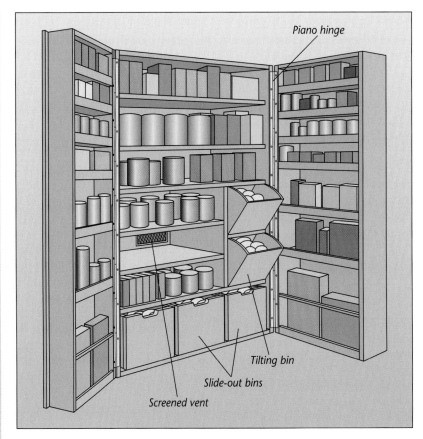

Building a larder

This built-in larder accommodates canned goods, grains, and bulk produce. Screened vents to the outside or a crawl space keep the temperatures low. Deep shelves hold canned and boxed goods; narrow lipped shelves on the double doors provide more accessible storage. Since the doors are very heavy when loaded, they are attached with piano hinges. The doors can roll on casters if you position the unit atop a kick base.

Slide-out and tilting bins hold fruits and vegetables. Units similar to the one shown are also available from kitchen cabinet manufacturers.

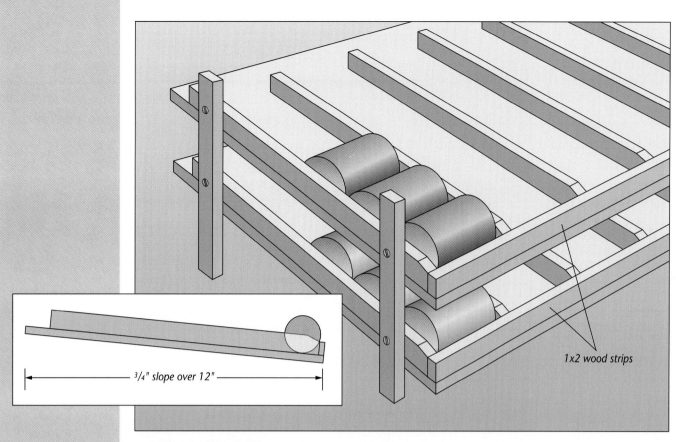

3/4" slope over 12"

1x2 wood strips

Building sloping shelves

Food shelves that hold only bulk canned goods can be sloped forward so that cans will roll to the front—saving you the trouble of digging for buried cans. Fasten 1x2 strips across the front and sides of the shelves to form channels that keep cans aligned, as shown above. Make the channels 1/8" wider than the height of the cans you're storing and, if possible, leave the back of the shelves accessible for loading. The shelves should slope 3/4" for every 12" of shelf depth *(inset)*.

BE PREPARED: EMERGENCY SUPPLIES

If you live in an area subject to natural disasters—floods, earthquakes, tornadoes—you should store emergency supplies in your home. Keep the supplies in a satchel or backpack that you can take with you if you need to evacuate. You should have a three-day supply of food and water for your household. Food can include canned and dried foods, as well as powdered milk. Most canned goods have a shelf life of about a year, so rotate the emergency supplies into your general food storage on a regular basis. You should have at least one quart of water per person per day. Water should be replaced every six months. Keep a pipe wrench or open-end wrench near the gas and water mains to shut the valves.

In addition to food and water, it's prudent to keep the following emergency supplies on hand:
• Portable radio
• Flashlight

• Extra batteries for radio and flashlight
• Whistle to attract attention
• Candles and waterproof matches
• First aid kit and instructions
• Medications needed by family members and, if applicable, special needs for babies and invalids
• Hygiene items—soap, toothpaste, toilet paper
• Metal can with tight-fitting lid or plastic garbage bags; either can be used to store human waste if sewage lines are damaged
• Extra clothing and walking shoes
• Blankets or sleeping bags
• Utensils, paper plates and cups
• Manual can opener
• Portable stove; charcoal should be used outdoors only and butane should not be used until it's determined that there's no gas leak in the area.

Building wine racks

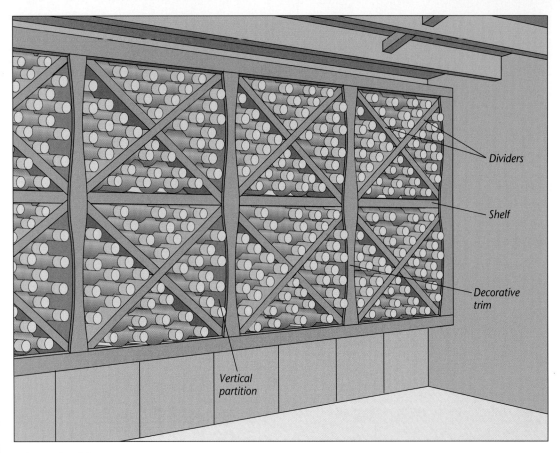

Dividers

Shelf

Decorative trim

Vertical partition

Triangular bins

For the bins shown above, build vertical partitions, then divide each section with a shelf made of two layers of ³/₄" plywood, or 2-by lumber. Cut diagonal dividers of the same thickness to span the compartments from corner to corner and join them with edge half laps (page 175). Cover exposed edges of the partitions with decorative trim. You can design the bins to hold about one case each.

Vertical slots

The slot system illustrated at right organizes bottles in vertical rows; the bottle sitting in the platform on top displays the contents of each slot below. In a 4' high unit, each row will hold a case of wine.

Assemble the platform from a piece of ³/₄" plywood, with two lips made of 1x3s; make semicircular cutouts to fit the bottle necks every 4" along the front lip.

Cut slats from 1x3s, shaping them at the top so that bottles will slide up and out. Fashion dividers from 1x10s or ³/₄" plywood. Nail the slats against the front edges of the dividers, then fix the platform to the slats and dividers, centering each slat between two semicircular cutouts in the lip, as shown. Nail a plywood base to the bottom of the slats and dividers.

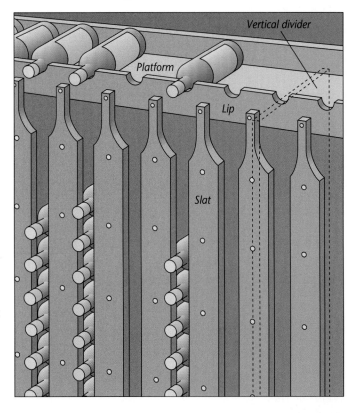

Vertical divider

Platform

Lip

Slat

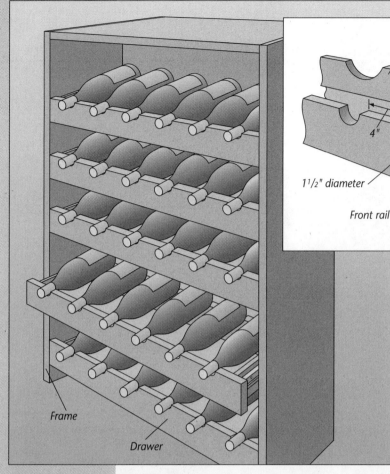

Frame

Drawer

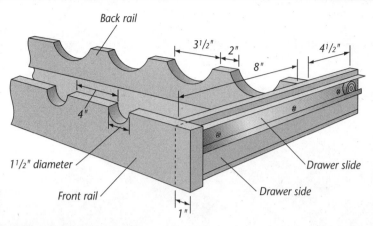

Back rail

$3^{1}/_{2}"$ 2" $4^{1}/_{2}"$

8"

$1^{1}/_{2}"$ diameter

4"

Front rail

1"

Drawer slide

Drawer side

Sliding drawers

The handy rack shown at left is like a chest of open drawers for wine. Start by shaping the front and back rails from 1x4s as shown in the inset, then connect them with plywood sides and add a bottom. Build a frame for the drawers from $3/4"$ plywood and fasten it to a wall or the ceiling for stability. Mount the drawers inside the frame with commercial slide runners, attaching the slides to the drawer sides and the runners on the inside of the frame. The drawers shown are 14" deep; they shouldn't be more than about 4' wide.

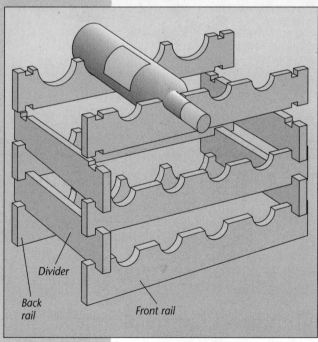

Divider

Back rail

Front rail

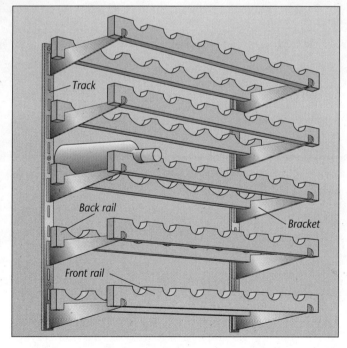

Track

Back rail

Bracket

Front rail

Racks that stack and hang

You can build simple wine racks by shaping boards as you would for sliding drawers *(above, top)*, and then stack the racks or mount them on shelf hardware. For a stacking rack *(above, left)*, cut dividers to separate the rails, and join the rails and dividers with edge half-lap joints *(page 175)*. For a shelf-mounted rack *(above, right)*, install a track-and-bracket shelf system on the wall *(page 179)*, then cut notches in the bottom edges of the rails to fit on the brackets.

READY-TO-USE WINE STORAGE UNITS

There are many creative ways to store wine bottles without resorting to buying a standard wine rack. This page shows a few examples.

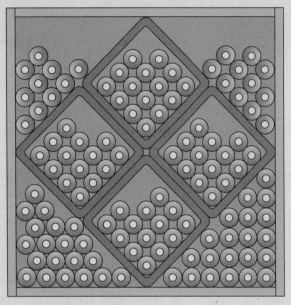

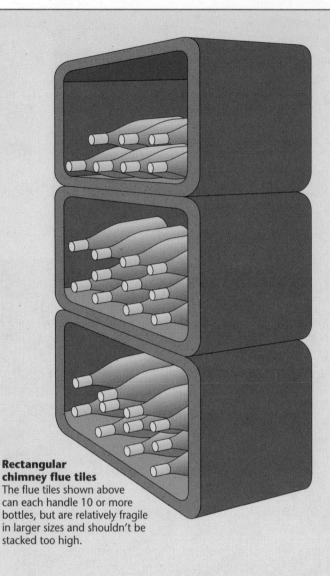

Square chimney flue tiles
To hold square chimney flue tiles in the diamond pattern shown above, build a case to fit tightly around them.

Rectangular chimney flue tiles
The flue tiles shown above can each handle 10 or more bottles, but are relatively fragile in larger sizes and shouldn't be stacked too high.

Drainpipes or mailing tubes
The tubes shown below pigeonhole individual bottles. Set on shelves and contained between concrete blocks, the tubes can be stacked. You can also store bottles on shelves without the tubes, but it will be harder to get at the bottles on the bottom.

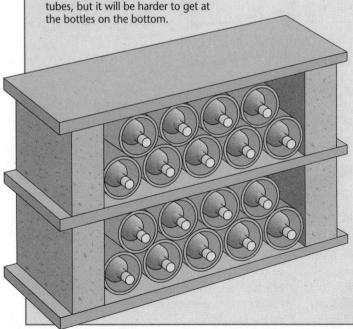

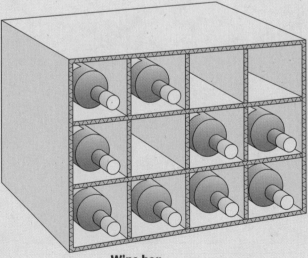

Wine box
The simplest solution for short-term storage is to turn a divided cardboard wine box on its side *(above)*. However, these are not strong enough to be stacked.

RECYCLING

Gone are the days when families loaded all of their food cartons, glass and plastic containers, and old newspapers into garbage bags and put them on the front curb so the sanitation workers could haul them away. Now, as recycling becomes more commonplace, we find ourselves separating glass, paper, and plastic into containers so they can be recycled. The first step in the recycling process should be to phone your municipality and find out what materials they can handle, as well as what sorting and preparation they require. In some areas, plastic bags and milk and juice cartons can also be recycled. In general, you should rinse cans and bottles. Some areas ask you to remove labels and caps from bottles, and all staples from paper and packaging.

Place both garbage cans and recycling bins in a well-ventilated area protected from the elements—a corner just inside the garage or carport door, or a small out-door shelter in your yard (check local building codes before constructing). Bins should be lightweight and made of plastic, metal, or painted plywood. An easy-to-carry container located in or near the kitchen will save you extra steps until you have a full load.

ASK A PRO

HOW CAN I SAVE ROOM IN MY RECYCLING BINS?

Soft drink cans normally take up a lot of room, but if you crush them before placing them in the bins, you'll be able to store them more compactly. Build a simple can masher from two lengths of 2x4 joined by a heavy-duty butt hinge. You can fashion a round handle at the front end of one pivoting 2x4, and you may want to fasten the device to a wall to keep it steady. Commercial versions are also available.

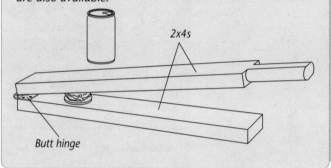

2x4s

Butt hinge

Hanging recycling bins

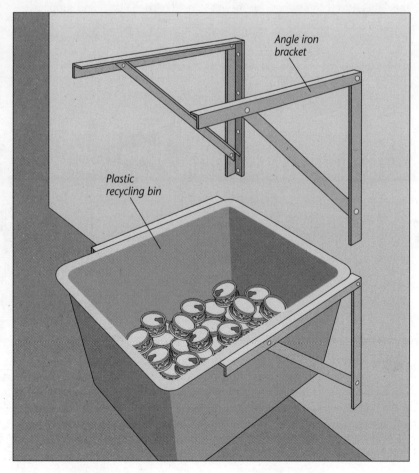

Angle iron bracket

Plastic recycling bin

Wall brackets

Hang plastic recycling bins one above the other to save space. On recycling days, the bins easily slide forward and out of the assembly. The brackets shown at left are made of angle iron, cut to length and reinforced with diagonal braces bolted in place. The bins will be heavy when full, so only hang them this way from a solid wall such as plywood or masonry, or use bins whose width corresponds to the spacing between studs. You can also attach drawer guides or runners inside an open cabinet frame to hold bins *(page 144).* If a more finished look is important, try a commercial stacking bin system.

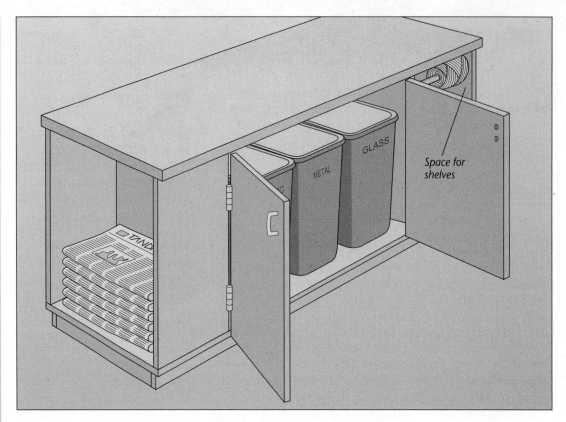

Plywood cabinet

The cabinet shown above provides space for newspapers and plastic recycling bins. A rod holds a spool of string for tying newspapers and there's space on the right—under the string—for shelves to hold garbage bags and supplies.

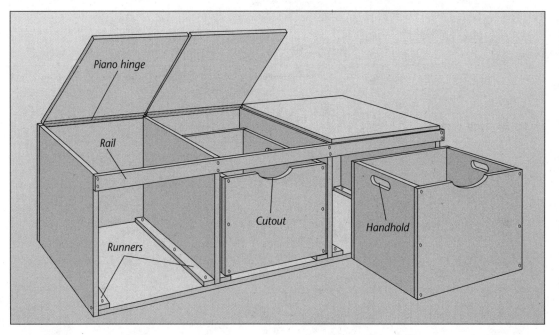

Sliding bins

The enclosed three-bin recycling system (*above*) can be modified for special needs. Side-by-side bins resting on runners hold different recyclable materials, such as plastic containers and metal cans. Construct the lids and bins from 1/2" exterior-grade plywood; the case from 3/4" plywood; the rail from 1x4 stock; and the runners from 1x2s. Use piano hinges to attach the lids to the back panel.

You can leave the lids open for easy access to the bins, or flip them down for instant extra counter space. On recycling days, slide each bin out easily by gripping the cutout on the front.

Storing newspaper

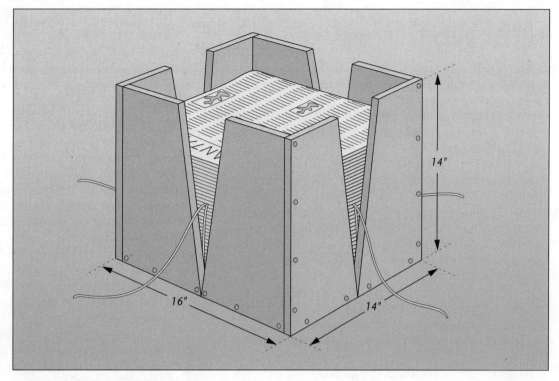

Building a newspaper box
Make a box from 3/4" plywood to fit around your newspaper—usually 14" by 16". The box shown above is 14" high, but you can customize your holder to store a week's worth of papers, if desired. Join the sides with glue and nails. Before stacking the papers, lay a length of string across the bottom of the box. Bundle the papers when the box is half full, then lay a new string across the stack, as shown.

GARBAGE DAY MADE EASY

Instead of lugging heavy garbage cans out to the curb and back, simplify your chore by mounting the containers on a wagon. Cut the base from 5/8-inch plywood large enough to hold two cans. Make the lip by attaching a frame of 2x4s around the perimeter of the base. Finally, fasten heavy-duty casters to the underside of the base at each corner of the wagon.

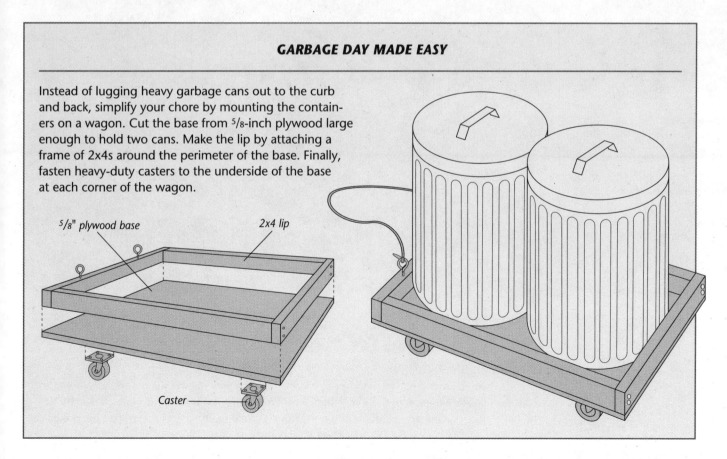

5/8" plywood base

2x4 lip

Caster

FIREWOOD

More and more, people are turning to firewood to supplement other home energy sources that are either expensive or in short supply. In many cases, firewood is being used as the primary alternative to these more costly sources.

If you buy dry, seasoned wood, you'll need to keep it dry, and if you buy unseasoned wood—lumber that has been felled recently—you'll need to season it by drying. Depending on the species, it can take anywhere from 15 days up to a full year for freshly harvested wood to dry. In both cases, store the wood so that air can circulate around it, and so that it is protected from rain, snow, and ground moisture. Keep wood that is stored outdoors off the ground, and sheltered under a shed roof. Don't seal it off completely, or you'll trap moisture and condensation inside the wood. The wood will dry faster if you split it before you stack it.

Wood can be stacked in either parallel or perpendicular (crisscross) rows. For safety and neatness, brace tall woodpiles with vertical supports.

ASK A PRO

HOW DO I PREVENT INSECTS FROM COMING INTO THE HOUSE WITH MY FIREWOOD?

Firewood can be infested with anything from ants to wood beetles. Help minimize or prevent this by keeping the wood off the ground. Never store wood up against your house, as insects can make their way inside through cracks in the foundation; storing wood at least 10 feet away is ideal. Bang the wood against the ground to get rid of as many insects as possible before bringing it inside.

To reduce the risk of having insects spread (should they make it indoors), only bring in wood as you need it; in general, don't store more than a day's worth of wood inside. As an additional precaution, you can surround the wood bin inside with sticky glue strips (available at your hardware store) to catch any insects that wander away from the wood; glue strips are more effective than bait traps, which only attract certain types of insects.

Storing firewood

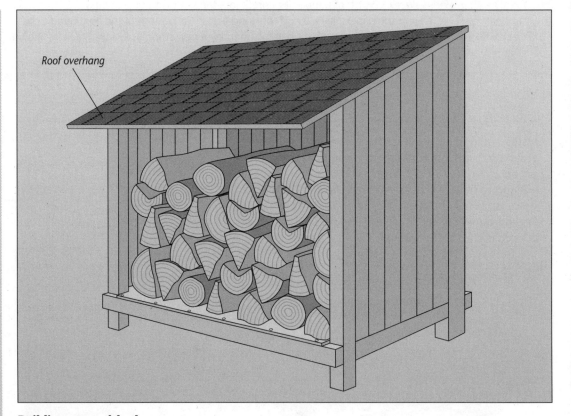

Roof overhang

Building a woodshed

Use pressure-treated lumber for the woodshed *(above)*. Raise the firewood off the ground and leave the shed open on one side to promote air circulation. A roof overhang keeps rain and snow off. CAUTION: Never cut pressure-treated wood indoors and don't burn it. Wear safety glasses and respiratory protection when cutting it, and long pants and sleeves and chemical-resistant gloves when handling it.

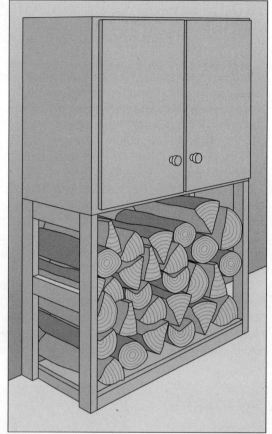

Finding nooks and crannies for firewood

Survey your garage, basement, carport, or attic for likely places to store firewood. You can easily stash a supply of wood under basement stairs *(above)* or beneath a carport or garage cabinet *(right)*.

ASK A PRO

HOW CAN I SAVE STEPS FROM THE WOODPILE TO THE FIREPLACE?

Instead of getting wood from an outside pile every day, try the following: Install a simple wood box through a wall to the outside of your house with an access door near your fireplace. The door will enable you to pass logs from the outside directly into the box, instead of making several trips through the house. The opening can be an attractive addition to the room, with a hinged door and a molded frame that projects from the interior wall (right).

If the wood box opens into a garage or carport, most building codes require that the opening have a solid-core self-closing door. In cold climates, insulate and weather-strip the door. To keep insects out of the home, line the wood box with sheet metal.

For a stylish variation on this pace-saving idea, store your wood under a fireside bench seat that can be loaded from the outside; when you need a log, just lift the carved or otherwise decorated seat. You can also set up a basement-to-fireplace dumbwaiter operated by cables and a hand winch to bring logs to the main floor. Make sure the mechanism is sturdy enough to handle the weight of the firewood.

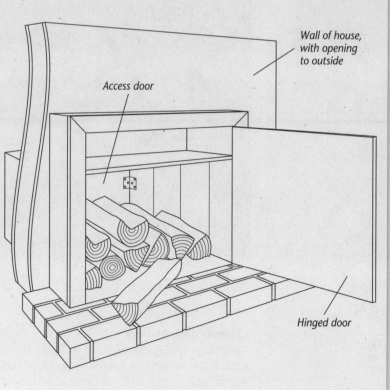

Wall of house, with opening to outside

Access door

Hinged door

WORKSHOP

onvenience should be your watchword when organizing a workshop. You'll need to have plenty of storage space to keep tools and hardware out of the way when you're working, but accessible when you need them. (For information on avoiding storage hazards in your workshop, turn to page 15.) Adequate wiring and outlets are also a must.

It's best to make a large, sturdy workbench the focus of your workshop. You have a choice of pre-made designs, or you can make your own from a 2x4 frame with a plywood or hardboard top. Ideally, the space beneath your workbench will provide room for drawers, cabinets, boxes, and shelves.

Grouping related tools and materials together makes them easy to find. Large power tools mounted on casters can be rolled out from a storage closet or cabinet, or away from a wall, then back again when the work is done. Wall cabinets best protect the blades and working parts of portable power tools from damage and keep them out of the reach of children. (Page 53 has more information on childproof storage.)

Properly storing hand tools can be a challenge. The popular perforated hardboard and hanger system provides the best means for visible, hands-on storage. You can also buy individual wall racks for small tools such as screwdrivers and pliers. Though less accessible, closed units like the one shown below protect tools from rust and dust; a light oiling prevents tools from rusting.

Besides tools and projects in progress, you'll want to store materials. Store leftovers in a rolling box with a hinged top. Shelf brackets fastened to every other wall stud will handle light lumber. For heavier loads, you can build a rack like the one shown on page 141. Ideas for storing plywood are also shown. Fiber storage tubes help protect lengths of pipe or moldings. For additional space, look to the rafters or ceiling joists.

Designing workshop storage

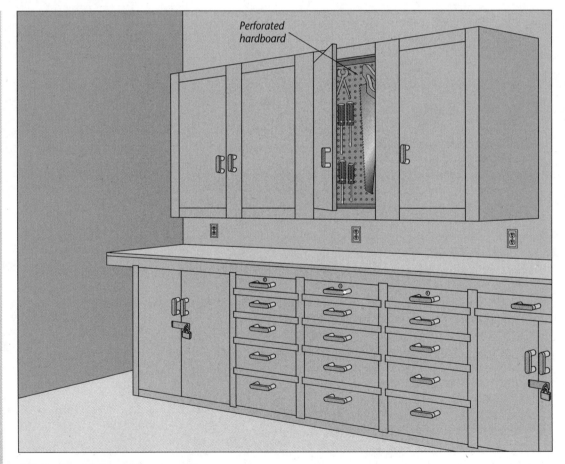

Perforated hardboard

Cabinets and drawers

The storage system shown above combines both cabinets and drawers with a work surface. The cabinets are lined with perforated hardboard for hanging tools; doors shield the tools from dust. The drawers and lower cabinet doors can be locked. The electrical outlets just above the countertop are handy for plugging in power tools.

Less-used storables, such as paint, brake fluid, and turpentine, can go on high shelves installed on the wall or suspended overhead or between ceiling joists. In an earthquake area, however, keep flammable liquids low—in a locked cabinet if there are children around. Size and space the shelves to fit the containers and make sure that their labels are visible.

Drawers are a blessing to any workshop owner. Build them into your work counters or in an open frame, or recycle old bedroom dressers or kitchen units. Drawers can hold a variety of small tools and supplies.

For hardware, you'll want small jars, boxes, or bins to hold each type of nail, screw, and washer. Labeling the contents of each container makes for easy use.

ASK A PRO

HOW CAN I STOP HOOKS FROM PULLING OUT OF PERFORATED HARDBOARD?
To prevent this, you can glue the hooks in place by applying adhesive to the end of each one with a glue gun. Of course, this means you can't easily change the layout of the hooks on the board. A more flexible solution is to use small plastic clips (right). Available at your hardware store, these fit over the hooks and lock them to the holes on each side. The clips can be pried off with a pocketknife if you wish to move the hooks. Otherwise, you can look for newer hooks, made with an anti-pullout design.

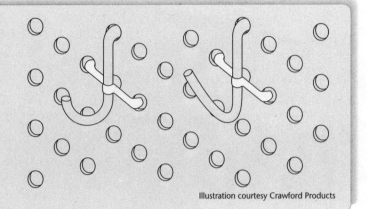

Illustration courtesy Crawford Products

Building a tool cupboard

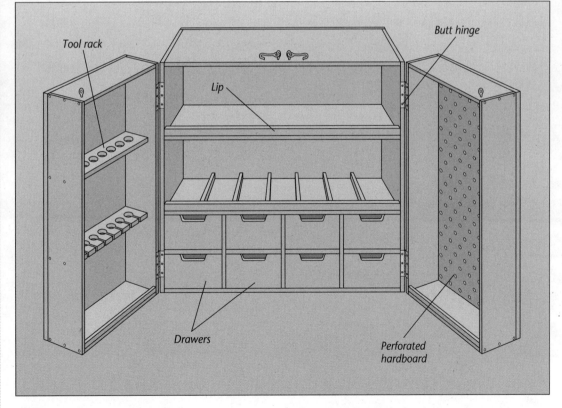

Tool rack

Butt hinge

Lip

Drawers

Perforated hardboard

Shelves, drawers, and racks
The cabinet shown above features double doors for storing hand tools, a main compartment with shelves for small power tools and drawers for supplies. Use the tool rack in one door to hold chisels and screwdrivers, and the perforated hardboard panel in the other door for hanging a hammer or saw. The lip along the front edge of each shelf prevents items from sliding off. Build the case from ³/₄" plywood and attach the doors with butt hinges. The unit can sit on a workbench or be hung from wall studs.

HOW DO I KEEP HAND TOOLS IN ORDER?

To make sure each tool goes back in its place on the wall, use silhouettes, as shown at right. The simplest way to make silhouettes is to hang your tools in the ideal order and outline each one with a broad-tipped indelible felt pen. Or, lay each tool on heavy white paper and trace its outline. Then cut out the silhouette and glue it to the wall. The glued-on silhouettes will last longer if you apply a coat of clear sealer over them.

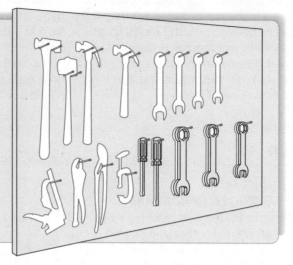

Keeping hand tools handy

Drawer dividers

To organize tools in a drawer and protect their edges, cut a series of wood blocks and screw them to the drawer bottom from underneath. Cut the blocks so a portion of the tool blades will be visible and space them to fit the blades *(right)*.

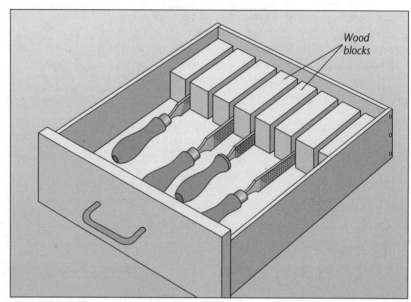

Wood blocks

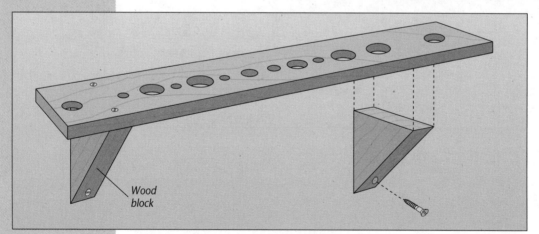

Wood block

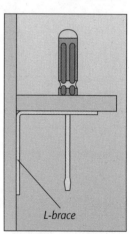

L-brace

Wall-mounted tool rack

A length of 1x3 stock with holes drilled through it makes an ideal rack for hanging tools such as screwdrivers and chisels.

Size the holes to fit the tool blades without allowing the handles to slip through. Fasten the rack to the wall with triangular wood blocks cut from 2x4 stock, screwing one edge of the blocks to the underside of the rack and an adjoining edge to the wall *(above, left)*. Alternatively, you can fasten the rack to a wall with L-braces *(above, right)*.

Tool cabinets

Metal tool cabinets, such as the one shown at right, are a good storage idea for anyone who owns even an average supply of tools. Made of sturdy, lightweight steel, they can withstand the wear and tear of heavy use, while taking up a relatively small amount of space in the garage or basement. The drawers are divided into two sets and vary in dimension, allowing tools to be stored by size. The model shown has perforations in the sides so items can be hung from hooks, and space for storage above the drawers. Similar models come equipped with casters.

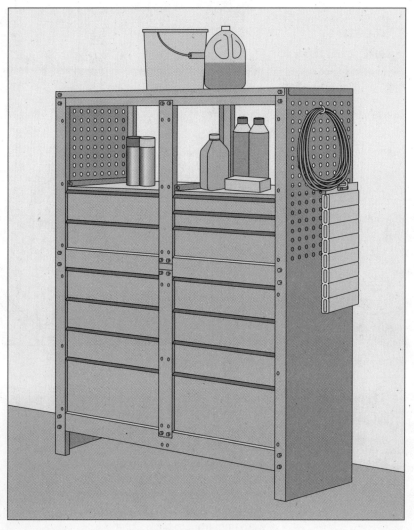

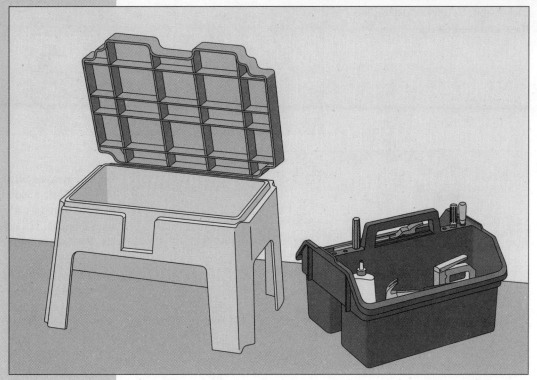

A smart tool box

The lightweight tool box shown at left provides storage for frequently used tools and doubles as a stepping stool. Easily toted from job to job, the tool box's lid flips open so a tool caddy can be removed. When the lid is closed, the stool can be used as a step to help get at hard-to-reach objects, such as light fixtures.

Storing bar clamps

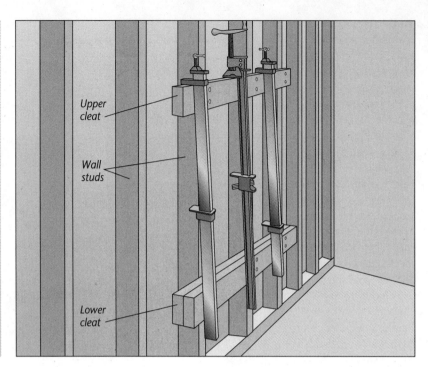

Upper cleat

Wall studs

Lower cleat

Building a wall rack
An unfinished basement or garage wall is a perfect space for storing bar clamps. Nail two cleats cut from 2x4 stock across the wall studs, positioning the upper one high enough to hold the clamps off the floor. Use a pair of 2x4s for the lower cleat to tilt the top of the clamps toward the wall. To store pipe clamps, you could use broom holders.

Storing blades and bits

Circular saw blades
Protect circular saw blades in a shelved box *(right)*. Build the box from 3/4" plywood. Before assembling the box, cut 1/4" wide dadoes *(page 176)* across the sides to accommodate the shelves. To tilt the shelves toward the back and prevent the blades from sliding out, angle the dadoes downward from front to back. Cut the shelves from 1/4" plywood and slide them into the box.

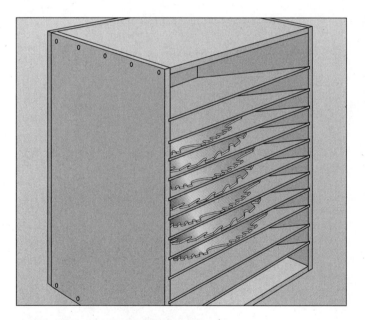

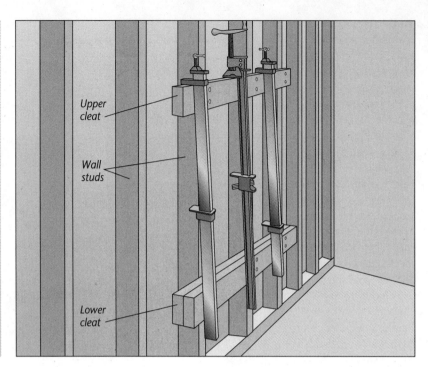

Wood block

Drill or router bits
Drill holes into a wood block to store bits and keep them visible *(left)*. Size the holes to fit the bit shanks snugly and space them so the bits will not touch each other and get nicked. Screw the block to a wall, making sure the fasteners do not intersect with holes for the bit shanks.

Building a rack for lumber and plywood

The rack shown below is designed to hold both boards and plywood. Lumber is stored on the shelves while plywood is stacked in the channel and secured to the front of the rack with the rope.

Cut the frame pieces from 2x4 lumber, making the verticals long enough to span from floor to ceiling, since they must be anchored with bolts to the joists. Bolt the frame pieces together, then fasten the cleats—cut from 1x4 stock—to the front edges of the vertical pieces. The frame pieces can also be joined with half laps *(page 175)*.

Cut the shelves from 3/4" plywood and fasten them to the top edges of the horizontal pieces. Next, assemble the channel and attach it to the rack. Drill a hole to attach the rope to the front lip of the channel.

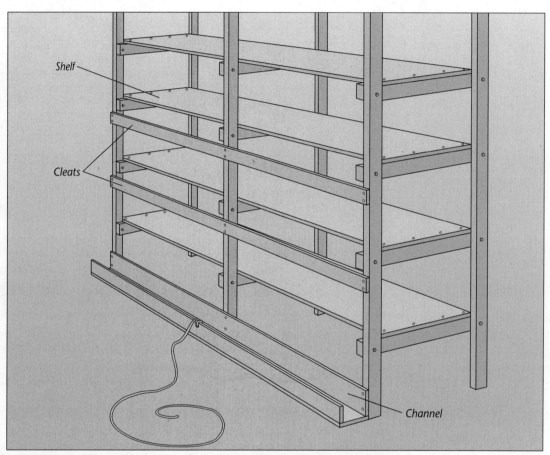

Shelf

Cleats

Channel

Using the spaces between joists

Store lumber and lengths of pipe in the gaps between ceiling joists. To fashion these overhead racks, fasten 3/4" thick furring strips across the bottom edges of the joists with screws, spacing them about 3' apart, as shown. Keep the screws clear of any wires or fixtures running along or through the joists.

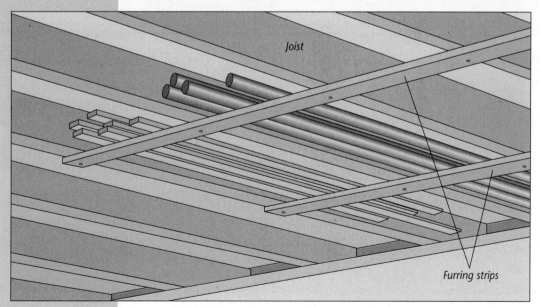

Joist

Furring strips

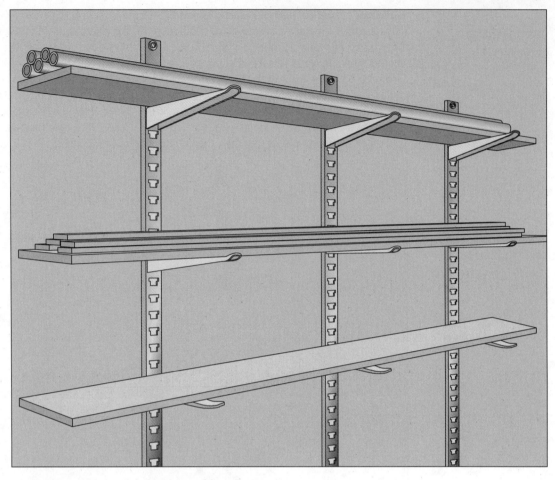

Storing materials with tracks and brackets

An adjustable storage rack, like the commercial one shown above, is handy for storing long pieces of lumber and other building materials. The rack is easy to assemble and, made entirely of metal, strong enough to hold a heavy load. The arms of the rack fit into slotted tracks bolted to wall studs. Note: The studs are concealed by gypsum wallboard in the example above.

When installing the tracks, make sure the slots line up laterally so that the metal arms can be set at the same height. Space arms as needed for efficient use of vertical space. Use lag screws and washers to secure the tracks to the studs. To secure the tracks to a concrete wall, you'll need to use special fasteners, see the tips below.

ASK A PRO

HOW DO I FASTEN A STORAGE RACK TO A CONCRETE WALL?

Due to the hardness of concrete, specialized screws and fasteners are needed when securing storage racks and shelves to concrete walls. Using lead anchors and lag screws is one common method, self-tapping concrete screws is another.

With lag screws and anchors, use a power drill fitted with a masonry bit to bore a hole into the concrete; the hole should be the same diameter as the anchor. Next, insert the anchor into the hole and push it in as far as it will go. Fit the screw inside the anchor and use a screwdriver to turn it into the opening. The anchor will start expanding against the walls of the hole as the screw advances, creating a firm hold. With self-tapping screws, the serrated threads simply bind against the concrete holding the fastener solidly in place. Always pre-drill when using these screws; use a masonry bit of a smaller diameter than the screw itself.

Keeping track of hardware

Building a cabinet for hardware bins

The hinged door on the shallow cabinet shown at right flips up to expose a bank of bins. Size the cabinet to fit the number of shelves, vertical dividers, and bins you will be installing. Fasten the door to the cabinet with a long piano hinge, then fix the cabinet to the wall. Label the bins as you fill them.

To hold the door open, attach hooks to the outside of the door and to the ceiling and use two lengths of chain. Close the door when you're finished with the cabinet to keep out dust. CAUTION: The cabinet on the floor should be kept locked if it contains anything toxic and there are children in the house.

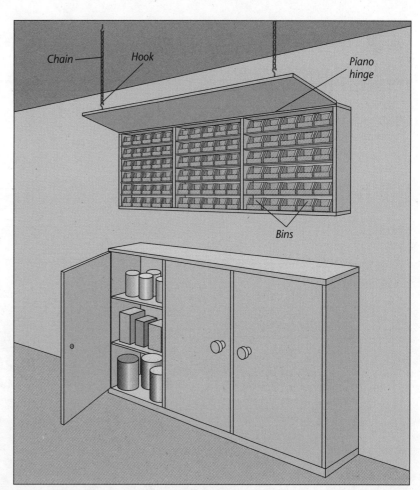

Chain Hook Piano hinge Bins

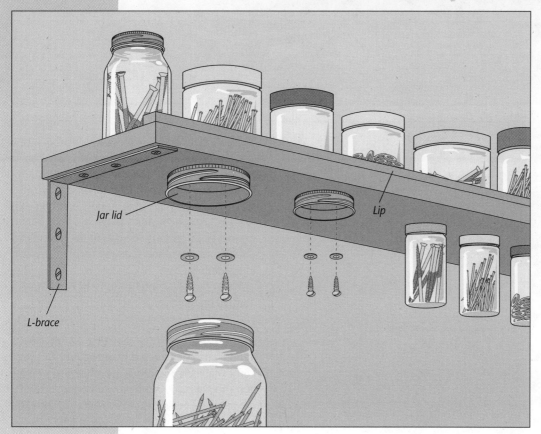

Jar lid Lip L-brace

Hanging jars under a shelf

Store fasteners in individual containers, labeling them unless they are glass or transparent plastic. To store jars on a shelf, attach a 1/2" by 3/4" lip along the front edge to prevent the containers from toppling off.

Mounting jars under the shelf will double the shelf's storage capacity. Fasten the jar lids to the shelf with screws and washers *(left)*, then screw the jars to the lids.

WHAT'S A SIMPLE WAY TO IDENTIFY THE CONTENTS OF BOXES OF FASTENERS?

Although clearly marked labels on containers is a popular option, there's a more effective method. Simply use hot-melt glue to fix a sample of the contents on the outside of the box.

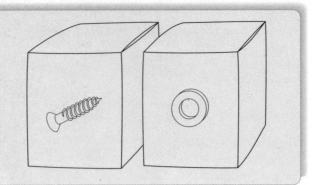

Storing supplies

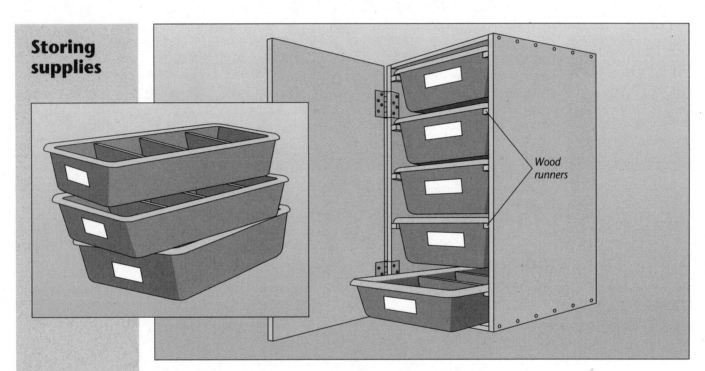

Wood runners

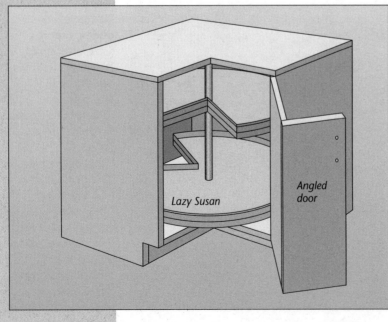

Lazy Susan

Angled door

Sliding bins

Available from office, restaurant, or school suppliers, sturdy plastic bins or cutlery trays are ideal for storing supplies. Those shown above are subdivided and have a lip around the top edges, which makes them easy to install inside a plywood cabinet. Fasten wood runners to the inside faces of the cabinet sides, spacing them to fit the bins. Hang the bins on the runners, sliding them in and out as needed.

To protect the contents from dust or simply conceal them, install a door on the cabinet.

Lazy Susan

A lazy Susan—a circular shelf that rotates around a rod—simplifies the task of accessing items in a corner cabinet. You can buy both the lazy Susan and cabinet ready-made. If you decide to build the cabinet yourself, make the door to match the L-shape of the cabinet, as shown at left.

LAUNDRY

An efficient laundry area needs storage space arranged around the washer and dryer. A long deep shelf—or shelves—placed directly above the machines adds room for frequently used supplies; consider a commercial unit like the one shown on page 117. Installing ceiling-high cabinets above the shelf provides a perfect spot for cleaning supplies, linens, and overflow storage.

Every laundry area needs counter space for folding, sorting, and mending clothes. A fold-down counter with an easy-to-clean laminate surface adds convenience in cramped quarters. Another useful feature is a sink for washing delicate garments or soaking out stains. Hang clothes for drip-drying on a metal or wooden closet rod over the sink. Mount a ceiling fan directly above it to help quicken the drying process and disperse the fumes from the soap and bleach.

Install cabinets or large-capacity storage bins below the counter. On the wall, attach a narrow cabinet or a rack for your ironing board. Adding walls around your laundry area hides clutter and muffles the noise of machines.

Storing an ironing board

In a closet or dedicated cabinet

A full-size ironing board can be stored near the laundry area either inside a storage closet or in a special shallow cabinet. In a storage closet, secure the board with a chain or strap, or build a narrow slot so that it stands upright (below, left).

If you're building a cabinet for your ironing board, you'll need to buy a fold-down board. Measure the board and allow several inches around it for access.

For extra convenience, add a sleeve board, a clothes hanger, and shelves inside the cabinet as well as an electrical outlet for an iron (below, right).

For simpler storage solutions, you can install an ironing board on the back of a door so that it folds down when needed, or simply fasten a commercially available ironing valet rack to a wall or door to hold the board and iron.

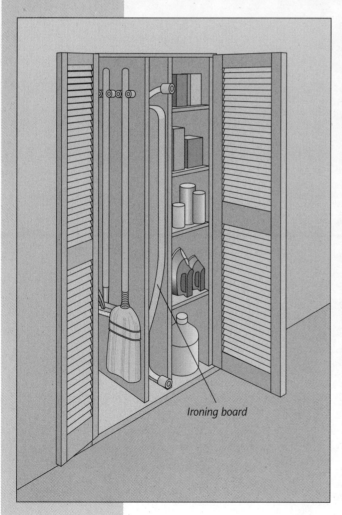

Ironing board

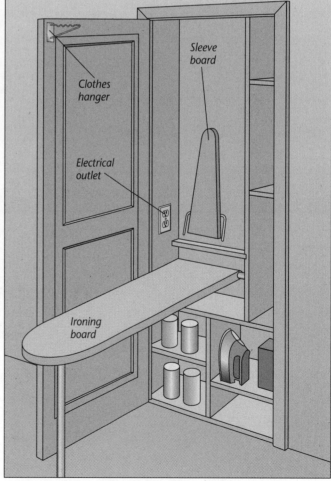

Clothes hanger

Sleeve board

Electrical outlet

Ironing board

Keeping clothes sorted

Using a divided drawer
Two options for sorting clothes for the laundry are shown below. You can build a cabinet with a single deep drawer and partition the drawer with plywood dividers into separate compartments for whites, colors, and permanent press items *(below, top)*. Another divider could be added, creating a compartment for towels or work clothes. Install the drawer with heavy-duty commercial slide runners. Alternatively, buy a commercial sorting tray with individual slide-out bins *(below, bottom)*. For added convenience and mobility, this model has casters.

If you have space under a counter, inside a free-standing island, or against a wall, you can simply stack sorting bins to keep clothes ready to go when laundry day arrives.

ASK A PRO

WHERE SHOULD I LOCATE A LAUNDRY CHUTE?
A laundry chute directs dirty clothes from your home's main or second floor to a laundry center in the basement or garage below. You can locate the chute opening in an inconspicuous but handy spot—inside a clothes closet in the master bedroom; in a wall, with a hinged or flap door; or inside a bathroom cabinet. If you have small children, be sure that the opening is raised high above the floor or measures no more than 12 inches across.

The best time to construct your laundry chute is when you're designing or remodeling your house. Build the chute from plywood, sheet aluminum, or 18-inch-diameter furnace heating duct, depending on what your local codes dictate.

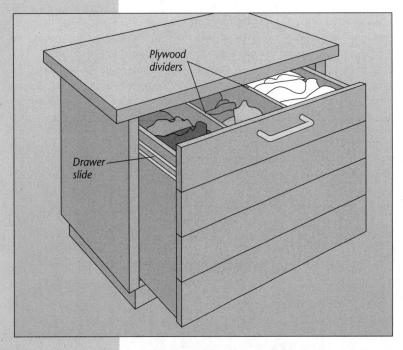

Plywood dividers

Drawer slide

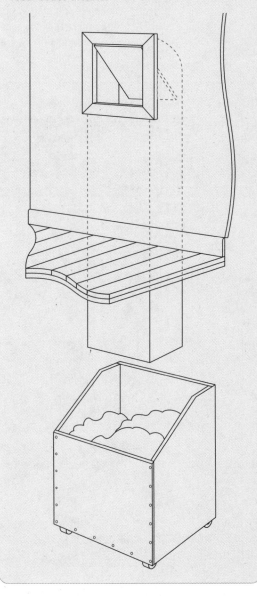

CLOTHING

Moisture, dust, and insects can threaten stored clothing. Moisture, either from condensation or seepage, is best controlled within the entire storage area; remedies are discussed on page 12. Damage from dust and insects can be controlled with tight-closing units. Built-ins are the most functional, but portable clothes closets, such as the one shown on page 148, are a simpler solution.

Moths are deterred by cedar-scented moth controlling substances placed in garment bags, chests, or closets; storing clothes in a cedar-lined closet or chest is a traditional option. To actually exterminate moths, you will have to resort to commercial mothproofing products, such as mothballs, to kill the moth larvae; keep in mind, however, that the odor can be unpleasant. These products require a tightly enclosed space to be effective. Because this can encourage the growth of mildew, some mothproofing products are combined with a mildew-inhibitor. To prevent mildew in a closed unit where you aren't using mothballs, vent it with finely screened openings. Always launder your clothes before storing them, since soilage will attract moths.

Keeping clothes moth-free

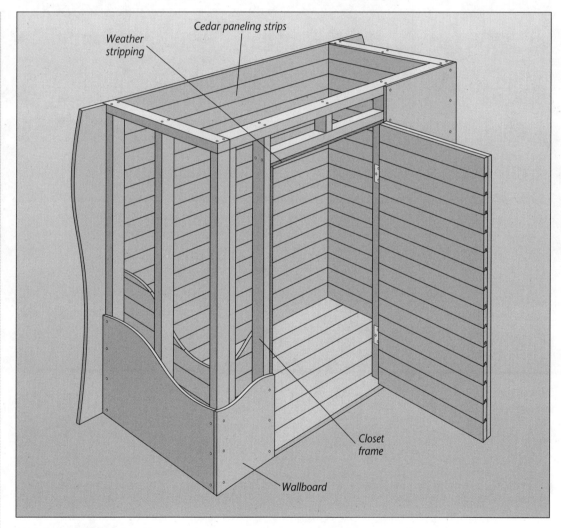

Cedar paneling strips

Weather stripping

Closet frame

Wallboard

Building a cedar closet

To fashion your own cedar closet—or convert an existing closet—line the interior of the closet frame with tongue-and-groove cedar paneling, available in kits from home centers. Cut the strips to length and install them edge to edge, one wall at a time, as shown above. For maximum protection, line the ceiling, floor, and door. Weather-strip the doorway tightly. (If you're building a closet, construct the frame from 2x4s and add 1/2" wallboard.)

Don't finish or seal the cedar—you'll lock in the fragrance, which negates its power to control the moths. To revive the fragrance, sand the surface lightly with fine sandpaper. Turn to page 148 for a method to store clothes under the rafters in an attic.

Hanging garment bags

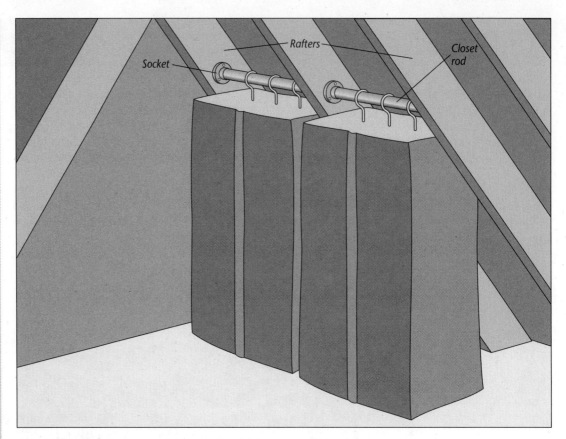

Between rafters

In an attic, hang garment bags from closet rods fastened between the rafters, as shown above. Rather than drilling holes through the rafters—which will weaken them—attach pole sockets to the rafters and fit the rods in the sockets. Garment bags are available in vinyl or fabric in several styles and sizes.

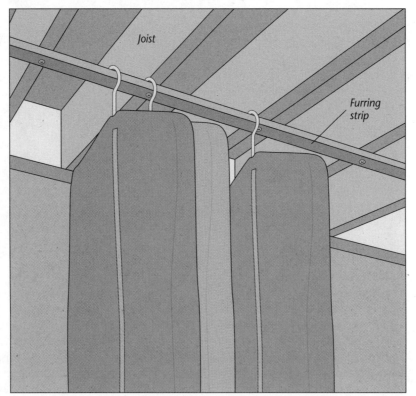

From ceiling joists

In a basement, hang garment bags from 1x2 furring strips screwed across the ceiling joists *(left)*. As with rafters, never bore holes through joists for closet rods.

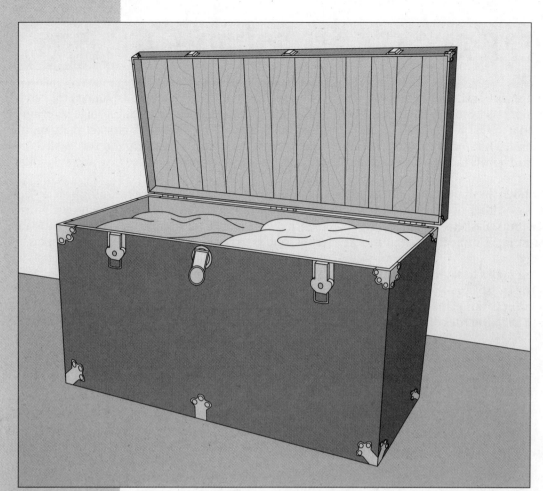

In a cedar-lined trunk

A handy place to store used children's clothes, out-of-season outfits, or even a wedding dress is in a sturdy metal trunk with an inner cedar lining, such as the one shown. A firmly closing lid protects the contents from the damages of dust, moisture, light, and insect larvae; a lock keeps out small children. These trunks, commonly sold at department stores or home centers, take up little space and can be easily stored under a basement staircase, for example.

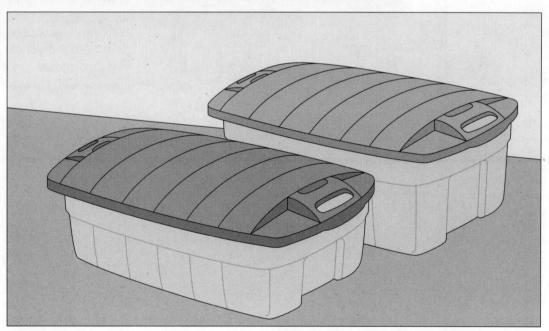

In plastic storage bins

When storing items such as clothing for the season, it's a good idea to keep them in containers that can be easily identified and accessed. One solution is to use the commercially available clear plastic bins shown above. Not only can the contents be viewed through the sides of the bins, but they are large enough to store an entire season's worth of outfits. Their wide handle grips make them easy to carry and they are sturdy enough to be stacked when stored. For added efficiency, plan to have one bin for each member of the family.

OUTERWEAR AND SPORTS EQUIPMENT

Keep your sports equipment at the ready by placing in-season items in more accessible storage, and out-of-season ones in areas that are more out of the way. Racks *(page 152)* or perforated hardboard provide handy places for baseball bats and tennis rackets, for example. Camping and fishing gear are made easily accessible by storing items in deep cubbyhole shelves near the garage door. Metal school lockers—either new or recycled—also make smart storage units. Basketballs, footballs, and sleeping bags can rest in a simple nylon hammock, hung overhead.

Hang bikes overhead on hooks to save space, or suspend men's bikes from the crossbar, as shown on page 155. Consider floor racks for parking, but for winter storage it's a good idea to keep the tires off the ground.

Skis are easily propped up by the pair or grouped in a rack. Turn to page 152 for other ski storage solutions. Snowshoes, skates, and small sleds are best hung on nails, spikes, pegs, or hooks. Toboggans and bigger sleds can rest atop raised platforms or on ceiling joists or collar beams in the garage *(page 153)*.

A mudroom provides space for donning and doffing outerwear without tracking dirt into the house. Furnish it with a long bench for removing wet boots and rain pants, and pegs or hooks and a long shelf for parkas, gloves, and hats. Equip the area beneath the bench with drawers or a storage chest for dry socks and shoes. A source of heat—an adjacent water heater or heating duct—can help clothes dry quickly. Make sure the floor can withstand moisture.

Equipping a mud-room

1x3s

Wire screen

Ledger strips

Ledger strips

Support post

Setting up drying racks

Dry items like skates and mitts on shelves. Make the shelves with wire screen or hardware cloth sandwiched in a frame of 1x3s; stagger the joints between the upper and lower frame pieces *(inset)*.

To install the shelves in a corner, attach ledger strips to the adjoining walls and a 2x4 post flush against the unsupported corner of the shelves. Fasten the shelves to the ledger strips and to the support post *(left)*.

To dry shoes and boots, drill angled holes into a 2x10 board and glue in dowels. Fasten the board to the wall *(below)*.

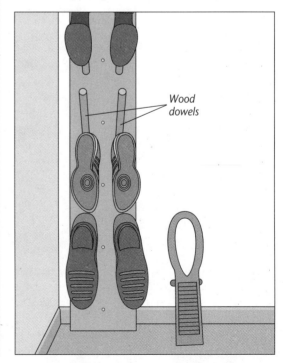

Wood dowels

Storing ski equipment

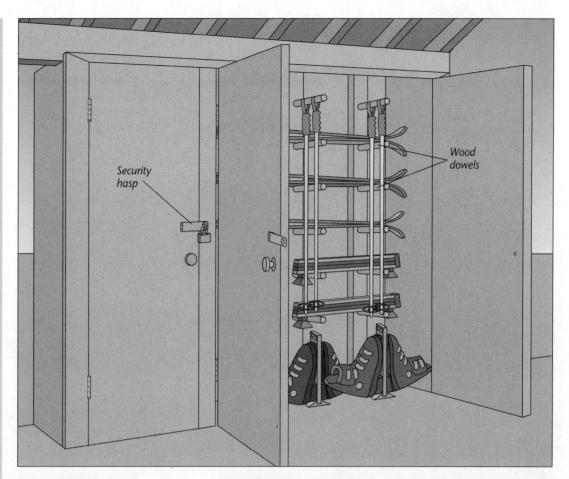

Security hasp

Wood dowels

In a carport
Provided there is sufficient clearance, a carport is a handy spot for ski equipment. Skis, poles, and a car ski rack rest on dowels in the long, shallow closet shown above. Boots can go on the floor—or inside your house in very cold climates.

For security, choose hinges with fixed pins, attach the hinges to the inside edges of the door and frame, and install a security hasp and padlock on each door.

On a landing
Boots and skis for a large family are easy to keep in order in the shallow compartments built on the stairway landing shown at right. Skis are propped up against the back of the closet wall with pegs to keep them from sliding sideways.

Poles are hung from dowels glued into a strip of wood, as shown opposite, which is then attached to the side of the cupboard.

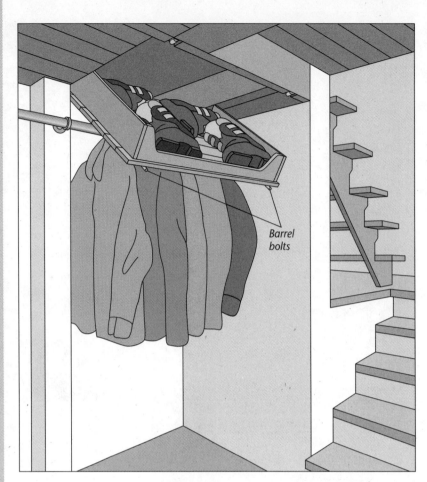

Barrel
bolts

An overhead compartment in the space between the joists in a finished basement is a convenient hiding place for ski boots or other gear. Use barrel bolts to keep the compartment closed.

The cupboard shown is kept from opening all the way by a closet rod; you can also attach a chain between the door and ceiling to hold the door partly open.

On a block and peg rack

With their curved tips, skis are easy to hang between blocks or pegs. Make the simple rack shown by fixing a pair of wood blocks to a runner board for every set of skis and fastening the runner along a wall.

Drill pilot holes in 2x4 blocks, then attach them to the 2x4 runner with glue and screws. Space the blocks 1 1/4" apart, rounding over and sanding their inside edges to follow the profile of the skis and prevent scratching them. Store ski poles by hanging their straps on dowels glued into holes drilled into the runner.

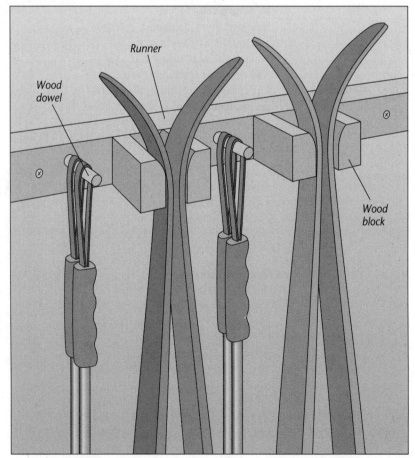

Runner

Wood dowel

Wood block

Stashing sleds

Joist

Using the space above joists

In some garages, there's usable storage space between the joists or collar beams overhead and the rafters.

As shown at left, this space provides a ready-to-use storage spot for sleds and other outdoor equipment.

Storing guns

Building a gun rack
The wall-mounted rack shown at right is made from 1-by lumber with notches cut in the uprights to support the gun stocks and barrels.

To store rifles out of the reach of children, install the rack in a lockable room, and be sure to keep the room locked at all times.

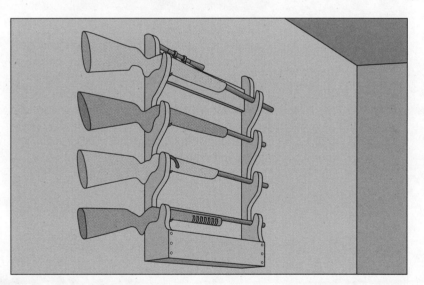

 PLAY IT SAFE

KEEPING GUNS SECURE
Improper storage of guns leads to accidents. Mishaps typically occur when a firearm is being cleaned, or when a child or burglar finds a gun in the home. Take the following steps to prevent firearm-related accidents and theft:
• For maximum security, keep guns in a locked steel cabinet or gun safe. If your guns are stored in a special room or closet, make sure it is locked; to prevent theft, you can add an interior steel door or curtain. A number of locking devices are available to prevent guns from being fired; these include trigger locks and locking cables that feed through the triggers.
• Always store guns unloaded and keep the ammunition in a separate, locked location. Store ammunition in its original labeled containers. Guns should be stored in a dry area and ammunition shouldn't be stored near heat sources.
• Make sure everyone in your household knows how to handle the guns safely. Your local police department can help with training programs.
• Teach children that guns aren't toys.

Storing weights

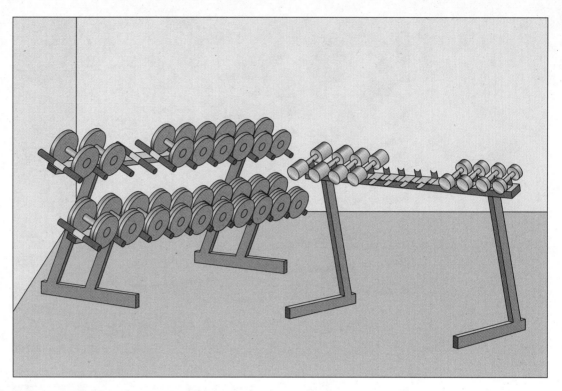

Using a weight rack

Garage and basement gymnasiums are becoming more and more popular these days. And as the workout space grows on the home front, so does the need for storage areas for fitness equipment. When storing dumbbells and other free weights, consider using commercial racks, such as those shown above. The racks are sturdy and hold the weights at knee or waist level—important for keeping the floor in the exercise area clutter-free and safe, and for taking the strain off your back when picking up the weights.

The racks can be left in a central area when the weights are in use. If you plan on storing the weights for a period of time, place the racks in a seldom-used corner along a garage or basement wall. You can purchase weight racks at most sporting goods or department stores.

Storing bicycles

Metal channel

Setting up a floor stand

Bicycle stands like the one shown at left are as convenient at home as they are at school or the park. You can buy a commercial rack or build your own from L-shaped slotted metal channel; assemble the stand using nuts and bolts.

Concrete bike blocks with a slot for the front wheel may be available from building suppliers. These blocks are heavy enough to stay put, but can be moved to suit changing needs.

Installing hanging racks

To hang a bike along a stud wall, fasten closet rod brackets like the one shown to two adjacent studs, then set the bike's crossbar in the notches *(left)*.

To hang bikes from a ceiling joist, build a T-shaped rack as shown below. Cut the vertical supports and brace from 2x4 stock and the crossbar holders from 1x3s. Notch the top ends of the supports to hug a joist and saw half laps at the bottom ends. Cut round notches into the top edges of the holders, then bolt the supports to the joist and holders. Nail the brace between the supports and place the bike in the crossbar notches. In a garage, size the racks so the bikes won't obstruct parked cars.

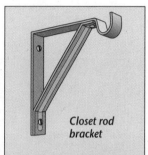

Closet rod
bracket

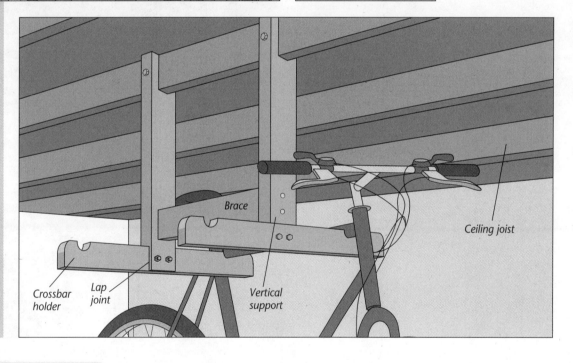

Crossbar
holder

Lap
joint

Brace

Vertical
support

Ceiling joist

ASK A PRO

HOW DO I STORE A BOAT?

Very light boats such as kayaks can be hung from an inside or outside wall in loops of rope. For heavier boats, build a simple rack fastened to garage wall studs. Use lag screws to attach a 2x4 to the side of a stud and then brace it with another 2x4 installed diagonally. Boats can also be hung from joists or collar beams—providing they can handle the weight. If you're unsure, check with a professional. You can also build a cradle with a pulley system (page 160).

FURNITURE AND OTHER BULKY ITEMS

Storing furniture, such as dining room tables and overstuffed chairs, is difficult due to their size and weight. You can attempt to get lighter furnishings up onto overhead platforms, but it is best to store them out of the traffic flow—in attic or basement corners and against walls—and in a compact arrangement. A rented storage locker will free up space at home, and can help solve long-term storage problems.

Protect your furniture from dust by covering it with old mattress pads or blankets; polyethylene sheeting, canvas, or even newspaper can also help keep it free from dust. Lamps, decorations, and breakables should be stored on heavy-duty shelves.

Hooks can support lightweight objects, such as outdoor furniture and folding chairs, on garage or basement walls; you could also place these on a loft platform or overhead rack, or inside carport storage units. Bulky outdoor items are best stored in a garden shed, patio storage unit, or garage extension.

To store card or Ping-Pong tables, model train or game boards, and suitcases during the off season, look for out-of-the-way ledges; or build enclosures specially tailored to their dimensions *(see page 159)*. Another way of storing large items is with a platform attached to a pulley system; you can even use it to pull an unwieldy table or trunk up out of the way.

Stashing bulky items

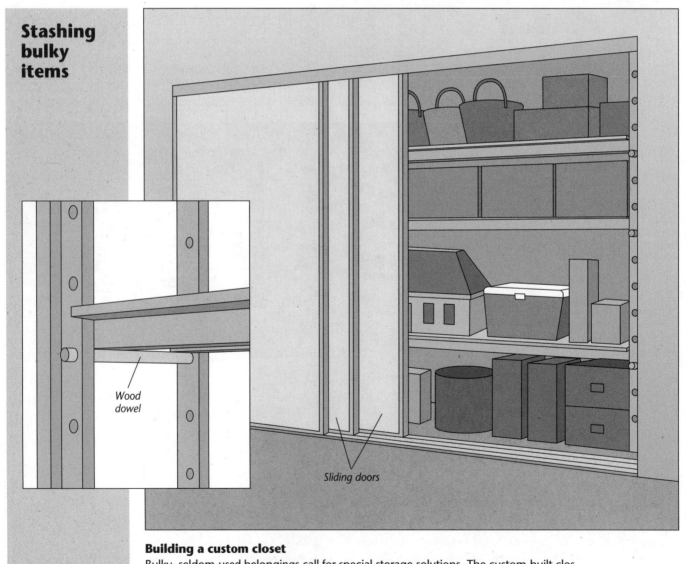

Wood dowel

Sliding doors

Building a custom closet
Bulky, seldom-used belongings call for special storage solutions. The custom-built closet shown above has three sliding doors that open two at a time, accommodating large items. Deep, sturdy shelves can be raised or lowered on adjustable dowels that fit into holes in vertical supports *(inset)*. This design can also be used for open shelving.

Storing carpets and quilts

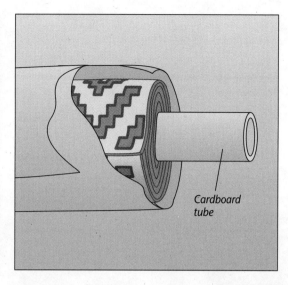

Cardboard tube

Rolling and wrapping

Roll a rug or carpet around a pole or cardboard tube, then loosely wrap the carpet in paper or plastic, leaving some air space *(left)*. Never fold a rug or carpet. Store the carpet in a space that is neither damp nor overly warm; excessive dryness is as harmful as mildew. Use mothballs or crystals to help keep insects away, but keep in mind that some fibers react adversely to these repellents. Consult a carpet expert before storing a prized carpet.

To store heirloom quilts and fine blankets, roll or loosely fold them, then wrap them in clean cotton pillowcases or sheets. Never store a quilt in a plastic bag; the fibers need to breathe. And keep quilts from direct contact with wood. Take your quilts out of their cases occasionally and refold them differently.

Propping up mattresses

Keeping mattresses upright

Store mattresses and box springs off the floor, and prevent them from sagging. Stand them upright against a wall on a plywood base propped up on bricks or blocks. Cover the mattress with plastic or a sheet.

To prevent the mattress from falling over, support it with a sheet of plywood or its own headboard and slats. Fasten eye hooks into the wall, wrap bungee cords around the mattress and attach them to the eyes.

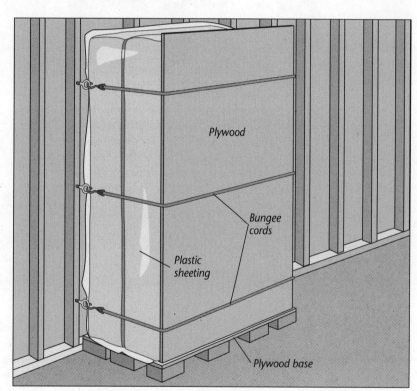

Plywood

Bungee cords

Plastic sheeting

Plywood base

ASK A PRO

HOW DO I KEEP CHRISTMAS LIGHTS UNTANGLED?

Save the cardboard tubes from rolls of gift wrapping paper and a few small-to-medium cardboard boxes. Cut the tubes to fit in the boxes lengthwise, then cut a V-notch into one end of each tube and secure a light strand plug in the notch. Coil the lights firmly around the tubes, as shown at right, by rotating the tube; tape the end in place. Then slip the tubes inside the box; a 12-inch-long box and tube will handle a strand of 35 to 50 small twinkle lights.

You can also wrap lights lengthwise around a long, flat piece of notched cardboard.

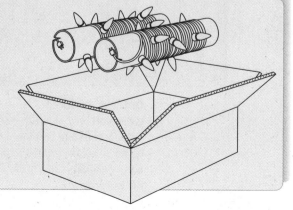

Hanging up furniture

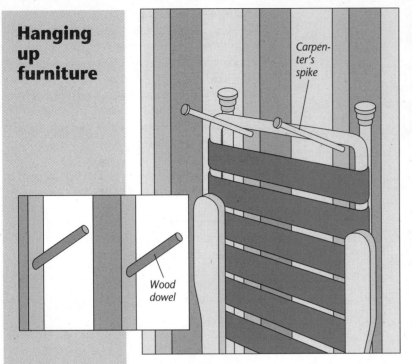

Carpenter's spike

Wood dowel

Shelf bracket

L-brace

Lawn chairs

Save precious floor space by hanging lightweight folding lawn chairs and recliners from wall studs, ceiling joists, or rafters. For simple supports, drive long nails, known as carpenter's spikes, into framing members; use two for each chair *(above, left)*.

You can also drill holes for ³/₄" dowels and glue them in *(inset, left)*. Shelf brackets *(above, right)* or L-braces *(inset, right)* will also get the job done. Yet another possibility is a simple track-and-bracket shelving system.

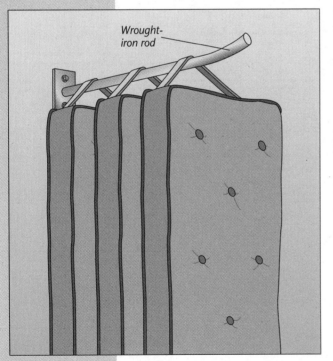

Wrought-iron rod

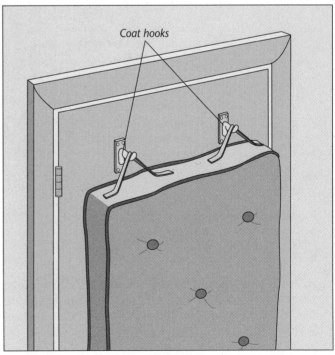

Coat hooks

Outdoor cushions

When bad or cool weather sets in, it's time to bring outdoor furniture cushions inside. Cushions should be stored off the ground to provide good air circulation, which promotes quick drying and prevents mildew problems.

Attach a wrought-iron rod to a wall stud *(above, left)* to hang several cushions from their hand loops or from loops you've sewn in place. You can also mount metal coat hooks on studs or on a closet door to hold individual cushions *(above, right)*.

Building wall racks

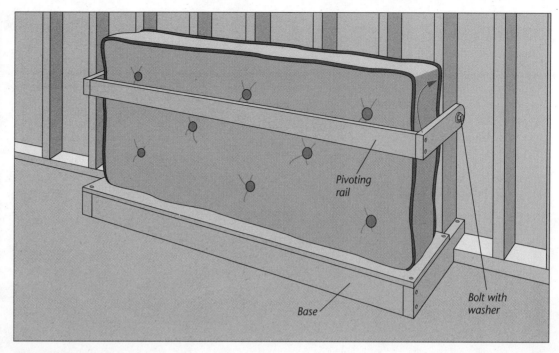

Pivoting rail

Bolt with washer

Base

Pivoting rail

The rack shown above will hold a mattress, or a Ping-Pong or game table. You can keep the object off the floor on a 2x4 base topped with a plywood shelf. For the rail, use 1x3 stock; leave the bolt or lag screw attaching the rail to the studs a little loose so you can pivot it.

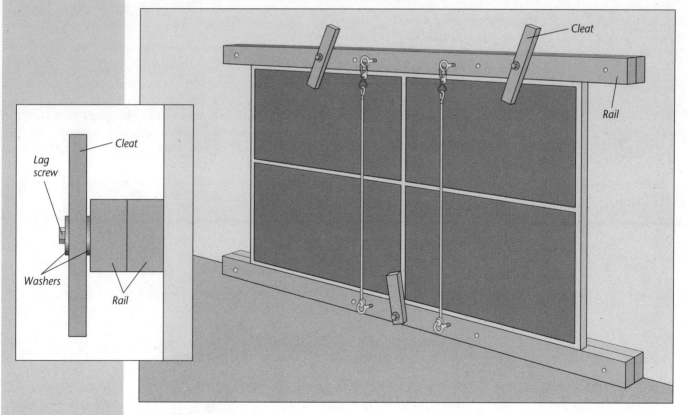

Cleat

Rail

Cleat

Lag screw

Washers

Rail

Swiveling cleats

To hold the top of a Ping-Pong table or game table against a wall, build a rack like the one shown above. For each rail, nail two 2x4s face to face to the wall; the space between the rails should equal the table width plus 1/4" for clearance.

Cut the cleats from 1x2 stock and fasten them to the rails using lag screws and washers *(inset)*; leave the screws loose enough so you can pivot the cleats. For extra security, attach a pair of ropes between the rails, fastening them to eye screws.

Using pulleys

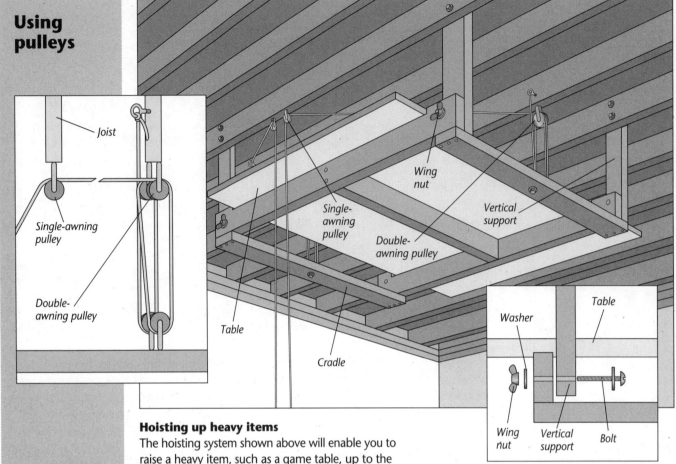

Joist

Single-awning pulley

Double-awning pulley

Single-awning pulley

Double-awning pulley

Wing nut

Vertical support

Table

Cradle

Table

Washer

Wing nut

Vertical support

Bolt

Hoisting up heavy items

The hoisting system shown above will enable you to raise a heavy item, such as a game table, up to the ceiling. Assemble a cradle for the table from 2x4 stock, then use a double-awning pulley—a device with a pair of side-by-side wheels—to link each side of the cradle to the joists. Attach two single-awning pulleys to a joist at one end of the cradle, then feed the hoisting ropes once around each wheel of the double-awning pulleys and over to the single-awning pulley *(inset, left)*. Pull on the ropes to hoist the cradle.

Once the cradle reaches the ceiling, anchor the ropes, and use a bolt and wing nut *(inset, right)* to attach the corners to vertical supports that are cut from 2x4s and bolted to joists. This will take the weight off the pulleys.

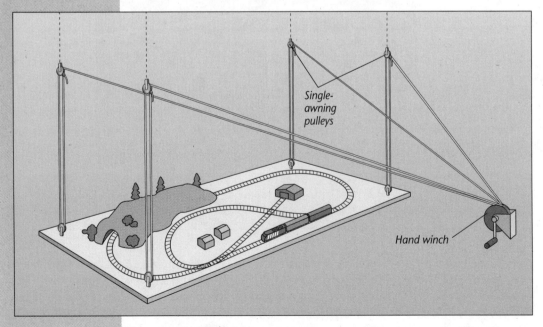

Single-awning pulleys

Hand winch

Raising lighter items

To hoist light items, such as a train board, single-awning pulleys are sufficient. At each corner of the board, use a hoisting rope and two pulleys, attaching one to the board and the other directly above to a joist *(left)*. Raise the board with a hand winch.

Creating storage off the ground

Garage platform

The platform shown below utilizes the space above your car hood in the garage. Cut the posts from 4x4s, the frame pieces from 2x6 stock, and the top from $5/8$" plywood. Size the pieces so the posts will straddle the car and the frame will extend above the hood without contacting the windshield (inset). Use nails to assemble the platform, then bolt it to the wall studs or to a masonry wall. You can also use the space above ceiling joists in a garage, as described on page 153.

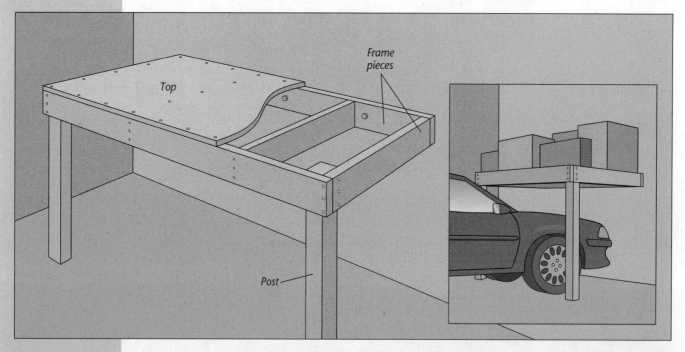

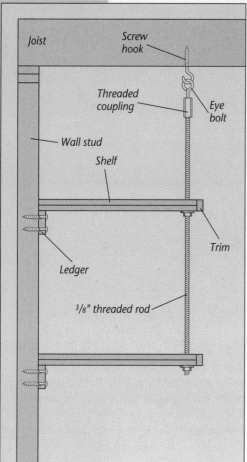

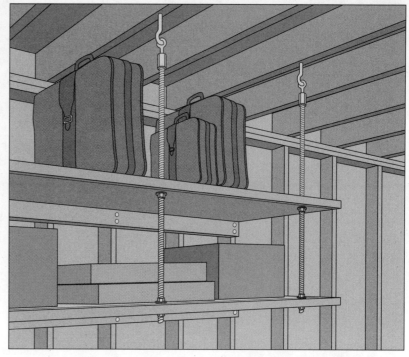

Hanging shelves

Fastened to wall studs and ceiling joists, the shelving shown above can hold heavy items. Make the shelves by gluing two $3/4$" plywood panels together; you can conceal the front edges by gluing on solid-wood trim. To support the shelves at the back, use 1x4 ledgers, screwing them to every second stud. For the front, drill a $3/8$" diameter hole through the shelf at every second joist, feed a threaded rod through the holes, and attach the rods to the joists (left).

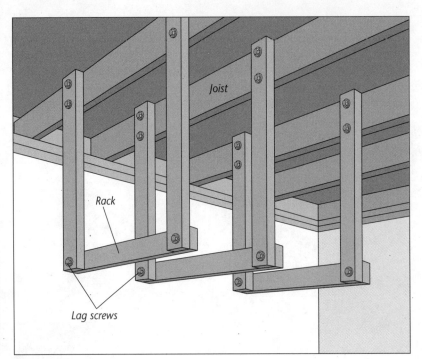

Ladder shelves

U-shaped racks made from 2x4 stock and attached to ceiling joists *(left)* are handy for keeping storm sashes, screens, window shades, and ladders out of the way.

Assemble the racks with lag screws or bolts, then bolt the uprights to the joists; use nails or screws for lightweight storage. Or, you can use half-lap joints instead of the simple butt joints shown. To store storm windows compactly, offset their hardware as you stack them.

Finding hidden space

Behind a cabinet

To slide narrow items like chairs or tables in and out of the back of a cabinet, install a door in the side panel *(right)*. This way, you won't have to unload the items at the front to remove a table from the back.

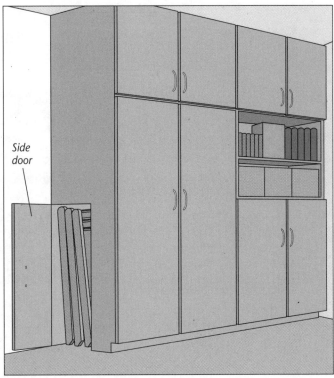

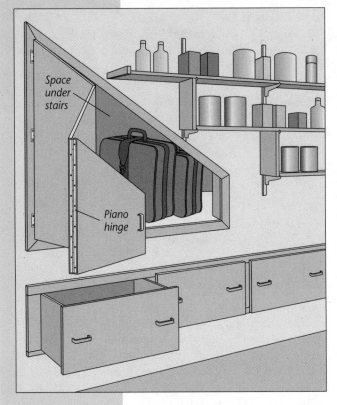

Under stairs

You can access the space under stairs—even if it's closed off by a wall. At the top of the space, cut a long, triangular hole for a door (being careful not to cut through any structural supports) and install a shelf below the opening. To avoid obstructions, make the door in three segments joined by piano hinges *(left)*. At the bottom of the space, install drawers. Ideas for storing firewood under stairs are shown on page 135.

Building a customized garage unit

A sloping cabinet

The tapered shape of the storage unit shown below takes advantage of storage space in the upper part of a garage without encroaching on a car's clearance space. Start by cutting the vertical supports so they will span from the sole plate to the ceiling above when angled forward at 15°. Bolt the bottoms of the supports to the wall studs and the tops to the ceiling joists; you may need to add blocking between the framing members to anchor the supports if the spacing between the studs and joists is not suitable for your needs.

Next, saw shelf brackets from 2x4s, bolting the back ends to the studs. At the front, notch the back edges of the vertical supports to fit the brackets. Cut the shelves from $3/4$" plywood and notch them to fit inside the studs at the back and the vertical supports at the front; the outside edges of the supports should extend 1" beyond the shelves. Cut the triangular side panels from $1/8$" plywood and nail them to the studs and supports. Cover the exposed edges of the shelves with 1" thick trim nailed in place.

To complete the unit, cut the doors from $1/2$" plywood, sizing them $1/8$" shorter than their openings and $1/2$" wider. The doors are not fixed in place; instead, they rest on the trim when closed and on 1x1 supports nailed to the shelf brackets when open.

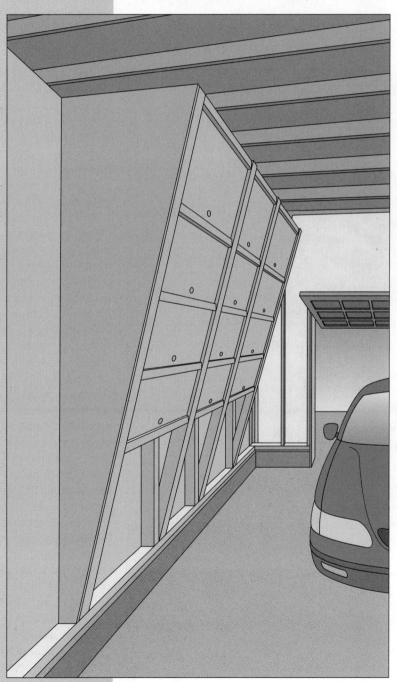

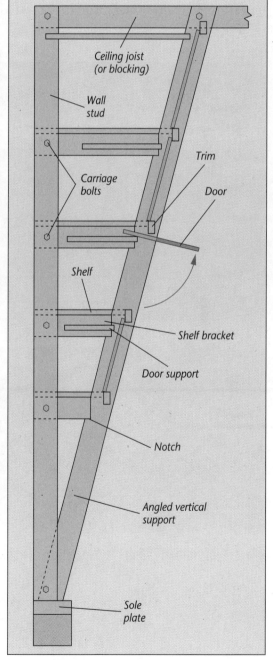

Ceiling joist (or blocking)

Wall stud

Carriage bolts

Trim

Door

Shelf

Shelf bracket

Door support

Notch

Angled vertical support

Sole plate

GARDENING TOOLS AND SUPPLIES

Garden tools need to be stored in a convenient place. Some options include building a garage extension or, if you don't have one already, you can construct a garden shed that houses a work center and potting benches *(page 166)*. Hang a chalkboard nearby for recording planting timetables and scheduling weekly gardening duties.

Large equipment, such as lawn mowers and garden tillers, need spacious floor storage and a clear path to the door. Equipment shouldn't block access to your potting bench. Make the door wide enough for your biggest piece of machinery. You may need to build ramps, if the door sills are high.

Smaller, lighter-weight tools and supplies can be hung handily on a rack made of perforated hardboard *(page 173)*. Garden poisons, sprayers, and sharp tools require extra storage precautions—use locked cabinets to keep children out. Seed packets and bottles can be stored on small shelves.

Remember that moisture can damage fertilizers, potting soils, and chemicals, so seal them inside tight-closing cans or bins. Consider metal containers to help keep rodents and insects out of grass seed and bird feed.

Avoid tangled hoses by wrapping them around a commercial hose reel *(opposite)* or a hose rack.

Finding hidden space

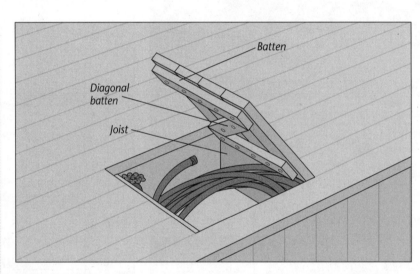

Batten

Diagonal batten

Joist

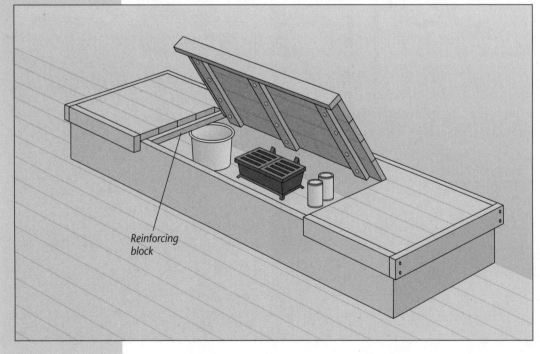

Reinforcing block

Under a deck
The space below the surface of most decks is ideal for storing garden tools or even a small barbecue. To install a trap door *(left, top)*, cut the decking so that the ends of the door rest on the center of a joist or beam. Build a compartment and attach it to the underside of the deck, drilling a hole in the bottom for drainage.

On the door's underside, fasten 1x3 battens offset from the ends and parallel to the joists or beams to keep the door securely seated. Add a third batten diagonally between the first two. Install a recessed pull on the door. You can simply set the door in place and lift it out as necessary, or use butt hinges to fasten one end to the deck.

Apply the same principles to install a door on a deck bench *(left, bottom)*, adding blocking to the underside of the seat to support the door's edge.

Quick fixes for garden storage needs

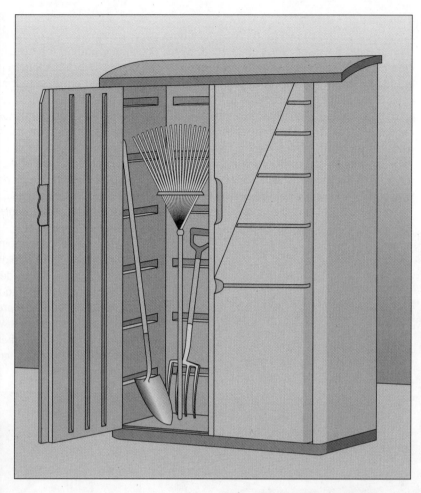

Instant outdoor storage

When storing backyard and garden maintenance equipment outdoors, consider a small shed such as the one shown. Made entirely of plastic, the shed is big enough to store most of the basic tools used in the garden and backyard, and small enough so as not to take up too much space. Some models come with wheels so they can be rolled around—or stored inside during cold winter months—with little effort. The sheds are available at home and garden centers.

Keeping hoses under control

It seems that no matter how carefully garden hoses are coiled, they always tangle or kink in storage. A commercial hose coiler, such as the one shown at right, helps prevent this by keeping the hose firmly wrapped round a drum. The hose feeds off of the drum when pulled out for use, and recoils when the handle is turned clockwise. Designed with wheels for easy mobility, the device can be moved to the source of water in the backyard or garden, such as an outdoor spigot, and returned to a garden shed, for example, when the watering is done.

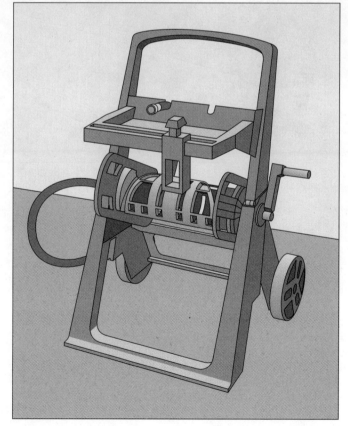

Building potting benches

Two garden centers

Either work center shown on this page will hold garden tools, pots, soil mixes and fertilizers efficiently. For either one, use exterior-grade plywood and apply a weatherproof finish if the cabinet will be located outside.

To build the fence- or wall-mounted cabinet *(below, left)*, start by making the cabinet and shelf from ³/₄" plywood, reinforcing the top corners with 2x4 blocks. Attach the cabinet back to the fence, then assemble the work surface, using ³/₄" plywood for the benchtop. Use pressure-treated lumber for the 1x3 stretcher and 2x2 legs.

Fasten the legs to the work surface with butt hinges, adding the stretcher. Attach folding leg braces to lock the legs in place and strap hinges to fix the benchtop to the cabinet, and add a handle to the outside face. To secure the bench in the folded-up position, attach swiveling cleats to blocks fastened to the cabinet top.

The freestanding work center *(below, right)* is basically a large cabinet with shelves, dividers, doors, and a fold-down work surface—all made from ³/₄" plywood. Use butt hinges to attach the work surface to the cabinet. Add a single leg with a butt hinge and folding leg braces.

Fasten hasps to the cabinet to hold the work surface in place when it is folded up. If you're storing soil or amendments inside the cabinet, you can drill ventilation holes into the sides.

CAUTION: Never cut pressure-treated wood indoors and don't burn it. Wear safety glasses and respiratory protection when cutting it, and long pants and sleeves and chemical-resistant gloves when handling it.

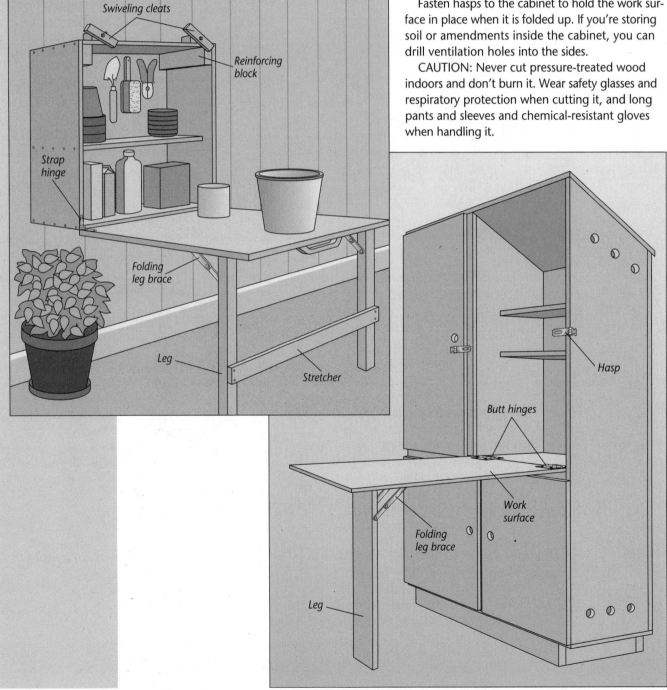

Swiveling cleats

Reinforcing block

Strap hinge

Folding leg brace

Leg

Stretcher

Hasp

Butt hinges

Work surface

Folding leg brace

Leg

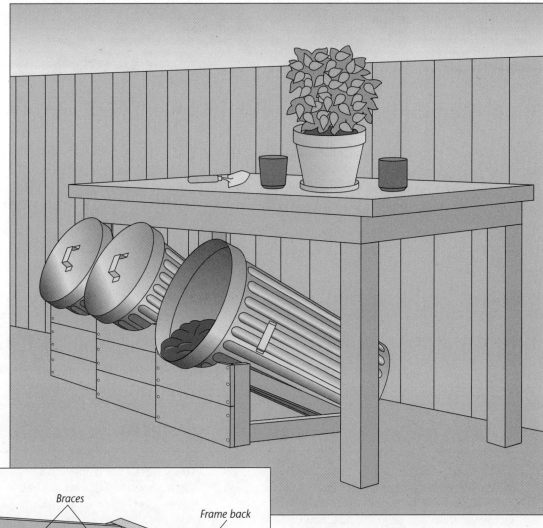

Storing soil mixtures

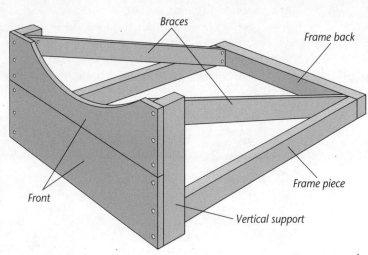

Braces

Frame back

Front

Frame piece

Vertical support

Garbage can racks

Metal garbage cans are ideal for storing peat moss, soil, and fertilizer. Build racks like these to hold the cans at an angle under a table.

Using pressure-treated lumber, cut the frame pieces and the vertical supports from 2x4s and the diagonal braces from 1x3 stock. Make the front from 1-by lumber to suit the angle of the can.

CAUTION: Never cut pressure-treated wood indoors and don't burn it. Wear safety glasses and respiratory protection when cutting it, and long pants and sleeves and chemical-resistant gloves when handling it.

MAINTENANCE TIP

KEEPING TOOLS RUST-FREE

If you're putting your garden center to bed for the winter, tools need an environment where they won't rust; a dry area or closed cabinet is best. If rust-producing dampness is a problem, treat tools with liquid rust cleaner, emery paper, or a wire brush; then oil any working parts and apply a light coating of oil to surfaces that are susceptible to rust.

Storing garden equipment

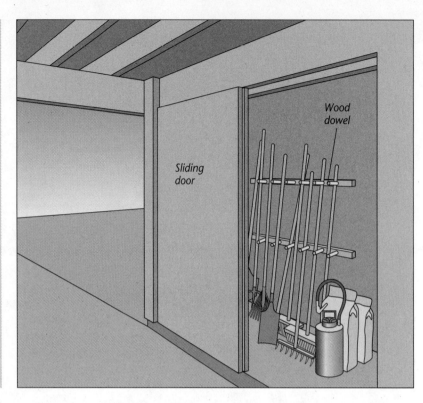

Sliding door

Wood dowel

Carport closet
To store brooms, shovels, and other garden tools vertically, drill holes in two wood strips for dowels and glue in the dowels. Fasten the strips along a wall, as in the carport closet shown at left.

Prop the handles of the tools against the strip, between dowels, leaving valuable floor space for other supplies.

You may be able to build a closet in your carport that is deep enough to store a lawn mower, but make sure you leave sufficient clearance for your car.

STYLISH BARBECUE STORAGE

The most durable barbecue is set into a freestanding unit built from brick, stone, or concrete blocks. If you're designing a barbecue area, be sure to make room for storage.

Below the barbecue or to the side, you can build in cabinets for utensils, accessories, starter fluid, and charcoal; keep briquettes in metal or plastic cans with tight-fitting lids to keep out moisture. The well-lighted countertop and double-door cabinets shown below make barbecuing as convenient as cooking in a kitchen.

In addition to cabinets, barbecue storage can include shelves, hanging pegs, and drawers for tongs, oven mitts, and other small accessories.

Portable barbecues rust quickly when exposed to dampness and precipitation. A deep cabinet to house a portable barbecue can be built against the house wall, protected beneath the eaves.

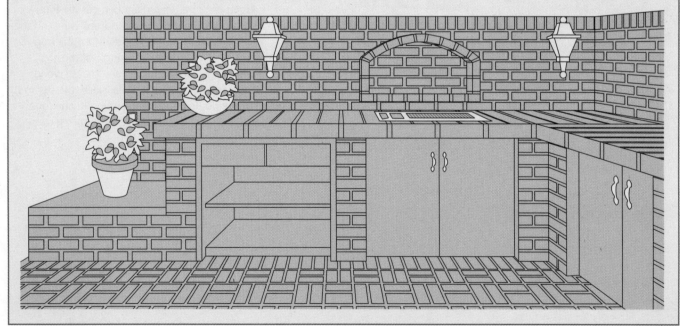

TOOLS AND TECHNIQUES

Making the most of your storage space is easy when you have the necessary tools and techniques to improve upon your home's available areas. Simple wall systems, boxes, cabinets, doors, and shelving are all easy to build yourself with basic know-how and information about the most commonly used tools and materials. This chapter will show you which tools and accessories are best suited for your building needs. Beginning on page 174, you'll learn about wood joinery—how to attach different boards in durable and attractive ways. Attaching solid shelves to walls, installing cabinets, and building and fitting drawers for furniture are all covered starting on page 177. Finally, to find out about the final touches that will make your projects as beautiful as they are solid, turn to page 187 for information about decorative wood edges, paints and stains, and other finishes.

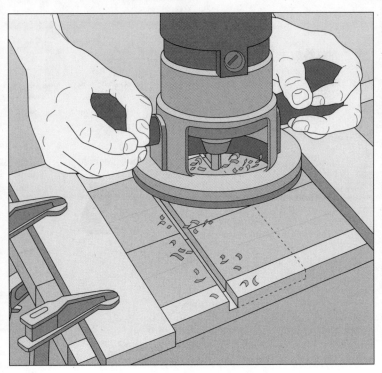

A knowledge of joinery basics is essential when building shelves, cabinets, and drawers. In the illustration above, a router is used to remove stock in the middle of a board to accommodate a lap joint. See page 175 for more on lap joints.

TOOLS

Having the right tools at hand is essential when tackling any home improvement project. It's best to stock your workshop with some basic tools and then purchase more specialized tools as the need arises. A collection of both is shown below. As a rule, buy the best quality tools you can afford, cheaper models won't stand the test of time and will end up costing you more money when you have to replace them. When using power tools, make sure to read the owner's manual carefully and follow all safety directions. Always wear proper safety equipment, including:

• Safety goggles or glasses when using power tools or a striking tool, especially when fastening into concrete.
• Gloves: Wear work gloves when loading or stacking wood, and rubber or plastic gloves when working with substances such as solvents or wood preservatives.
• A respirator when using adhesives, paints, and other substances that give off toxic fumes.
• A dust mask when sanding, sawing, or otherwise creating sawdust.
• Earmuff protectors or earplugs if you're using power tools for extended periods.

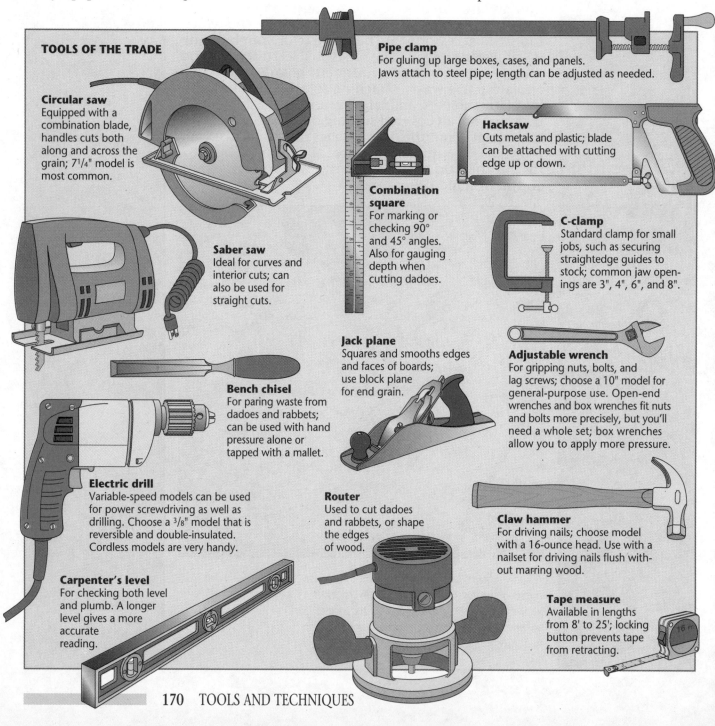

TOOLS OF THE TRADE

Pipe clamp
For gluing up large boxes, cases, and panels. Jaws attach to steel pipe; length can be adjusted as needed.

Circular saw
Equipped with a combination blade, handles cuts both along and across the grain; 7¼" model is most common.

Hacksaw
Cuts metals and plastic; blade can be attached with cutting edge up or down.

Combination square
For marking or checking 90° and 45° angles. Also for gauging depth when cutting dadoes.

Saber saw
Ideal for curves and interior cuts; can also be used for straight cuts.

C-clamp
Standard clamp for small jobs, such as securing straightedge guides to stock; common jaw openings are 3", 4", 6", and 8".

Jack plane
Squares and smooths edges and faces of boards; use block plane for end grain.

Adjustable wrench
For gripping nuts, bolts, and lag screws; choose a 10" model for general-purpose use. Open-end wrenches and box wrenches fit nuts and bolts more precisely, but you'll need a whole set; box wrenches allow you to apply more pressure.

Bench chisel
For paring waste from dadoes and rabbets; can be used with hand pressure alone or tapped with a mallet.

Electric drill
Variable-speed models can be used for power screwdriving as well as drilling. Choose a ³⁄₈" model that is reversible and double-insulated. Cordless models are very handy.

Router
Used to cut dadoes and rabbets, or shape the edges of wood.

Claw hammer
For driving nails; choose model with a 16-ounce head. Use with a nailset for driving nails flush without marring wood.

Carpenter's level
For checking both level and plumb. A longer level gives a more accurate reading.

Tape measure
Available in lengths from 8' to 25'; locking button prevents tape from retracting.

FASTENERS

The most beautifully crafted storage units would be useless without proper fasteners; namely, glue, nails, screws, and bolts. (Some of the most common fasteners are illustrated below.) Generally speaking, adhesives alone are not enough. Use them in conjunction with fasteners such as nails and screws. Nails are easy to use, but screws provide more strength. Set nails with a nailset and cover them with wood putty so they don't show. Bolts, the strongest of all the fasteners, pass completely through a material and are fastened in place with a nut threaded onto the end. For most bolts, use washers on each side of the material to keep the bolt and nut tight or to distribute the load. Carriage bolts require only one washer placed between the nut and the wood.

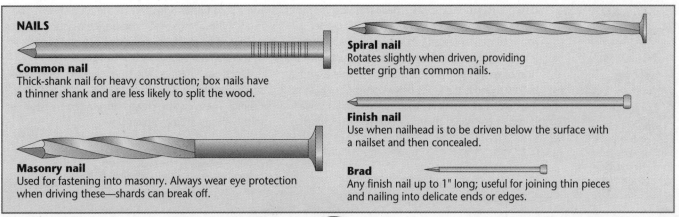

NAILS

Common nail
Thick-shank nail for heavy construction; box nails have a thinner shank and are less likely to split the wood.

Masonry nail
Used for fastening into masonry. Always wear eye protection when driving these—shards can break off.

Spiral nail
Rotates slightly when driven, providing better grip than common nails.

Finish nail
Use when nailhead is to be driven below the surface with a nailset and then concealed.

Brad
Any finish nail up to 1" long; useful for joining thin pieces and nailing into delicate ends or edges.

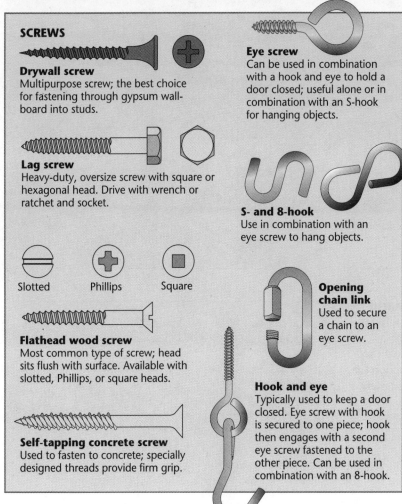

SCREWS

Drywall screw
Multipurpose screw; the best choice for fastening through gypsum wallboard into studs.

Lag screw
Heavy-duty, oversize screw with square or hexagonal head. Drive with wrench or ratchet and socket.

Slotted · Phillips · Square

Flathead wood screw
Most common type of screw; head sits flush with surface. Available with slotted, Phillips, or square heads.

Self-tapping concrete screw
Used to fasten to concrete; specially designed threads provide firm grip.

Eye screw
Can be used in combination with a hook and eye to hold a door closed; useful alone or in combination with an S-hook for hanging objects.

S- and 8-hook
Use in combination with an eye screw to hang objects.

Opening chain link
Used to secure a chain to an eye screw.

Hook and eye
Typically used to keep a door closed. Eye screw with hook is secured to one piece; hook then engages with a second eye screw fastened to the other piece. Can be used in combination with an 8-hook.

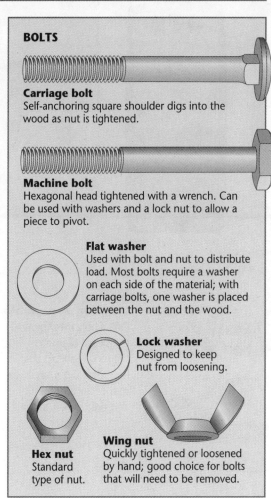

BOLTS

Carriage bolt
Self-anchoring square shoulder digs into the wood as nut is tightened.

Machine bolt
Hexagonal head tightened with a wrench. Can be used with washers and a lock nut to allow a piece to pivot.

Flat washer
Used with bolt and nut to distribute load. Most bolts require a washer on each side of the material; with carriage bolts, one washer is placed between the nut and the wood.

Lock washer
Designed to keep nut from loosening.

Hex nut
Standard type of nut.

Wing nut
Quickly tightened or loosened by hand; good choice for bolts that will need to be removed.

FASTENING TO WALLS

When storing items on shelves or bookcases, it's often necessary to secure the unit to a wall first. This prevents the unit from toppling over in the event the load is unbalanced or top-heavy.

For attachments to masonry walls, use an expansion shield *(bottom)*. With wallboard or plaster, drill a hole and install either a spreading anchor or a toggle bolt *(opposite page)*. You might consider installing perforated hardboard rather than shelving for easy storage and access to hand tools.

Fastening to wall studs and ceiling joists

TOOLKIT
• Stud finder (optional)
• Screwdriver or electric drill
• Tape measure

Locating and attaching to studs and joists

When securing a storage unit to a wall or ceiling, fasten it to studs or joists. These framing members are usually spaced 16" or 24" apart on center (from center to center), as shown below. The trick is locating the first one. Knock on the wall with the heel of your hand. A solid sound indicates a stud; a hollow sound is the space between.

You can also look for the fasteners in your wallboard or paneling; they most likely correspond to the location of a stud. If you can't see the fasteners, use a stud finder *(inset)*. With the type shown, the red light indicates when the device reaches a stud or joist. If all else fails, drill small exploratory holes in the wall or ceiling.

Once you've found the studs or joists, use drywall screws to attach your storage unit to the wall or ceiling. These can be power-driven into the stud or joist without drilling a pilot hole.

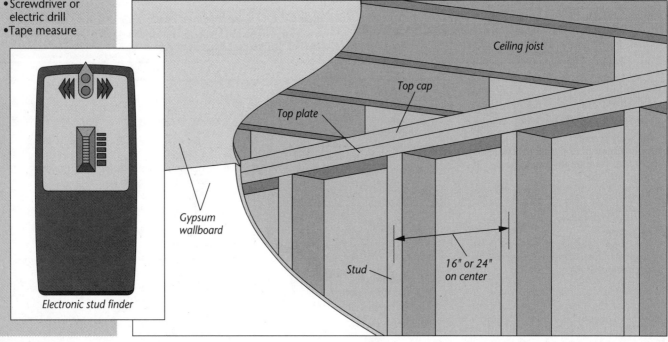

Electronic stud finder

Ceiling joist

Top cap

Top plate

Gypsum wallboard

Stud

16" or 24" on center

Fastening to masonry

TOOLKIT
• Electric drill with masonry bit
• Hammer
• Adjustable wrench or open-end wrench

Installing an expansion shield

Drill a hole into the wall equal to the the sleeve diameter—but slightly longer—then tap the sleeve with your hammer. Slip a lag screw through the part of the storage unit to be fastened and tighten it into the sleeve *(right)*.

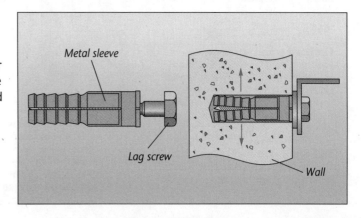

Metal sleeve

Lag screw

Wall

Fastening to wallboard or plaster

TOOLKIT
• Electric drill
• Screwdriver

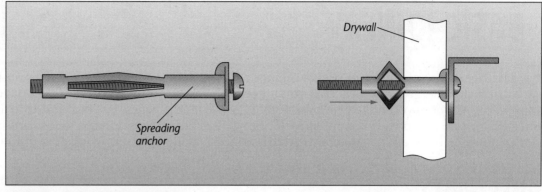

Drywall

Spreading anchor

Installing a spreading anchor

Drill a hole in the wall with a bit sized as per package instructions. Slip the screw through the object to be attached and thread it into the sleeve.

Tap the sleeve into the wall and tighten the screw; the sleeve will expand against the back of the wall, as shown above.

Installing a toggle bolt

Drill a hole through the wall so that the screw and retracted toggle will slide through easily. Decide on what part of the storage unit you will attach to the wall, then slip the screw through and thread on the toggle; make sure the screw is long enough to go all the way through the wall. Pass the fastener through the hole—the spring-loaded toggle will open once it clears the wall.

Tug on the screw as you begin tightening it; this will pull the toggle up against the back side of the wall *(left)*.

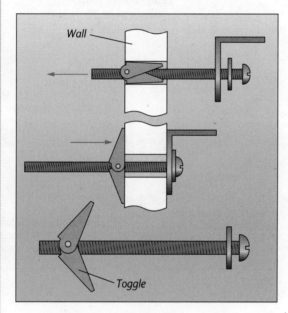

Wall

Toggle

 ASK A PRO

HOW DO I INSTALL PERFORATED HARDBOARD?

The trick with perforated hardboard is to install it with a space behind it so the pegs or hooks can fit through. To do this, slip a spacer over the screw before threading it into the anchor or toggle. The spacer will hold the board out from the wall, as shown at right.

Alternatively, you can fasten furring strips to the wall behind the board, and attach the board to these strips.

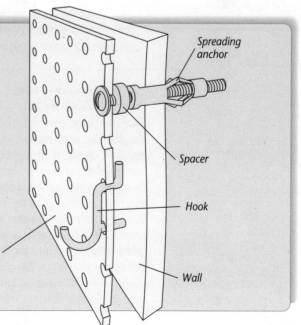

Spreading anchor

Spacer

Hook

Perforated hardboard

Wall

BASIC JOINERY

Whether you're planning an ornate cabinet or a basic storage rack, it's likely that you'll need to join pieces of wood to complete your project. Shelves, frames, and boxes—the building blocks of do-it-yourself storage units—are constructed using basic joinery methods. Tips on how to make three basic joints—butt, lap, and dado—are covered on these pages. Use butt joints to assemble frames and boxes, lap joints to join boards that overlap, and dado joints to fix shelves to the inside of cabinets.

BUTT JOINTS

When a project calls for attaching the face or edge of one board to the face, edge, or end of another, the easiest joinery method is a butt joint—the two pieces simply butt up against each other.

Some butt joints need only be glued together, such as in the edge-to-edge joint shown *(right)*; the glue bond along the joint lines will be stronger than the wood fibers themselves. Clamp the pieces together while the glue dries.

Butt joints involving end grain require additional reinforcement. The simplest way to strengthen end-to-face joints is to use nails or screws, which should be more than twice as long as the thickness of the piece they are passing through.

Other ways of reinforcing butt joints include glue blocks, fluted or spiral-groove dowels, and plate joints (wood biscuits).

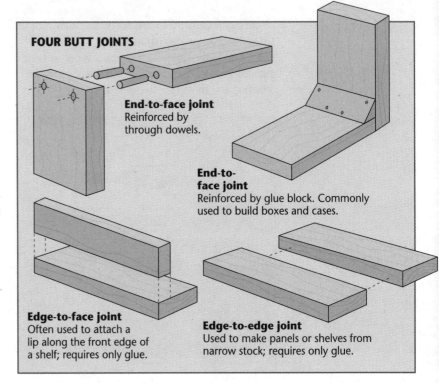

FOUR BUTT JOINTS

End-to-face joint
Reinforced by through dowels.

End-to-face joint
Reinforced by glue block. Commonly used to build boxes and cases.

Edge-to-face joint
Often used to attach a lip along the front edge of a shelf; requires only glue.

Edge-to-edge joint
Used to make panels or shelves from narrow stock; requires only glue.

Reinforcing corners with through dowels

TOOLKIT
- Tape measure
- Table saw or radial-arm saw or circular saw and straightedge guide
- Backsaw and miter box
- Clamps
- Drill
- Mallet
- Sanding block
- Router with straightedge bit
- Chisel or block plane

1 Preparing the stock
When making an end-to-face joint, be sure to cut the pieces so their ends and edges are perfectly square to each other. Cut the boards on a table saw or radial-arm saw.

Alternately, you can use a circular saw, but you'll need a straightedge to guide the cut. If your stock is narrow enough, you can cut the wood with a backsaw and miter box.

2 Reinforcing with through dowels
Glue and clamp the joint. Then, once the glue has cured, remove the clamps and drill holes through the face of one piece and at least 3/4" into the end grain of the adjoining piece. Bore two holes per joint. Cut the dowels slightly longer than the depth of the holes. Coat the dowels sparingly with glue and tap them into the holes with a mallet *(right)*. When the glue has cured, saw off the excess dowel then sand the surface flush.

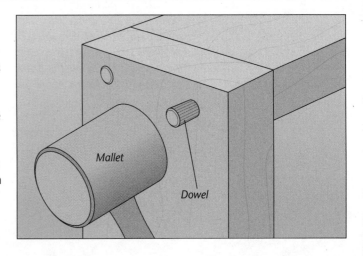

Mallet

Dowel

LAP JOINTS

Lap joints, used to join two pieces of overlapping wood, are formed by cutting recesses across the grain of one or both of the boards. When these recesses are at the end of the piece of wood, they're referred to as rabbets. When located in the middle of the wood, they're called dadoes. See the next page for more on dado joints.

You may need to reinforce end and T half-lap joints with nails, screws, or dowels. Simply glue and clamp full-, edge-, and cross half-lap joints—the extra shoulder helps lock the pieces in place.

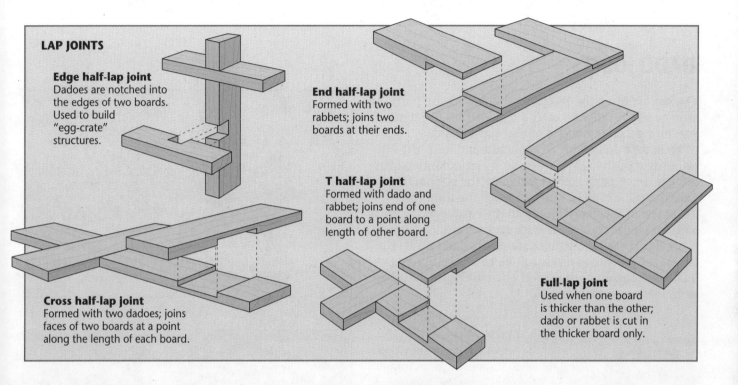

LAP JOINTS

Edge half-lap joint
Dadoes are notched into the edges of two boards. Used to build "egg-crate" structures.

End half-lap joint
Formed with two rabbets; joins two boards at their ends.

T half-lap joint
Formed with dado and rabbet; joins end of one board to a point along length of other board.

Cross half-lap joint
Formed with two dadoes; joins faces of two boards at a point along the length of each board.

Full-lap joint
Used when one board is thicker than the other; dado or rabbet is cut in the thicker board only.

Cutting a lap joint

TOOLKIT
• Clamps
• Router with straight bit
• Bench chisel and mallet
• Block plane (optional)
• Tape measure

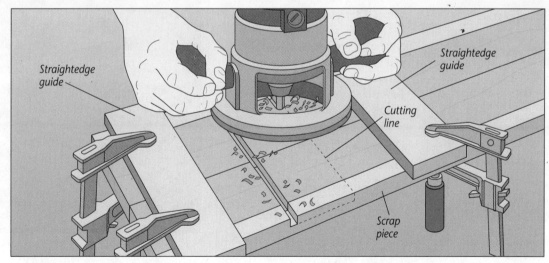

Straightedge guide

Straightedge guide

Cutting line

Scrap piece

Making a cut in the middle of the stock

To cut a wide dado, mark both edges of the recess. Clamp the stock to your workbench, adding a scrap piece along each edge to prevent the edges from splintering. (For a cross half-lap joint, you can cut both pieces at once, provided they're exactly the same width.)

Adjust the router so the depth of cut is exactly half the stock's thickness. Set two straightedges by measuring the distance from the edge of the bit to the edge of the base plate and clamping the straightedge at this distance from your cutting lines. Next, make two cuts just to the waste side of the lines to define the outline of the dado; keep the router's base plate against the guides. Remove any waste with passes down the middle, and then smooth the bottom of the dado with a chisel, if necessary.

DADO JOINTS

Dadoes are often used to join a shelf or vertical partition to the inside of a case. A dado joint is easily made by cutting a groove across one face of a board.

To make a dado joint, first measure and mark the outside edges of the wood. Then set a combination square for the depth of the recess and mark the bottom of the cut. The cut should be one-quarter to one-third the thickness of the board. To make the cuts, you can use a circular saw, as shown below, or a router, as shown on page 175. If you're cutting dadoes to attach shelves to a case, clamp the two sides of the case together and make the cuts in both sides at once to ensure that they will line up correctly.

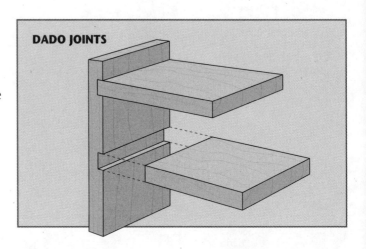

DADO JOINTS

Making a dado joint

TOOLKIT
• T-square
• Circular saw
• Bench chisel and mallet
• Jack plane or sanding block (optional)

1 ▶ **Making the cuts**
Screw two pieces of wood together at right angles to form a T-square. Clamp the T-square across a scrap of wood, set the circular saw's depth of cut at ⅜", and notch the T-square as shown. The notch can then be aligned with cut lines on the workpiece to ensure perfectly square dadoes that are exactly the right width.

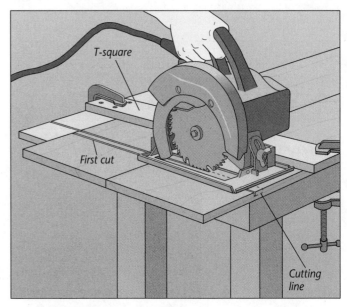

T-square

First cut

Cutting line

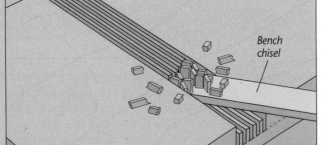

Bench chisel

◀ 2 **Chiseling out the waste**
Hold a chisel, bevel side down, at a point about half the dado's depth; tap it lightly with a mallet to remove waste. Work toward the center, gradually lowering the depth of your cuts.

When you reach the bottom, turn the chisel over and, holding it flat, smooth the bottom of the dado. Check the fit of the second board; it should slide in with light hand pressure or a few taps with a mallet. If the fit is too tight, plane or sand the second board rather than making the dado wider.

BOXES, BINS, AND CASES

The three basic storage units that you can make yourself are all based on the same construction principles. Boxes, bins, and cases are all built using five basic pieces—two sides, a back, a top, and a bottom; shelves are optional. Butt joints are probably the most common and easiest way to join the separate wood pieces. See page 174 for more on butt joints. If you plan to place items on top of the unit, make sure the top piece is well supported by cutting it to overlap the sides. If you plan to move or lift a filled storage box, make sure the bottom is sturdy—attach it to the inside of the sides so it doesn't pull off when the box is lifted off the floor. If you want a kick space below a box or case, attach the bottom to the sides with dadoes, as shown at right.

Assembling a standard box is a straightforward task. Reinforce the joints by putting glue in the dadoes and attaching the two sides to the bottom, then attach the top. Finally, attach the back—fasten one edge, then square the box and fasten the other edge.

Rabbet joints attach the top to the sides in the case shown *(right)*, although butt joints are also acceptable. You can attach the shelves with reinforced butt joints *(page 174)* if your load won't be too heavy; dado joints will make your unit sturdier and easier to assemble. Cut dadoes in both sides at the same time so they line up. Your best bet is to use a router to cut both the dadoes and rabbets *(page 175)*, but you can use a table saw or a radial-arm saw with a dado blade. Alternatively cut dadoes with a circular saw and a T-square *(page 176)*.

Spread glue in the rabbets and dadoes, then lay one sidepiece on a worktable. Slip top and shelves in place and fit the other side on top. Use two pipe or bar clamps for each joint to secure the assembly while glue dries. Reinforce joints with nails or screws.

Ledgers are another way to attach shelves *(page 179)*. For adjustable shelves, install tracks with clips *(page 179)* or drill two vertical rows of dowel holes on the inside faces of the sides; the shelves rest on dowel pegs that can be moved as needed. Adding a door to a case *(page 180)* yields a cabinet.

Use 1-by lumber or $3/4$-inch plywood; $1/4$-inch plywood or hardboard is fine for backs.

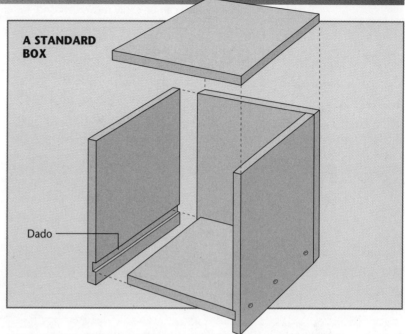

A STANDARD BOX

Dado

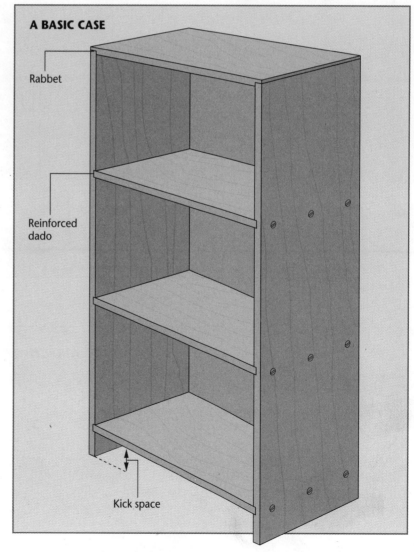

A BASIC CASE

Rabbet

Reinforced dado

Kick space

Adapting the basic box

Tilting and rolling bins

Attach a box to a counter with hinges to create a tilt-out bin *(below, left)* for convenient access to areas under the counter or at the bottom of a cabinet or closet. To create a rolling bin which can be easily moved around, fasten casters to a box *(below, right)*.

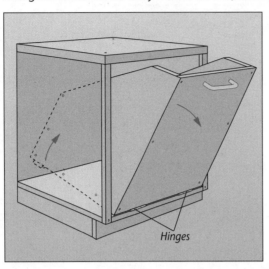

Hinges

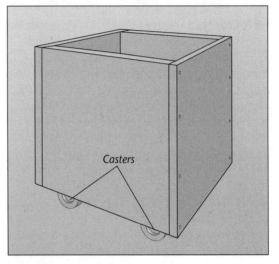

Casters

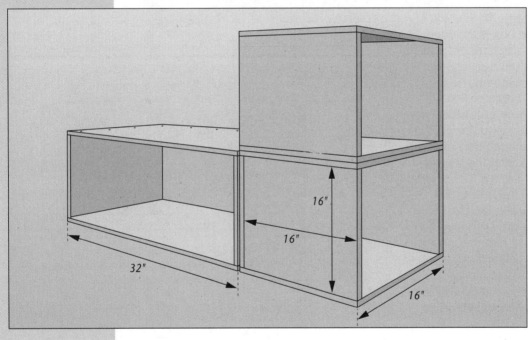

32"

16"

16"

16"

Modular boxes

To build a set of stacking bins, construct several boxes of the same size, or make rectangular units that are twice as long as square ones *(left)*. For extra support and safety, bolt high stacks of boxes together or to a wall *(page 172)*.

READY ROD ATTACHMENTS

To install a rod inside a cabinet or closet, use pole sockets *(near right)*. First, screw one socket in place, then insert the rod and level it before fastening the other socket. You can provide additional support to a very long rod by fastening a hook to the top of the case near the middle of the rod. This will keep the rod from sagging when loaded.

You can also suspend a rod from the bottom of a shelf using closet rod brackets *(far right)*.

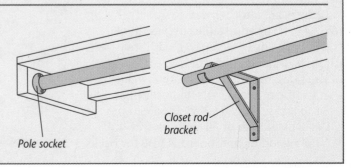

Pole socket

Closet rod bracket

SHELVES

Building shelves to maximize your wall storage space can be as easy as picking up simple materials from the hardware store and spending a few hours in your workshop. Choose from among solid lumber—pine, fir, and other softwood—plywood, or particleboard for your shelf material. Particleboard, though inexpensive, tends to sag over time. Plywood is stronger than particleboard, but weaker and less expensive than solid wood. Plywood and particleboard come with a melamine or laminate covering. For deep shelves use plywood or solid boards edge-glued together *(page 174)*.

The many different brackets available for attaching shelves to walls include shelf brackets, L-braces, track-and-bracket systems, and Z-brackets *(below)*. See page 172 for information on fastening shelves and other objects to walls according to storage weight and wall type.

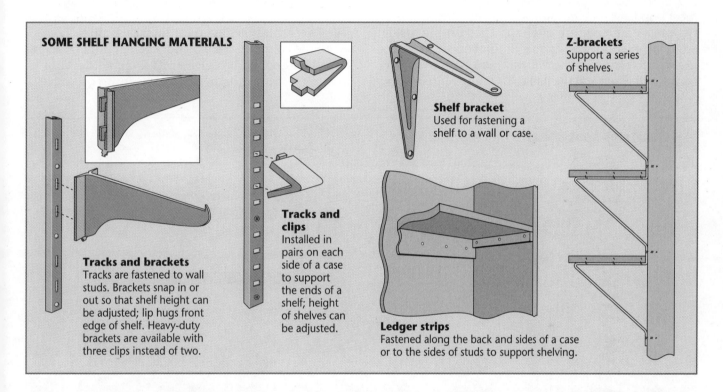

SOME SHELF HANGING MATERIALS

Tracks and brackets
Tracks are fastened to wall studs. Brackets snap in or out so that shelf height can be adjusted; lip hugs front edge of shelf. Heavy-duty brackets are available with three clips instead of two.

Tracks and clips
Installed in pairs on each side of a case to support the ends of a shelf; height of shelves can be adjusted.

Shelf bracket
Used for fastening a shelf to a wall or case.

Ledger strips
Fastened along the back and sides of a case or to the sides of studs to support shelving.

Z-brackets
Support a series of shelves.

Mounting tracks and brackets

TOOLKIT
- Tape measure
- Hacksaw
- Stud finder (optional)
- Electric drill
- Screwdriver
- Carpenter's level

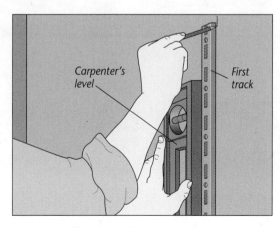

Carpenter's level

First track

1 Installing the first track
Cut the tracks to fit with a hacksaw, aligning the slots. Center one track over a wall stud, drill a pilot hole through a track hole, then loosely drive in a screw. Once plumb, mark a line alongside the track *(above)*, then drive the remaining screws.

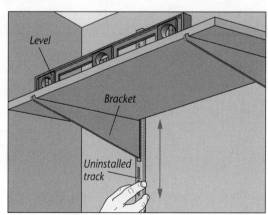

Level

Bracket

Uninstalled track

2 Installing the second track and the shelf
Insert brackets in the corresponding slots of both the anchored and the uninstalled track. Hold the unsecured track against the wall, place a shelf across the brackets and check for level *(above)*. Mark the position on the wall and screw the track in place.

DOORS

oors fulfill a variety of functions, including concealing clutter inside cabinets and closets. The illustrations below depict the three most popular types: hinged, sliding, and bifold. Whereas plastic or canvas roll-up doors are an economical alternative, they're not as durable or protective as the others.

Your choice of hinges used to attach the doors depends on the type of unit, the attachment point, and the kind of door, among other factors. Some of the most popular types are shown opposite. Butt hinges, the most common, are often installed on the inside edges of the door and frame; unless you set the hinge leaves into mortises, you will have to leave a wide gap between the door and the frame. To hang a hinged door, fasten one leaf of each hinge to the door. Then hold the door in position and mark the top screw holes in the free leaves on the cabinet. Install the top screws, check the swing and alignment of the door, then install the bottom screws.

The type of catch used also may vary. Some common types are shown opposite. Fasten the catch to the cabinet frame for overlay doors, or mount them on fixed shelves at the top or bottom of flush doors. In earthquake areas, choose a catch that won't shake loose; see page 16 for information on earthquake security. To secure the contents of a closet or cabinet from children, install childproof catches (page 53). To protect against theft, use a security hasp like the one shown on page 16.

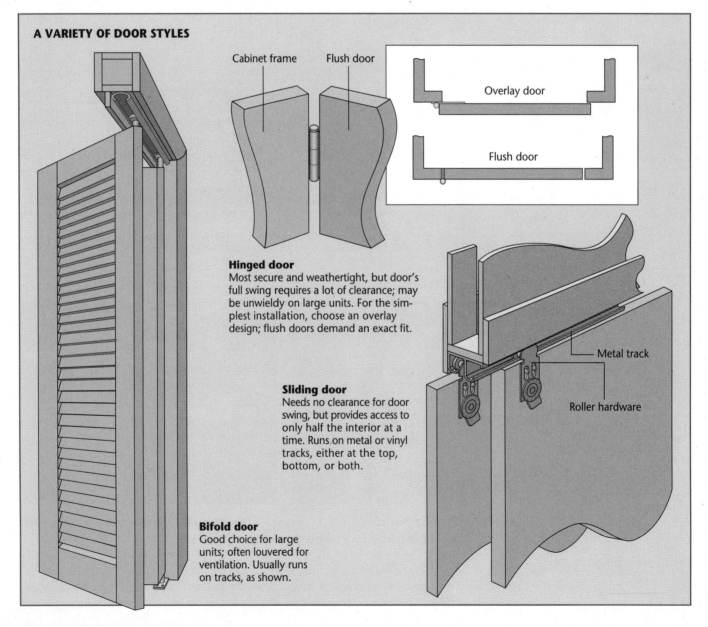

A VARIETY OF DOOR STYLES

Cabinet frame   Flush door

Overlay door

Flush door

Hinged door
Most secure and weathertight, but door's full swing requires a lot of clearance; may be unwieldy on large units. For the simplest installation, choose an overlay design; flush doors demand an exact fit.

Sliding door
Needs no clearance for door swing, but provides access to only half the interior at a time. Runs on metal or vinyl tracks, either at the top, bottom, or both.

Metal track

Roller hardware

Bifold door
Good choice for large units; often louvered for ventilation. Usually runs on tracks, as shown.

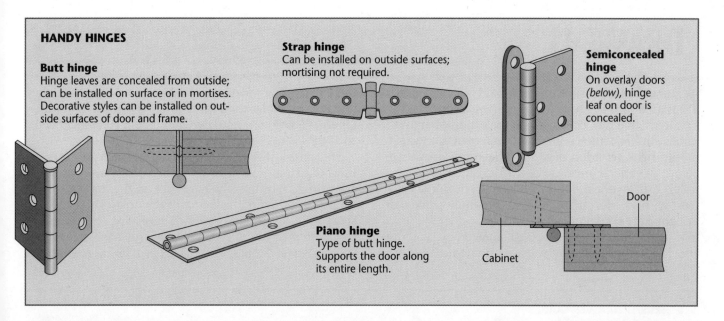

HANDY HINGES

Butt hinge
Hinge leaves are concealed from outside; can be installed on surface or in mortises. Decorative styles can be installed on outside surfaces of door and frame.

Strap hinge
Can be installed on outside surfaces; mortising not required.

Semiconcealed hinge
On overlay doors *(below)*, hinge leaf on door is concealed.

Piano hinge
Type of butt hinge. Supports the door along its entire length.

Door

Cabinet

Chiseling out a hinge mortise

TOOLKIT
• Sharp knife
• Bench chisel
• Mallet

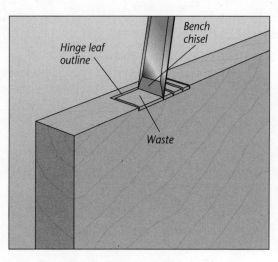

Hinge leaf outline

Bench chisel

Waste

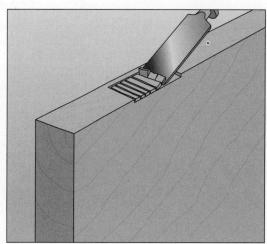

1 Scoring the hinge outline
Outline the hinge leaf on the surface, then score your marks using a sharp knife. Holding a bench chisel vertically—bevel facing the waste— tap it lightly with a mallet to deepen the scored lines to the full depth of the mortise; use a chisel of the same width as the mortise. Then make a series of cross-grain cuts every 1/4" from one end of the outline to the other *(above)*.

2 Chiseling out the waste
With the bevel facing down, chip out the waste wood using hand pressure alone *(above)*. (For a mortise that goes right to the edge, as shown, you can also hold the chisel horizontally and cut the waste away by keeping the flat side of the blade against the bottom of the mortise.) Clean up the mortise holding the chisel flat, bevel up, and working across the grain.

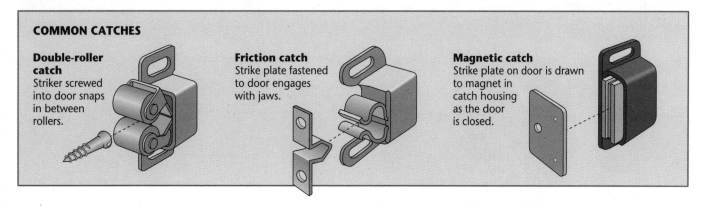

COMMON CATCHES

Double-roller catch
Striker screwed into door snaps in between rollers.

Friction catch
Strike plate fastened to door engages with jaws.

Magnetic catch
Strike plate on door is drawn to magnet in catch housing as the door is closed.

DRAWERS

Although it is possible to design and build drawers to fit your storage units, this can be a tricky task. An alternative is to choose from a selection of manufactured drawers, which come with their own hardware for mounting. A selection of commercial models is shown below. In general, metal guides with ball bearings or rollers usually operate most smoothly, but simpler systems with wooden strips or plastic channels work well in light-duty situations.

When building the frame for a storage unit, you must allow for an opening that will accommodate the size of the drawer. The opening should be about 1/4 inch higher and 1/8 inch wider than the drawer. If you're installing commercial side-mounted guides, you'll generally need to allow 1/2 inch on each side.

The guides and runners on most commercial systems have one or more elongated screw holes that allow for adjustment. Position the hardware on the drawer and cabinet, then mark the center of the holes. Drive the screws and test fit the drawer. If necessary, loosen the screws slightly and reposition the hardware. Once everything fits as it should, drive in the remaining screws.

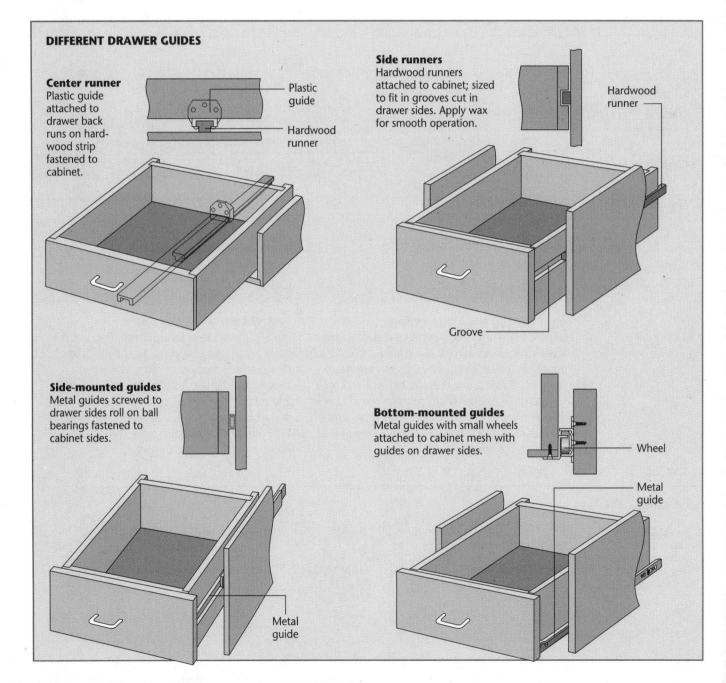

DIFFERENT DRAWER GUIDES

Center runner
Plastic guide attached to drawer back runs on hardwood strip fastened to cabinet.

Plastic guide

Hardwood runner

Side runners
Hardwood runners attached to cabinet; sized to fit in grooves cut in drawer sides. Apply wax for smooth operation.

Hardwood runner

Groove

Side-mounted guides
Metal guides screwed to drawer sides roll on ball bearings fastened to cabinet sides.

Metal guide

Bottom-mounted guides
Metal guides with small wheels attached to cabinet mesh with guides on drawer sides.

Wheel

Metal guide

CABINETS

Once your kitchen or bathroom cabinets are built, it's time to install them. The following pages will give you a few tips on the installation process for both wall-mounted and floor-based units. Illustrations of both are shown below. Although it is possible to handle installation yourself, it's much better to have a second set of hands to make the process run more smoothly.

As shown on page 184, the first step in mounting both upper and lower cabinets is to prepare the wall. As much as possible, try to ensure that the wall is flat by filling in any holes and sanding off bumps. (A long straightedge will help you locate any high spots.) Be sure to remove any baseboard, moldings, or vinyl wall base that might interfere with the placement of the lower cabinets.

Once the imperfections are corrected, use a chalk line to mark the top and bottom lines for the upper cabinets. Next, use a stud finder *(page 172)* to mark the center of each stud along the wall. Alternatively, you can use a small nail to make exploratory holes in the wall to locate the studs. If you need to cut an access hole in the cabinet's back or bottom for plumbing lines or electrical boxes, do so before mounting the cabinet. Ensuring that the units are plumb and level on the wall is a crucial step when installing cabinets.

Before securing them in place, it's best to have a helper hold them up to the chalk lines as you check for level *(page 184)*. Shims between the cabinets and the wall help to even out any discrepancies. A scribing tool, such as the one shown on page 185, will help when filling in the space between the edge of a cabinet and an uneven wall. Scribing will also be necessary when fitting countertops on the lower cabinets to walls, which are rarely perfectly straight *(page 186)*.

Cutting a hole in a countertop to fit a bathroom or kitchen sink is also shown on page 186, as is the final step, securing the top to the cabinet.

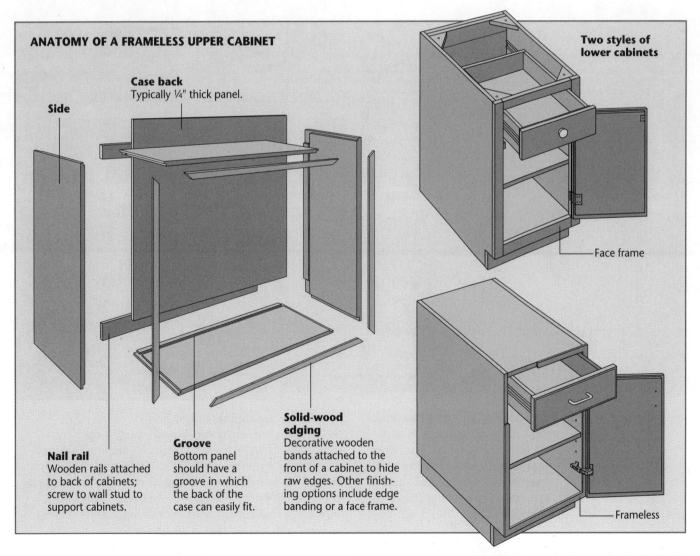

ANATOMY OF A FRAMELESS UPPER CABINET

Side

Case back
Typically ¼" thick panel.

Two styles of lower cabinets

Face frame

Frameless

Nail rail
Wooden rails attached to back of cabinets; screw to wall stud to support cabinets.

Groove
Bottom panel should have a groove in which the back of the case can easily fit.

Solid-wood edging
Decorative wooden bands attached to the front of a cabinet to hide raw edges. Other finishing options include edge banding or a face frame.

Installing cabinets

TOOLKIT
- Tape measure
- Drill with $1/8$" bit
- Carpenter's level
- Mallet
- C-clamp
- Knife or sharp chisel
- Scribing tool (optional)
- Jointer plane (optional)

1 Preparing the walls
Before you can attach anything to your walls, you must make sure they're smooth, level, and clean. First check the flatness of the walls using a long straightedge. Apart from sanding down bumps and bulges, you can work around any irregularities with a scribe rail *(page 185)*. Your next concern is locating the wall studs and marking them. Use a stud finder, as shown on page 172, to help you. Use a pencil to mark all the stud positions above the top of floor cabinets and above and below the proposed location of the wall cabinets. Make sure that the marks won't be covered by the temporary rail.

2 Placing the first cabinet
Mark lines on the wall for the tops and bottoms of the cabinets. Screw a temporary support rail to the wall, its top edge aligned with the mark indicating the bottom of the cabinet. Have a helper hold the first cabinet in position, then drill pilot holes through the back of the cabinet or the nail rail into the studs. Screw the cabinets to the wall, using $1^1/2$" screws; check for level *(right)*.

3 Shimming and fastening
Check the edges of the cabinet for plumb. If out of alignment, back off the screws and drive wood shims between the cabinet and wall as needed *(above)*. Check for plumb again and refasten the screws.

4 Fastening cabinets together
As you install each cabinet, secure it to the one beside it with a C-clamp. Make sure the cabinets are shimmed out the same distance from the wall. Drill two $1/8$" pilot holes through the sides of the front frame and into the preceding cabinet; holes should be one third and two thirds of the way from the top. Drive $2^1/2$" screws into the holes and pull the cabinets together. For lower units, place screws at the frames' top and middle.

5 ▸ Shimming for level and plumb

Before you add shims to the lower part of the cabinet, particularly a corner cabinet, you may want to add scribe rails along its length. (For more on scribe rails, see below.) Position the cabinet so the scribe rail touches the wall or the cabinet edge is against the wall. Level the cabinet by placing shims underneath, or, for lower cabinets with legs, by adjusting leg height. Make sure adjoining cabinets are plumb.

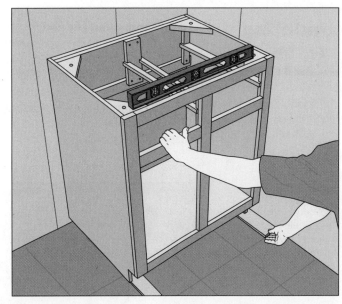

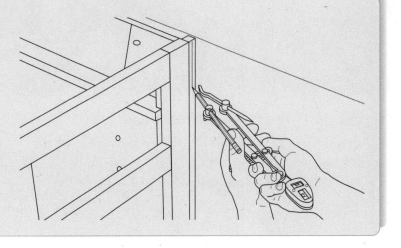

6 ◂ Fastening to walls

Once the cabinet is level and plumb, and the scribe rails are firmly against the wall, drive screws through the shims into the wall studs. Use a knife or a sharp chisel to trim any excess material from the shims. Repeat the steps to install the remaining units.

 ASK A PRO

WHAT'S A SCRIBE RAIL?

It's likely that the walls to which you fasten cabinets will be irregularly shaped, with rough surfaces and the occasional bump. To compensate, you could attach a scribe rail—a length of wood cut and shaped to fit between the wall and the edge of the unit. A scribing tool will help trace the wall's irregular pattern onto the scribe rail, so the fit will be tight. Plane the edge of the rail down to the marked line, making sure to tilt the tool slightly toward the rear of the cabinet to ensure a snug fit against the wall. It's best to scribe the rail before fastening the cabinet to the wall, but after the unit is level and plumb.

1 **Laminating the end**

Once the end of the premade countertop is cut to fit your particular space, you will need to laminate the end to cover the exposed wood. Crosscut a section of plastic laminate larger than needed, using a router with a flush-trimming bit. The old and new laminate should fit seamlessly; gaps will be noticeable.

Attach the laminate onto the counter edge with contact cement; press it with a roller. When the cement has cured, hold the router flat on the counter and ease it into the laminate, trimming it flush. Work against the bit rotation direction. Square inside corners with a chisel, then remove excess cement with a scraper.

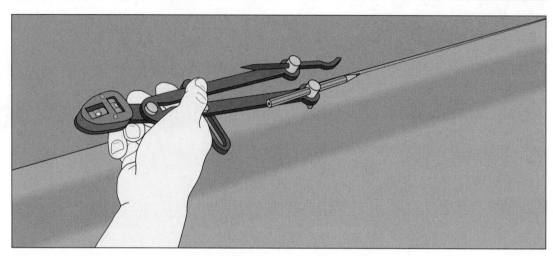

2 **Adjusting the fit**

If your walls are not perfectly smooth, or if they have irregular bumps, you will need to match the counter to the shape of the wall. In this case, you could choose to skip the scribe rail option (page 185), and instead sand down the high spots with a belt sander. The scribing tool should be set slightly wider than the distance between the wall and the counter lip. Drag the scribe along the wall, above the point where the wall meets the counter's backsplash. Then, hold the belt sander at an angle, and gently sand the counter down to the scribed line; because the backsplash isn't very thick, usually about $3/4$ inch, it should be fairly easy to shape. The lower part should be sanded more than the top, so the counter and the wall fit together securely. If necessary, do the same for other walls.

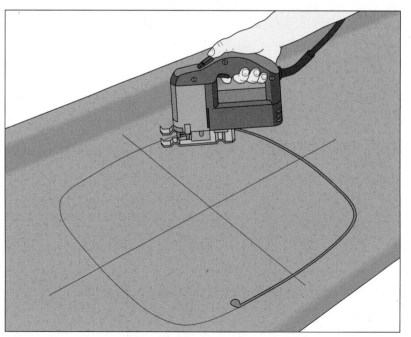

3 **Cutting a sink opening**

Mark the position for your new sink, making sure you will not be cutting into any screws or plumbing pipes. Drill a $1/2$" access hole, then cut out the sink form using a saber saw and combination blade. Alternatively, use a plunge router with a panel pilot bit—it may burn the edge, but the sink will hide the mark. Once this is finished, install the sink, according to the manufacturer's instructions.

FINISHING TOUCHES

Once your storage units are built, you may want to add a few finishing touches to their design to make them fit the surrounding decor. Of course, this may be more of a concern for the bedroom or bathroom, for example, than it is for the garage, attic, or basement. Finishing the edges and adding a paint or stain are two easy ways to spruce up a cabinet or shelf.

This section will show you how to use a router to mold a profile to an edge (below). An almost endless

selection of router bits allows you to choose between a wide range of profiles, from Roman ogee to a rounding-over bit.

On page 188, you'll see how to band the edges of your units and apply trim by hand. See page 189 for the final touches: painting and staining.

Remember to wear eye protection when routing and hammering, and rubber gloves and a respirator, if necessary, when applying stains or paints.

Routing the edges

Using a router
Although edge banding and trim strips (page 188) add a finished look to storage cabinets, cases, and shelves, you might want to finish up your project with decorative, molded edges. You can accomplish this task quite nicely with a router. Depending on the type and style of bit you use, the router can be used to shape edges,

decorative grooves, recesses, and even make woodworking joints. Various guides make routing easier and improve accuracy. Use either the accessory edge guide, a straightedge or circle guide, or a template. Special piloted bits are used to rout edges. Always unplug the router when installing or changing a bit.

Routing

TOOLKIT
- Edge-shaping bit with ball-bearing pilot
OR
- Edge guide for your model router
OR
- Straightedge guide and clamps

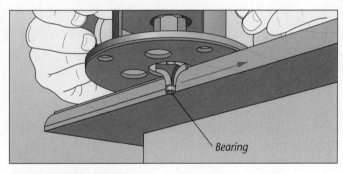
Bearing

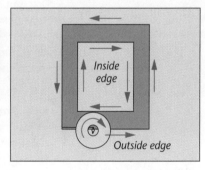
Inside edge
Outside edge

Using a piloted bit
For edge-shaping, choose a self-piloting router bit; its bearing runs along the edge being shaped, guiding the router (above, left). If you're shaping all four sides of the storage unit, begin with the end grain on one side, then continue from left to right, follow-

ing the path shown (above, right) for an outside or inside edge. If you're routing the ends only, work from the outside corners in, or clamp a wood block flush against the far edge to prevent the end grain from tearing as the bit exits the stock.

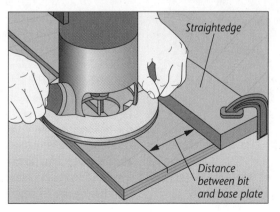
Straightedge
Distance between bit and base plate

Making a groove cut
To guide a cut near an end or edge, use the accessory edge guide available for most routers. Attach the guide loosely to the base plate, line up the bit with a reference line on the stock's edge, then tighten the guide. If the cut is further in from the edge, clamp a straightedge to the stock, to the left of the cutting line, for the base plate to follow (left). To locate the guide, measure the distance from the bit's outside edge to the edge of the base plate; or test cut against the straightedge and check the distance from the cut to the guide.

Wood edging

TOOLKIT
- Tape measure
- Circular saw
- Claw hammer
- Drill
- Router with laminate trimmer or a block plane

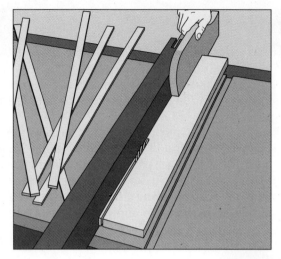

1 ▶ Cutting the strips
Using your table saw, rip hardwood edging strips ¼" thick and slightly wider than the edge that is to be concealed. Rip all the strips you'll need at one time; for safety, feed the board into the blade with a push block *(left)*.

2 ▶ Fastening them in place
Measure the height and width of the cabinet, cutting edging strips a bit longer than the measurements. Then, use a miter box and backsaw to cut the ends of the strips at 45°. Spread glue along one cabinet edge, then place the edging, pressing lightly. Drill pilot holes in the edging and fasten with finishing nails *(right)*. Trim any excess wood until the edging fits neatly in place. Glue, nail, and trim the rest of the pieces in the same way.

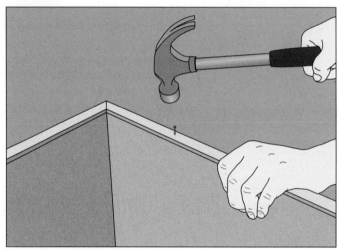

3 Routing off the edge
Once the glue has dried, install a laminate trimming bit in your router and trim the edges of the strips flush with the cabinet sides. (You can also do the job with a block plane.) Position yourself so you will be pulling the router toward you. Hold the router away from the edge to be trimmed and feed the bit into the stock when the motor is at full speed. Move the router in a clockwise direction, working at a slow, even pace. Set the router down only after the bit is at full stop.

Edge banding

TOOLKIT
- Tape measure
- Backsaw
- Iron
- Chisel
OR
- Edge trimmer
- Sandpaper
OR
- Smooth file

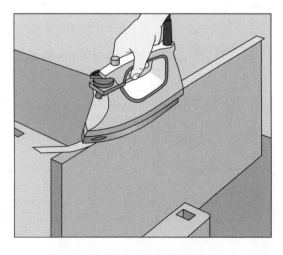

1 ◀ Applying trim by hand
Edge banding—fastening strips of thin plastic laminate that match the color of your melamine or plywood—is an alternative to adding solid wood edgings. You can rent a commercial bander, but an iron will do just as nicely. As above, cut the banding a bit longer than needed, then place it on the edge of the unit. Set the iron on its highest heat level and gently run it over the trim; this will melt the adhesive on the back of the strip, causing it to adhere to the edge. Use quick, even strokes so the trim doesn't scorch or bubble. When the banding has cooled and set, trim the edges with a chisel or edge trimmer. Finish with a smooth file.

PAINTS AND STAINS

If you're constructing your storage units out of natural wood, you'll want to add a protective finish once they're built and installed. Generally, there are two types of finishes to choose from: those that penetrate, such as natural oils and oils fortified with synthetic resins, and finishes that sit on the wood's surface, such as shellac, lacquer, varnish, enamel, and paint. This is not to say that polymerized tung oil won't build up on the surface, or a thinned-down varnish won't penetrate the wood's pores when used as a sealer. To achieve a natural-looking wood finish, your best bet is to use a penetrating finish; for more complete protection and a glassier appearance, you're better off using a surface finish. The chart below can help you decide which finish is best for your project.

Buying the appropriate finish can be difficult, since product packaging is often confusing. Products that are oil finishes by name, for example, may contain polymers, resins, and driers, giving them the qualities of varnish and other more durable finishes. To determine exactly what you are getting, it's always best to read the label on the can carefully before buying. As a rule of thumb, you can determine the finish type by examining the list of solids in each—better finishes will have a higher percentage of the resin or oil that gives the product its name. You might also want to ask your paint dealer or hardware store clerk for more help. As well, it's a good idea to talk to friends and neighbors who may have used the particular finish you're considering—chances are that their experience will help you avoid any pitfalls.

Before you begin to work with any finishing product, take the necessary safety precautions, such as storing supplies in locked metal cabinets. Wear a respirator when exposed to fumes, and allow for adequate ventilation with flammable products. For information on storing hazardous products, turn to page 15.

TYPE OF FINISHES	
Penetrating finishes	**Characteristics**
Boiled linseed oil	Lends warm, slightly dull patina to wood. Dries very slowly; requires many coats. Moderate resistance to heat, water, and chemicals. Easily renewable.
Mineral oil	Clear, viscous, nontoxic oil; good for cutting boards and serving and eating utensils. Leaves soft sheen; easily renewed. For better penetration, heat in double boiler before applying.
Tung oil	Natural oil finish; hard and highly resistant to abrasion, moisture, heat, acid, and mildew. Requires several thin, hand-rubbed applications (heavy coats wrinkle badly). Pure tung oil has low sheen; best with polymer resins added. Polymerized tung oil also builds a surface finish.
Penetrating resin (Danish oil, antique oil)	Use on hard, open-grain woods. Leaves wood looking and feeling "natural." Easy to apply and retouch; doesn't protect against heat or abrasion. May darken some woods.
Rub-on varnish	Penetrating resin and varnish combination; builds up sheen as coats are applied; dries fairly quickly. Moderately resistant to water and alcohol; darkens wood.
Surface finishes	**Characteristics**
Shellac	Lends warm luster to wood. Easy to apply, retouch, and remove. Excellent sealer. Lays down in thin, quick-drying coats; can be rubbed to a very high sheen. Little resistance to heat, alcohol, and moisture.
Lacquer	Strong, clear, quick-drying finish in both spraying and brushing form; very durable, but vulnerable to moisture. Requires three or more coats; can be polished to a high gloss. Available in less-flammable water-base form, similar to standard type, but slower drying time; nonyellowing.
Alkyd varnish	Widely compatible oil-base interior varnish; produces a thick coating with good overall resistance. Dries slowly and darkens with time. Brush marks and dust can be a problem.
Phenolic-resin varnish (spar varnish)	Tough, exterior varnish with excellent weathering resistance; flexes with wood's seasonal changes. To avoid yellowing, product should contain ultraviolet absorbers.
Polyurethane varnish	Thick, plastic, irreversible coating; nearly impervious to water, heat, and alcohol. Dries overnight. Incompatible with some stains and sealers. Follow label instructions to ensure good bonding between coats. Water-base type less resistant than solvent type.
Water-base varnish	Water base makes for easy cleanup but raises wood grain. Not as heat- or water-resistant as alkyd varnish, nor as chemical-resistant as polyurethane.
Enamel	Available in flat, semigloss, and gloss finishes in wide range of colors. May have lacquer or varnish (alkyd, polyurethane, or acrylic) base.
Wax	Occasionally used as a finish, but more often applied over harder top coats. Increases luster of wood. Not very durable, but offers some protection against liquids when renewed frequently.

INDEX

ACKNOWLEDGMENTS

The editors wish to thank the following:
Amerock, Rockford, IL
Artwire Creations, Pennsauken, NJ
Clairson International, Ocala, FL
ClosetMaid, Ocala, FL
Ekco Consumer Plastics, Worcester, MA
Elfa Corporation, Lodi, NJ
EMPAK, Consumer Products Division, Shakopee, MN
Frem Corporation, Worcester, MA
Grayline Housewares Inc., Carol Stream, IL
Hold Everything, San Francisco, CA
IKEA Home Furnishings, Burlington, Ont.
Iron-A-Way, Morton, IL
LeeRowan, a Newell Company, Fenton, MO
The Loft Bed Store, Woodbridge, VA
Rev-A-Shelf, Jeffersontown, KY
Rubbermaid Inc., Home Products Division, Wooster, OH
Sears/Craftsman, Hoffman Estates, IL
Sears Roebuck and Co., Hoffman Estates, IL
Spacemaker Ltd., Mississauga, Ont.
The Step 2 Company, Streetsboro, OH
Suncast Corporation, Batavia, IL
Universal Gym Equipment Inc., Cedar Rapids, IA
U.S. Consumer Products Safety Commission, Washington, DC
Windquest Companies Inc., Holland, MI

Picture Credits

p. 17 Crandall & Crandall
p. 18 *(both)* Crandall & Crandall
p. 19 *(both)* Crandall & Crandall
p. 20 *(both)* Crandall & Crandall
p. 21 *(upper)* Rubbermaid Inc.
p. 21 *(lower)* Tom Wyatt
p. 22 *(upper & lower left)* Tom Wyatt
p. 22 *(lower right)* Crandall & Crandall
p. 23 Crandall & Crandall
p. 24 *(both)* Crandall & Crandall
p. 25 Russ Widstrand
p. 26 *(both)* Crandall & Crandall
p. 27 *(both)* Crandall & Crandall
p. 28 Stephen Marley
p. 29 *(upper)* Crandall & Crandall
p. 29 *(lower)* Iron-A-Way
p. 30 *(upper)* Artwire Creations
p. 30 *(lower)* Rev-A-Shelf
p. 31 *(upper)* Rev-A-Shelf
p. 31 *(lower)* Rubbermaid Inc.
p. 32 *(both)* Rev-A-Shelf
p. 72 Crandall & Crandall
p. 73 *(upper, both)* Philip Harvey
p. 73 *(lower)* The Loft Bed Store
p. 74 *(upper left)* © Inter IKEA Systems B.V.
p. 74 *(upper right)* Philip Harvey
p. 74 *(lower)* LeeRowan, a Newell Company
p. 75 *(left)* Crandall & Crandall
p. 75 *(upper right)* Norman McGrath
p. 75 *(lower right)* Philip Harvey
p. 76 *(upper left)* Stephen Marley
p. 76 *(upper right)* LeeRowan, a Newell Company
p. 76 *(lower)* Stephen Marley
p. 77 *(upper)* Windquest Companies Inc.
p. 77 *(lower)* Philip Harvey
p. 78 *(upper)* Philip Harvey
p. 78 *(lower)* Philip Harvey
p. 79 *(left)* LeeRowan, a Newell Company
p. 79 *(right)* Artwire Creations
p. 114 Spacemaker Ltd.
p. 115 *(upper)* Frem Corporation
p. 115 *(lower left)* Frem Corporation
p. 115 *(lower right)* © Inter IKEA Systems B.V.
p. 116 *(both)* © Inter IKEA Systems B.V.
p. 117 *(upper left)* Elfa Corporation
p. 117 *(lower left)* LeeRowan, a Newell Company
p. 117 *(right)* Iron-A-Way
p. 118 *(upper left)* The Step 2 Company
p. 118 *(lower left)* Spacemaker Ltd.
p. 118 *(right)* ClosetMaid
p. 119 *(all)* LeeRowan, a Newell Company
p. 120 *(upper)* Spacemaker Ltd.
p. 120 *(lower left)* Rubbermaid Inc.
p. 120 *(right)* Windquest Companies Inc.
p. 121 *(upper)* Spacemaker Ltd.
p. 121 *(lower left)* LeeRowan, a Newell Company
p. 121 *(lower right)* The Step 2 Company